ONCE A PAULINA...

Once a Paulina, always a Paulina
Janet Gough, High Mistress 1992–8

ONCE A PAULINA...

A HISTORY OF
ST PAUL'S GIRLS' SCHOOL

HOWARD BAILES

JAMES X JAMES

For Susan

First published 2000
© St Paul's Girls' School 2000

ISBN 0 907 383 351

Project Editor and Designer: Eleanor Hayes
Printed and bound by Butler & Tanner, Ltd, Frome

Published by James & James (Publishers) Ltd
Gordon House Business Centre
6 Lissenden Gardens
London NW5 1LX

FOREWORD

On 19 January 2004, St Paul's Girls' School will celebrate its one hundredth birthday. Although it arrived late on the scene by comparison with other successful girls' schools, it was destined to play a leading part in the education of women in the twentieth century. Conceived as a school of the 'highest rank', its very foundation bespoke a new educational vision and widening opportunities for women. The history of St Paul's Girls' School coincides with the century which was to see an unparalleled increase in the rights and status of women. Generations of Paulinas reflect these changes and the new career paths opening up for them. They also bear testimony to the excellence of the education they received, an education rooted in the liberal traditions of English public schools, combining intellectual enquiry, rigour and breadth of activities.

As the school approaches its centenary, this new history is timely in bringing the story up to date. Howard Bailes has spent 16 years of his teaching career at St Paul's and has looked after the archives since 1995. He has used his extensive knowledge of the school to write an illuminating and delightful account from the foundation to the appointment of the eighth High Mistress at the turn of the century. The book is illustrated with a fascinating selection of photographs and other images of school life from the extensive archive collection.

In getting to know the school as that eighth High Mistress over the last eighteen months, I have been privileged to read the book as it has been written, almost chapter by chapter. I am immensely grateful for the insights it has given me into this unique story and so many of the characters who have helped to shape it. I am sure it will stir memories for former Paulinas and engage the interest of present and future generations as well as the many others who hold the school in high regard.

Elizabeth M. Diggory.

Elizabeth M. Diggory
June 2000

CONTENTS

ACKNOWLEDGEMENTS

Many people have helped me with this book. I owe a particular debt to Miss Janet Gough, our High Mistress from 1992 to 1998, who asked me to take on the delightful task of looking after the archives of the school and preparing its history. I have benefited from her wise advice at every stage of the project. My colleague Clare Sharp generously spared time from her crowded professional life to read the text. Anne-Veronica Burrows was a warm-hearted supporter of my early forays into the archives. Mrs Jacqueline Childs, during her many years as Librarian (1982–95), added greatly to the school's records and helped me to become familiar with them. Numerous Paulinas, former staff and people associated with St Paul's Girls' School have agreed to be interviewed or have sent me information, and I have endeavoured to show my debt to them in the text. I have used many manuscript and published sources. We decided to dispense with footnotes as inappropriate for a book of this kind, but the bibliography records my chief sources. My comments on the Clarendon Commission rely heavily on its definitive and excellent history by Colin Shrosbee, cited in the bibliography. I am grateful to the Mercers' Company for giving me access to its archives and to the archivists, Dr Anne Sutton and Miss Ursula Carlyle, for their frequent assistance. Queen Mary and Westfield College, University of London, is thanked and acknowledged for permission to quote from the Constance Maynard Diaries. My thanks go to Mr Edmund Gray for sending me a fascinating extract from his mother's memoir, *My Life*, by Nicolete Gray, *née* Binyon. Dr Diane Greenwood, Director of Education in the Diocese of Rochester, allowed me to quote a substantial part of her novel, *Holy Terrors* (Headline, 1994).

Dame Alison Munro, High Mistress from 1964 to 1974, and the Baroness Brigstocke, High Mistress from 1974 to 1989, have been wonderful sources of insight and information. Kate Perry, the archivist of Girton College, Cambridge, helped me with her knowledge of Chrystabel Procter and sent St Paul's substantial portions of Chrystabel's manuscript autobiography. Mr Roger Tanner also gave me some fascinating material about Chrystabel and her sister Jane. My colleague Liza Coutts, who has written the entry on Frances Gray in the *New Dictionary of National Biography*, shared with me her knowledge of Miss Gray's career. Many thanks to Adam Ford for drawing my attention to the origins of the hymn 'I vow to thee, my country' and for telling me about the stone steps of the Mercers' Building. At short notice, Alan Owen took some splendid photographs of the school in the Spring of 2000 and the results of his work are handsomely displayed in some of the colour plates. Mrs Christine Sehgal, as Secretary of the League, 1992–99, was an enthusiastic collaborator in the entire project and helped me on innumerable occasions with her knowledge of Paulinas past and present. Miss Audrey Norris, for many years High Mistress's Secretary and School Secretary, has been a source of information and excellent advice.

Earlier compilations, the *St Paul's School Book* of 1925 and the fine centenary volume of 1954, contain valuable material. Miss Etain Kabraji's collection of school memoirs, *Looking Back* (privately printed, 1994), which caught so many vivid memories before it was too late do so, is indispensable. Mrs Irene Cockcroft has made available her expert knowledge of Dr Hermia Mills and of Hermia's mother Ernestine, the great enamellist, and all information relating to them is courtesy of Mrs Cockcroft. Alan Gibbs allowed me to read his scholarly article on Jane Joseph, whose untimely death in 1929 robbed Kensington of a distinguished young composer, in advance of its publication in *Holst Among Friends*, (Thames Publishing, 2000). Mrs Jenifer Glynn has provided the school with much information on the life and scientific work of her sister, Rosalind Franklin. Over the last three years, I have enjoyed a steady correspondence with Miss G. Murray, who joined the Classics department in 1945 and served as Second Mistress from 1971 to 1978. I have treasured her witty, expert and ironical memories of St Paul's. An alternative history in manuscript, they are preserved in the archives for the interest of future generations. Her reading of my drafts has saved me from many errors of fact and ambiguities of expression. I am grateful to Hamish MacGibbon and Eleanor Hayes at James & James for their expert guidance at every stage. To my wife Susan, who has read the text and provided me with many ideas and with unfailing support, special thanks.

Howard Bailes
June 2000

1

THE FOUNDATION

If wisdom be desirable on its own account, if virtue, to deserve the name, must be founded on knowledge, let us endeavour to strengthen our minds by reflection till our heads become a balance for our hearts; let us not confine all our thoughts to the petty occurrences of the day, or our knowledge to an acquaintance with our lovers' or husbands' hearts.

MARY WOLLSTONECRAFT: *A Vindication of the Rights of Women*, 1792

Miss Jenkyns wore a cravat, & a little bonnet like a jockey-cap, and altogether had the appearance of a strong-minded woman; although she would have despised the modern idea of women being equal to men. Equal, indeed! she knew they were superior.

ELIZABETH GASKELL: *Cranford*, 1851–3

THE OPENING

A Friday afternoon on 15 April 1904 produced much excitement along Brook Green in Hammersmith or, as its more gentle residents preferred to call it, West Kensington. At the gates of the newly built St Paul's Girls' School a cadet corps from its counterpart, St Paul's School, formed a guard of honour. A temporary dais in the Great Hall (for a permanent oak platform would come later) was banked with flowers, ferns and palms and carpeted with royal blue. In the body of the Hall, some sixty Paulinas, all dressed in white, were outnumbered by a multitude of adults. For many years to come Paulinas would wear white dresses, stockings and ribbons for Governors' Day. Promptly, at 3.30 p.m. HRH Princess Mary arrived, dressed in black velvet with jet sequins, with her husband, HRH George, Prince of Wales. That St Paul's had the honour of a royal opening

*John Williams Watson,
Master of the Mercers'
Company, and Chairman of
the Governors at the
Opening in 1904.*

testified to the intended status of the school. Their visit had, indeed, nearly been disrupted. As early as June 1903 the Master of the Mercers' Company had requested the Princess of Wales to open the school. Sir Arthur Bigge, private secretary to the Prince of Wales, had replied in the affirmative in January and offered 23 March 1904 as the date. Then the sudden death of the Duke of Cambridge, the Queen's first cousin and former Commander-in-Chief, required their Royal Highnesses to cancel the engagement. This did not prevent the *Westminster Gazette* from publishing an account of the opening of the school. The Master, afraid that the Prince and Princess had been offended, successfully demanded that the *Westminster Gazette* publish an apology. No offence, however, seemed to have been taken by their Royal Highnesses. Miss Frances Gray, the Head Mistress, hoping 'that we may have some lovely weather' and Sir John asked the Master to approach the Princess again. So the date was rearranged for 15 April, though there were, in fact, a few showers.

The ceremony within was distinctly cheerful. Applause from the crowd greeted their Royal Highnesses as they arrived at the school gates. The Blue Viennese Band played a medley of lollipops, including, inappropriately, selections from *La Traviata* and, more in keeping with the occasion, Sousa's *Imperial Edward*. After a bouquet of Alexandra orchids had been presented to the Princess by his daughter Joyce, the Chairman of the Governors (John Williams Watson, the Master of the Mercers' Company) gave his address. This dwelt on John Colet and his foundation, in 1509, of St Paul's School and then expressed his hope that 'the shield in this school, though it might be but a blank at present, might, under the guidance of Miss Gray and those who were destined to succeed her, bear in time its own honoured names, the names of noble women who had served their generation'. After rising to more applause, the Princess said simply: 'I have great pleasure in declaring the St Paul's Girls' School open.' This was greeted with cheers. The Prince of Wales, after a short and unremarkable speech, proposed a remedy (an occasional holiday), which was received with 'hearty "hurrahs"' from the girls according to *The Times*, with 'shrill cheers' according to the *Morning Post* and with the '"Rah, rah" of young ladies', according to the *Standard* (all 16 April 1904). During the ensuing tour of the school, the Prince appeared to be in a jocular mood. This caused Miss Gray some anxiety. Bracingly, he remarked that the marble could cause accidents ('it might be a broken arm or a broken leg, and that would be quite enough for once'), found a jar in the cookery room empty ('Oh, they have eaten all the sugar!'), commented on the Swedish Gym Mistress's pronunciation of the word 'march' ('saying to himself, "mersh"') and observed that the cane seats in the Great Hall would not last for long ('That one has begun to go already'). Helpfully, he then suggested that a strip of canvas be nailed across the damaged seat. Meanwhile, the Princess of Wales charmed her audience. She praised the girls' drawings, expressed surprise at the 'cheapness' of the cost of education in the school (the fees were then £7 a term) and laughed 'heartily' at the girls climbing ropes in the Gym, declaring 'I wish I could do that!' Miss Gray presented the finest gymnasts, all wearing white girdles, a badge of honour that immediately became a school tradition. In the Library, the Princess complimented the future first Head Girl, Mary Mackenzie, on her macaroons, before signing the Visitors' Book with her husband. Then the royal party left to a 'hearty reception' from the crowds gathered outside.

Sir John Watney, the Clerk of the Mercers' Company, had supervised the whole occasion and had good reason to be gratified by a day 'memorable in the annals of women's education'. The Head wrote generously to Sir John: 'from beginning to end the burden of the whole affair was yours . . . throughout the year your kindness has never failed me'. Sir John returned the tribute, declaring that he had been helped greatly by Miss Gray and also by the architect, Gerald, whom the Clerk had deluged with instructions: 'Mr Horsley to make plan for seating accommodation. Mr Horsley to arrange for flag staff to be put up.' It was Horsley who persuaded Maples to lend furniture and a fine blue carpet for the Library, while Miss Gray ensured the delivery of silver cutlery from Mappin & Webb. The extant newspaper reports of the opening are uniformly complimentary and carry no hint of resistance to the Mercers' 'lofty aim, which is nothing less than affording in St Paul's School for Girls the very finest and most advanced educational establishment of its kind in the kingdom' (*Daily Telegraph*, 13 April 1904). F. W. Walker, the High Master, who opposed the notion of a such an institution and visited the

Sketch of the opening ceremony of St Paul's Girls' School with the Prince and Princess of Wales. Published in The Graphic *16 April 1904.*

Princess Mary (above) *and Prince George* (below) *at the turn of the century.*

girls' school only on its formal opening, seems to have been in a distinct minority by 1904. We might now, however, notice the dominance of men at the formal ceremony. It was the Princess of Wales who agreed to open the school but it was her husband who gave the royal speech. Of the twenty-eight people on the dais, twenty were men. Of the eight women, four were there in their own right: the Princess, Miss Gray and two Governors, Mrs Eleanor Sidgwick, the Principal of Newnham College, Cambridge and Mrs Frances Mary Wells. The High Master sat on the central and main row, behind the royal couple and the Master; the Head Mistress (who received the title 'High' in February 1910) was placed to his left and in a third row, behind the Bishop of Kensington. In his vote of thanks to their Royal Highnesses, Dr Pye Smith praised St Paul's School for 'training boys in generosity, strength and manliness' and hoped that its counterpart would 'train girls in all that was gentle and womanly' (*Saturday Post*, 16 April 1904). There was therefore a contrast between the official opening and the actual beginning of the school. This had already occurred on 19 January 1904.

On that day, the Master of the Mercers' Company rang the school bell to summon the school to prayers for the first time. The bell seems to have caused the neighbours considerable annoyance. One original Paulina recalled the many encounters of W. G. Ruthven, the first porter and caretaker, 'with agitated inhabitants of the surrounding houses who arrived to deplore the frequent sound of the school bell'. Miss Gray, therefore, later switched to a smaller one: 'We are trying a handbell. It is a terrible infliction to ourselves.' (*Paulina*, December 1924). Fifty-three Paulinas were assembled, a small company in what seemed to be a vast edifice. They sat on a few rows of chairs before the temporary platform, sang 'O God of Bethel' to the harmonium and then quietly left for the Form rooms either side of the Great Hall. Over the next few days the new Paulinas, unfamiliar with the school's topography, were seen to be following their Form Mistresses everywhere. For the first academic year, girls went upstairs only for the Art rooms or the kitchen. After a morning spent on an entrance examination, the new Paulinas gathered again for more prayers, met Miss Gray and then went down to the dining room (now the Studio Theatre and Seminar Room) for a formal dinner. The staff to pupil ratio has never been bettered, since there were fourteen full-time assistant teachers on the staff and four Music teachers, headed by Mrs Norman O'Neill, a Medallist of the Paris Conservatoire and a pupil of Clara Schumann.

January 19 was a day of profound significance to Frances Gray. For much of the previous eight months, since her appointment on 2 April 1903, she had been based at the Grosvenor Crescent Club, seeing prospective parents and interviewing possible staff. The Governors themselves held formal meetings and kept minutes from January of that year. Her letters to Sir John Watney carry an unmistakable tone of exhilaration and testify to the keen public interest in the new school. 'I have dealt with over 120 genuine applications

for posts', Miss Gray wrote (passing through Nottingham) 'and still they come.' Miss Constance Flood Jones, the school's first Art Mistress, proudly pasted professional recommendations and congratulations upon her appointment in her beautiful scrapbook. From the Grosvenor Club Miss Gray dashed off an appeal for prospectuses and examination papers: 'People are clamouring for the scholarship papers, so I hope to receive them soon.' Shortly after the school opened, she told the Clerk: 'We need prospectuses very badly; the last supply was nearly all exhausted the first day. People call at the door and carry them off.' It was a proud moment in October when, having used various letterheads during the year, she wrote for the first time on St Paul's Girls' School notepaper. Almost daily, too, from spring to winter 1903, she wrote to Gerald Horsley or saw him about some aspect of the building and furniture. But this burst of activity covered only the last staging post of the school's long road from its origins to its opening.

The west front of St Paul's School as seen from Hammersmith Road circa *1900.*

THE CONTEXT

The original inspiration for such a school was the reforming nature of Victorian society itself. For St Paul's was a second-generation girls' school, entering upon a broad highway rather than a narrow and pioneering path. By the turn of the century, a formidable amount had been done for the education of girls and women. Much of what was achieved was driven by economic and social necessity. Between the truly affluent, whose daughters did not need to work, and those close to subsistence, whose whole family were expected to earn, lay a broad social range wherein women, especially if unmarried, would need to earn something. These were the governesses of Charlotte Yonge's *The Clever Woman of the Family* (1865) and a hundred other Victorian novels. Insofar as the scanty information about Frances Gray's family allows one to judge, it appears that she was one of those women who had either to earn or to face virtual indigence, living with a father on a small official salary. Hand in hand with economic need went the excitement of new opportunities for formal education. Intellectual women born in the previous century – Mary Wollstonecraft or Madame de Staël – could win their status without concern for formal qualifications. Once high schools and colleges for girls and women developed, however, intellectual credibility required proper qualifications. Expectations of marriage were gradually balanced by the exciting chance, or sober need, of secondary or higher education. 'When a girl asks herself that question – what shall she do with her life?' muses Trollope's heroine in *The Vicar of Bulhampton* (1870), 'it is so natural that she should answer it by saying that she will get married, and give her life to somebody else.' But Jessica Morgan in Gissing's *The Year of Jubilee* (1894) 'nourished ambitions . . . to become a graduate of London University . . . To become BA, to have her name in the newspapers, to be regarded as one of the clever, the uncommon women.' That Gissing has his anti-heroine turn hysterical and fail her finals is merely a measure of the obstacles faced by late Victorian feminists.

Victorian reform in general, not only of women's education in particular,

Hammersmith Road around the time of the foundation of St Paul's Girls' School.

14

provided the direct impulse for the foundation of St Paul's Girls' School. During the nineteenth century, the movement to examine the funds of charitable institutions slowly gathered pace. Anxieties about the 'condition of England', the struggle between Anglicans and Nonconformists over the control of schools and Benthamite concerns with the public usefulness of charitable funds all fused to create the first Charity Commissioners (1818). These were, in the words of their originator, Henry Brougham, 'persons not only of incorruptible integrity, but of stern disposition'. Over the next twenty-five years they turned their critical attention to hundreds of charities and schools, finding, in Harold Perkins's apt quotation, 'empty walls without scholars, and everything neglected but the receipt of salaries and emoluments'. The disquiet aroused by their successive volumes of reports led to the Charitable Trusts Act, passed during Lord Aberdeen's brief ministry, which established the modern Charity Commission and brought England's ancient charities under legal control (1853). By Victoria's second decade, therefore, any ministry was likely to support the public examination of an established charity. In 1873, the Mercers' Company and the John Colet Foundation came under such scrutiny.

The Mercers' Livery Hall set up for dinner, c.1890–1900.

In the 1860s, three Royal Commissions into the nation's education were appointed. It was tempting at the time, and has been ever since, to see these as corresponding to a simple view of Victorian society: élite or aristocratic, bourgeois and working class. The first Commissioners, under the Duke of Newcastle, examined elementary education in order to 'report what measures, if any, are required for the extension of sound and cheap elementary education to all classes of the people'. Their report (1861) is not directly relevant to our story. A second Royal Commission, under the Earl of Clarendon, enquired into what were purported to be the nine great public schools of England. Their report (1864) and its sequel are profoundly important to the history of St Paul's Girls' School. The Clarendon Report recommended that the nine schools investigated should form a distinct élite, designed to educate the governing classes of Great Britain and set apart from the grammar schools.

To achieve this end, provisions for local foundation boys were to be gradually removed and access to the schools was to be overwhelmingly by the payment of fees. The first Public Schools Act, 1864, gave legal status to the newly defined public schools. A further Public School's Act, in 1868, was concerned with the government of seven of the nine Clarendon schools. In the austere judgement of Colin Shrosbee, the historian of the Clarendon Commission, the 'public schools were left confirmed by legislation in the status and privileges they had acquired by tradition and appropriation'.

The Merchant Taylors and the Mercers' Company managed to persuade the Commissioners and then some members of the House of Lords' select committee that their schools should be exempt from the 1868 Public Schools Act. Their evasion of the act did not, however, blunt the social significance of the Clarendon Report. The 'nine' were now seen as the great public schools of England. Depending on their status, other schools could aspire to this standard or were debarred from it. It was assumed, therefore, that a school created to be the girls' counterpart of one of the nine would also be an élite school, set apart from the newly founded high schools. The Clarendon Commission set a template for the future St Paul's Girls' School and the gravitas of its report is to be felt during the ensuing debates between the Mercers' Company and the Endowed Schools Commissioners and Charity Commissioners.

Finally, the enquiry under Henry Labouchere, Baron Taunton, surveyed a vast range of schools not considered by either of its predecessors. Its report appeared in 1868. Only after Emily Davies had appealed to Matthew Arnold and Henry Roby, then second master of Dulwich College and secretary of the Commission, were girls' schools included amongst the 942 investigated. The precise proposals of the Taunton Commission – to create three tiers of lesser schools corresponding to the social standing of the pupils – were largely ignored and would probably have proved unworkable in any case. But their report had direct effects upon girls' schools. First, the overwhelming evidence of the misuse of charitable funds and scanty provision of education for girls aroused national attention. Against over 800 endowed schools educating boys, the Commissioners set only twelve similar schools providing education for girls. Secondly, the Commissioners included committed reformers, such as Henry Roby, who were prepared to approach charities directly and to demand that they contribute to girls' education. Finally, the report led directly to the Endowed Schools Act of 1869. This empowered charitable foundations

Girton College.

of women. What to him was a literary conceit:

> The Princess Ida seemed a hollow show
> Her gay furred cats a painted fantasy
> Her college and her maidens, simply masks

was a historical reality a century later.

THE FOUNDATION OF ST PAUL'S GIRLS' SCHOOL

Within this remarkable era of girls' education lay the origins of St Paul's. Some parallels can readily be drawn between this school and others. The impetus to found such an institution came in the wake of the Taunton Commission; the Clarendon Report provided the terms of reference for the kind of school St Paul's was to be, while the Endowed Schools Act enabled an ancient foundation to use funds to this end. There were also differences between St Paul's and other girls' schools. The pathway from the original proposals to the School's opening was unusual in its length (thirty-one years) and complexity. Also, St Paul's Girls' School was unique in one respect: it was the first modern girls' school to be founded and funded by a City Livery Company, and that the oldest.

If one individual has to be chosen as the only begetter, it is Baron Lyttelton, who headed the new Commission for Endowed Schools. His reputation as a reformer and his status as a peer made such an appointment unremarkable, quite apart from Gladstone's approval of his brother-in-law's activities. In 1872, Lyttelton approached the Mercers' Company and asked whether they would consider diverting some of the funds of the John Colet Foundation towards a girls' school. In 1509, or possibly in 1508, John Colet, the Dean of St Paul's, had directed his vast fortune towards forming a boys' school, entrusting the endowment, in Erasmus's celebrated words, 'not to the clergy, not to the bishop, not to the chapter, nor to any great minister at court, but amongst married laymen, to the Company of Mercers, men of probity and reputation'. This was just the sort of foundation to which the Endowed Schools' Commissioners were turning their vigilant gaze. In an arch reference to a revolutionary period of English history, the Commissioners called their suggested scheme the Heads of Proposals (the demands of the Army Council laid before Parliament on 1 August 1647). The four 'heads' were: to move St Paul's from the city to a more spacious site in the metropolis and to divide it into modern and classical schools; to use a third of the Colet Foundation to create and to fund a girls' school; to allocate nine places on the governing body of twenty to non-Mercers; to divide the 153 scholarships between the boys and girls on a two to one ratio. If the idea of two boys' schools were realised, then the arithmetic easily lent itself to a pro-

John Colet, the Dean of St Paul's Cathedral (1467–1519).

posed tripartite division. The scholarships did likewise: fifty-one each.

The Company's records in its Acts of Court do not suggest that the Mercers were affronted by these proposals. Indeed, the Commissioners and the Company negotiated with a genial mood and goodwill on both sides. Lyttelton and his colleagues presented an 'invitation', a 'private and confidential communication' to the Mercers, not a demand. Lyttelton reassured the Master that the Commissioners would 'gladly receive and consider any Scheme which the Company may submit'. There was, however, little chance of immediate action, because the question of a girls' school was overshadowed by the disputes about the status and location of St Paul's itself. By early 1874, the Court of Assistants sensed that they were about to succumb to a plan which was seductive in its radical simplicity: a new boys' school, a new girls' school, a clear division of funds. Once the Mercers started to object to the scheme on broad grounds, then the cause of girls' education was in danger, or at least in suspension. As the Master put it to the Commissioners, the Company would be ' delighted' to found a girls' school, but only if 'the funds would admit of it'. The Master and Lord Lyttelton occupied essentially the same ground: Lyttelton claimed 'that in the abstract Girls should be . . . as well educated as Boys but recognised that boys' education was bound to be more expensive and therefore should have a certain priority'. Another Commissioner, Henry John Roby, was less muted in his response. A former fellow of St John's, Cambridge and a former master at Dulwich College, he had made his name in educational reform as secretary of the Taunton Commission. Roby remarked, rather sharply, that 'there were very large funds' and that (in a nice reference to the Mercers' original craft) the Company 'must cut their coat according to their cloth', meaning, presumably, that there was plenty of it. He spoke of the 'great dearth' of good girls' schools and declared that the Mercers could well set up two or three of such establishments. These interviews ended a little uneasily. The Mercers had made it clear that the girls' school must wait upon the provision of a new St Paul's School. Moreover, as the Master had objected to 'the diversion of so large a part as a third' for a girls' school, the Commissioners agreed that the proportion should be reduced to a fourth. Nevertheless, it was a triumph for the Commissioners to win the Mercers' agreement to the principle of a girls' school. This commitment was formally stated in the Schemes of the Charity Commissioners, March 1876 and July 1879. Once the Company took on such a responsibility, it would be impressively discharged.

Roby's throwaway comment flung into conflict the opposing concepts of girls' schools. Were the Mercers to set up an élite school in the Clarendon mode, or one or more populist schools, in the Taunton tradition? But the whole question fell into abeyance for more than a decade after the critical interviews of 1874 between the Endowed Schools Commissioners and the Mercers. There is no evidence that the delays were deliberate. The governing body of St Paul's School and the Court of Assistants were intensely engaged

W.G. Ruthven was the first porter and caretaker at St Paul's Girls' School.

The North view of the proposed school by Reginald Blomfield, published in The Builder, *23 October 1897.*

during these years, first over the proposed division of the school into classical and modern and then with the move from the City to Hammersmith. Moreover, pressure on the Mercers temporarily relaxed when Disraeli's new administration of 1874 put the Endowed Schools Commission under the guillotine (31 December 1874). Their functions were then absorbed by the Charity Commissioners. Lyttelton himself, the reforming gadfly, left the scene. He had long been troubled with manic depression and had been watched closely by his servants. In April 1876 he broke away from an attendant and precipitated himself down the stairwell of his house in Park Crescent. Gladstone, as Professor Matthew shows, managed to persuade himself that his brother-in-law did not commit suicide, 'but fell in a too rapid descent, over the banisters'. These were extenuating circumstances for the delays. Nonetheless, there is remarkably little on the planned girls' school in the Acts of Court and the St Paul's School Minute Book from 1874 to the early 1890s.

By the early 1890s, the Charity Commissioners picked up matters where their Endowed Schools predecessors had left off. In 1892 they submitted a draft scheme which proposed that two schools should be set up and of an inferior grade to St Paul's. These proposals were a diplomatic compromise. The Governors had managed, in 1879, to preserve St Paul's from division. To suggest that the Mercers create two new schools, but set apart from St Paul's, was a way of scattering the benefits of the Colet Foundation without damaging the integrity of John Colet's own school. Nonetheless, this draft awoke the opposition of the High Master, F. W. Walker, and Col. Montagu Clementi, then Master and therefore Chairman of the Governors. It was not the revived proposal of a modern school that caused their hostility, as the new plan did not, unlike that of 1879, threaten to split St Paul's asunder between classical and modern institutions. Indeed, Clementi was an enthusiast for developing a modern 'department' within St Paul's and in April 1892 told the Chief Charity Commissioner that 'he would wish to complete St Paul's School before beginning a girls' school'. The real anxiety now amongst the conservatives, as George Cannell shows in his indispensable article, was engendered by the Commissioners' proposal to allocate a third of the 153 scholarships to boys from endowed or state elementary schools. This would, Clementi said crossly at Apposition in 1893, bring to St Paul's many 'newcomers with their defective and alien learning'. The High Master declared that this scheme would deliver St Paul's 'defenceless into the hands of the despoiler'. A flurry of debate therefore was developing over four entangled issues. Should there be another boys' school? What should be the status of the girls' school? Could the Mercers afford to launch the boys' school before the girls'? How should scholarships be allocated if there were another boys' school and/or another boys' and girls' school? Indeed, the Governors told the Commissioners that the Mercers would be prepared to set the question of a girls' school aside until the matter of a Modern school had been settled. Perhaps that was just playing for time, but to stall on the question of a modern school as a way of protecting St Paul's proper also meant further delays for the girls' school: 'that untravell'd world, whose margin fades'. 'Could not,' plaintively wrote the Commissioners in 1892, 'the provision of two new schools be pushed forward simultaneously?' After months of debate, the Governors at last agreed to this. The school committee was asked, in October 1892, to 'settle the area required for a Boys' Modern School and a Girls' School'.

This resolution cleared the field for some debate over the girls' school's status, which had been rather obscured by the gunsmoke produced by the battle over St Paul's and its scholarships. The Charity Commissioners' draft scheme of 1892 had suggested that the two institutions should be called 'Dean Colet's Boys' School' and 'Dean Colet's Girls' School'. The girls should be given a 'liberal education'. This meant, in effect, not a classical one. St Paul's was to be assured of £8,000 p.a. from the Foundation, while 'Dean Colet Girls' School' was to receive £2,500 p.a. The Head Mistress would be granted a modest stipend of £200 p.a. and the fees were to be correspondingly low, £12–20 p.a. It is a tribute to the Colet Foundation that when St Paul's was opened, as a grand school, the fees were hardly above this figure: £7 per term. Therefore, the scheme protected the status of St Paul's as an élite, Clarendon school while the girls' establishment would be a different and lower order. This point was picked up by *The Times*, 8 May 1893, which characterised the two putative schools as 'devoted to a more popular and democratic education than that which is carried on no matter how admirably by St Paul's School'.

Brook Green in the early 1910s.

At this point, when the Surveyor was already searching for a suitable site and had, in July 1893, recommended two acres in west Hampstead, on the Kidderpore Estate, a crucial turn to the debate was given by Joshua Fitch, one of the university Governors. Fitch had an enthusiasm for women's education scarcely rivalled amongst his male contemporaries. He had served on the Taunton Commission, was a founding member of the North of England Council for the Higher Education of Women (1866), had helped to establish the Girls' Public Day School Company and to secure the 1878 Charter which opened the University of London to women. By the time he turned his attention to 'Colet Girls' School', Fitch had a formidable and international reputation: he had been knighted, been awarded an honorary LLD by the University of St Andrews and had been created a Chevalier of the Légion d'Honneur by the Third Republic. His opinion commanded respect. In January 1894 he presented a powerful memorandum which argued that the girls' school should be cast in the Clarendon mould. London and its suburbs, he wrote, were already well supplied with 'intermediate' schools. The Governors should abandon the notion of a modest Colet Girls' school and commit themselves to 'a school of the highest type, splendidly endowed and equipped'. It would therefore be 'worthy in all respects to rank as the sister institution to St Paul's'. As is to be expected, given the period, Sir Joshua's argument had class overtones. He warned that if a large proportion of scholarships was reserved to children from state institutions, then parents of some status would shy away from such a 'Dean Colet's'. They would see it as inferior, 'even', to an ordinary high school. Later in that year, Professor Jowett (who died on 1 October 1893) and Baron Hannen (who died in March 1894) were quoted *d'outre-tombe* as advocates of a Clarendon school for girls. Their posthumous support, and Fitch's plea for the Mercers not to lose a

25

'great opportunity' to render 'this unique service to the higher education of women', turned opinion within the governing body. The Mercers immediately appealed to the Charity Commissioners and asked them to support a girls' school of 'the highest educational rank'. In response to a formal request from the Court of Assistants, the Charity Commissioners withdrew their draft scheme for a lesser school in June 1894.

Sir Joshua Fitch's intervention could not have been more opportune for the future of St Paul's Girls' School. To turn back briefly to the boys' school: a few months before this critical decision of June 1894, a new Royal Commission on Secondary Education had been announced (February 1894). The Governors had immediately seized their chance and asked for the whole idea of creating 'modern' schools to be dropped. And so it was. A new scheme of 1894 (April) produced a fresh legal wrangle between the Mercers and the Charity Commission, chiefly over whether the conscience clause of the Endowed Schools Act applied to St Paul's School. This issue was taken to the Judicial Committee of the Privy Council. The Commissioners blinked first. In 1898 they relinquished their insistence on the conscience clause. By the end of the century, when a new Scheme was agreed between the two parties, the proposed 'inferior' boys' school had simply disappeared from view. Not so the girls' school. For by adopting the Charity Commissioners' initiative, and transforming it into their own preference for a school in the Clarendon mode, the Mercers had made the idea of a girls' school their own. It was now a Company venture, and they would do it proud. The Governors and the Court of Assistants demanded that plans for a girls' school 'of the highest grade' be included in the new scheme that was eventually published in 1900. Without the turn given by Fitch to the debate, the idea of a girls' school might have vanished in the campaign to protect the status of St Paul's itself. Paulinas owe much to Sir Joshua Fitch, and it is a pity that he did not live to see their school open.

As far as the particulars of finance were concerned, the Mercers' reluctance to spend on 'Dean Colet's' largely disappeared now that it was to be St Paul's Girls' School, the name formally adopted on 9 April 1897. In the Scheme of 1900, it was resolved that two-thirds of the Foundation should be directed to the boys' school and one-third to the girls, with the proviso that St Paul's should have a minimum of £14,000. As Greville Palmer put it on 1 December 1897: 'The Girls' School is a modern idea. We should be following Dean Colet's wishes if we think first of the Boys' School.' 'I quite understand,' the Chief Charity Commissioner replied. This stipulation remained academic, since two-thirds of the Foundation's income did not fall below £14,000. The thirty-nine scholarships given to the girls' school did not affect those already granted to the boys'. Ironically, in view of the quarrel of the 1890s with the Charity Commission, the Scheme included the conscience clause.

From the mid-1890s, the pace of events accelerated. The Surveyor advised against the site off Finchley Road, briefly considered an existing school near

Miss Harriet Jones, Head Mistress of Notting Hill School around 1900.

Addison Road, Kensington, and then alighted upon the two and a half acres of the Grange and its garden in Brook Green, Hammersmith. By the winter solstice of 1895, the Mercers had bought the freeholds of the Grange, End House and Zion House from the Hall family. Only two years after Fitch's great memorandum, the Company was searching for an 'architect of eminence' to design their school. Three leading Head Mistresses were asked to form a consultative committee. They were Miss Dorothea Beale of the Ladies' College, Cheltenham, Dr Sophie Bryant of North London Collegiate, famous for holding the first D.Sc. to be awarded to a woman, and Miss Harriet Morant Jones of Notting Hill High School. It is curious to find, in the midst of these moves, the High Master proposing that a copy of the Torrigiano's bust of Colet be made as a present for what he was still calling 'Dean Colet's Girls' School'. Two more years were absorbed by manoeuvres between the Mercers and the Charity Commissioners over the wording of the new Scheme and the cost of the new building, but by the spring of 1901 the architect, Gerald Horsley, was inviting tenders from building firms.

Miss Dorothea Beale circa *1900.*

Just over thirty-one years since Lord Lyttelton asked trustees of the Colet Foundation to form a girls' school, its Governors met for the first time, in the Mercers' Hall (23 January 1903). Sir Joshua Fitch was there. A first decision was to apply to the Mercers for one-third of the Foundation's income. This resolution, and the formation of this body, before the school was completed, incensed Col. Montagu Clementi. Writing just after the school opened, he declared that it had been in effect illegal to form a new governing body before the school opened. The application for funds from the Mercers he characterised as 'effrontery, not to say stupidity'. In an intemperate memorandum of June 1904 he argued that St Paul's School had undeniable claims upon the £73,000 that had been used on the Brook Green site. 'It was not until after the lavish expenditure on the Girls' School, out of funds belonging to St Paul's School', he wrote, 'that the Govenors were at last shamed into attending to some of these long-standing grievances affecting the latter School.' At least the Colonel beat the retreat with all his Lee-Metfords blazing. The battle had been won for the girls' school, and its governing body carried on imperturbably. Other members of the Clementi family were to be good friends of the new school. Three Clementi-Smiths, all clergymen, were on the first governing body. In 1918, the Reverend Percival funded the Muzio Clementi prize, to be awarded each year for a 'critical essay on some work by Clementi'. Alas, Clementi experts amongst Paulinas proved hard to find. With the family's approval, the terms of the prize were broadened in 1951 so that it could be given for a fine performance on the pianoforte.

Interlocked spheres of influence were shown by the four women Governors of St Paul's. With Miss Elizabeth Blakesley came literary culture and a link with the City. She was a sister of the then Master and the daughter of Joseph Blakesley, the scholarly cleric who was one of Tennyson's early friends and became Dean of Lincoln (1872–85). Mrs Frances Mary Wells

Mrs Eleanor Sidgwick, Vice-Principal of Newnham College, and one of the first Governors at St Paul's Girls' School.

brought in the weight of Oxford academic tradition: she had been one of the early scholars of Lady Margaret Hall and was married to J. B. Wells, a Fellow of Wadham and subsequently Warden and Vice-Chancellor. The new career woman was exemplified by Miss Lillian Faithful, who carved a formidable course from a First at Somerville, Oxford, to posts at the Oxford High School, Royal Holloway College and the Women's Department of King's College, London, to the headship of the Ladies' College, Cheltenham. With Eleanor Sidgwick came an already legendary mix of politics, aristocracy and radical reform in women's education: she was the sister of Arthur Balfour, Prime Minister when the Governors first met, niece of Lord Salisbury and the Principal of Newnham College, Cambridge. To Frances Gray, Mrs Sidgwick had been the revered Vice-Principal (as she was from 1879 to 1892) who 'was able to give a reproof such as anyone might well dread, though I do not think it was ever conveyed by words, and if it was by a glance it never suggested anger'. When an anxious Frances faced the algebra part of 'Little-Go' in order to be admitted to the Tripos examination, it was Eleanor Sidgwick who took her step by step through quadratic equations. Helen Fowler writes, in *Cambridge Women*, that Nora Sidgwick 'is always described as shining like a star in any gathering'. Amongst the first Governors of St Paul's Girls' School, she was indeed the star.

By the turn of the century, therefore, the school proposed in 1872 had just what its warmest advocates could have wanted: the support and finance of the oldest City Livery Company, a splendid site and a declared aim to be 'of the highest educational rank'. The Mercers' Company may have taken some time to arrive at the summit, but, once there, they were determined to hold it on behalf of St Paul's Girls' School.

2

THE ARCHITECTURE
OF THE SCHOOL

Within this sober Frame expect
Work of no *Forrain* Architect
MARVELL: *Upon Appleton House*

A contemporary observer might find the old buildings of St Paul's Girls' School to be deeply traditional. Their strawberry-pink brick, their Portland stone dressings, the marble and oak of the entrance and Great Hall evoke classical antecedents. To some degree, these appearances are misleading. Gerald Horsley, the architect (1862–1917), did intend his building to convey a reassuring sense of tradition. In many aspects of its design and materials, however, the school was distinctively modern. Even its aesthetic was fashionable. Horsley was an exponent of the Queen Anne revival, the Sweetness and Light of Mark Girouard's famous book on the subject. Like his master and teacher Norman Shaw, Horsley liked hand-made glazing with its slight imperfections, small-paned windows, light colours, English brickwork, deep gables, alcoves, wrought iron, and relief sculpture on white stone. When St Paul's Girls' School was completed, in 1903, the school provided a piquant comparison with the nearby St Paul's School. Alfred Waterhouse had designed that in a severe ecclesiastical style during the early 1880s, using, writes Hugh Mead in *A Miraculous Draught of Fishes*, a 'hard and reddish-purple brick'. Waterhouse's aim, as when building Girton in the previous decade, was dignity and grandeur. Horsley's school, Queen Anne and domestic in tone, stood in deliberate contrast to its imposing counterpart. If Basil Champneys in Cambridge played his Newnham College off against Waterhouse's Girton, then Gerald Horsley did likewise in Hammersmith with his girls' school against St Paul's.

To his architecture Horsley brought an artistic temperament and background. His father, John Callcott Horsley, was a successful painter and Royal

Gerald Horsley, architect of the school.

29

*William Morris
(1834–1896), leader of the
Arts & Crafts movement.*

*Norman Shaw, architect
and teacher of Horsley.*

Academician. In 1847, Fiona MacCarthy relates in her *William Morris* (1994), he had joined the group of artists gathered by Henry Cole to combine 'the best Art with familiar objects in daily use'. As a young man, Gerald met Edward Burne-Jones, Walter Crane and William Morris and was excited by their ideas. From them, Horsley derived a fascination with the texture and appearance of materials. Arts and Crafts were to have a direct influence upon the architecture of St Paul's. He also developed as a fine artist and draughtsman: his obituary in the RIBA Journal (1917) describes his 'studies of sculptural detail in which the most sensitive accuracy was combined with soft, refined texture'. The beautiful water-coloured floor plans and elevations for the High Mistress's house and Music School exemplify his skill. After Kensington School, Horsley went straight to Norman Shaw's office as a pupil and spent eight years there learning his profession (1879–87). There, too, with four colleagues, he formed the Art Workers' Guild, devoted openly to the ideas of William Morris. From Norman Shaw's practice, Horsley won an RIBA studentship, spent a year travelling in Italy and Sicily and returned enthusiastic about Italian art but still determined to build in an English idiom. By the time the Governors were seeking an architect for their projected school, Horsley had contributed to a school in Arundel, designed a church organ case, built the west block of Bedford Court Mansions and a chapel in Westminster. This was not a great deal for a successful architect in his mid-thirties and the St Paul's Girls' School commission therefore made a major contribution to his practice.

By 1896, the Mercers were ready to find their architect. They invited Norman Shaw to ask three practitioners to submit competition plans and to choose the best. It was not surprising that Shaw was appointed to judge the three plans. He was an 'architect of eminence', to use the Mercers' phrase, and from 1877 he had become architect to the Bedford Park estate, 'the Healthiest Place in the World'. Hundreds of 'Queen Anne' houses had been built in this showpiece suburb, within walking distance of Brook Green. John Belcher, Reginald Blomfield and Horsley were asked to submit designs. Belcher (1841–1913) was in his mid-fifties and well known; Blomfield was a lively exponent of Queen Anne and, like Horsley, a disciple of Shaw. An elevation indicating Blomfield's design was published in the *Builder* (23 October 1897) and shows an attractive building but more stocky than Horsley's and without its soaring gable front. The master, praising Horsley's design for its 'excellence and compactness', nominated his pupil as the architect of St Paul's Girls' School (16 January 1897). Belcher consoled himself with a commission for Colchester's Town Hall.

Seven years elapsed between choosing the Brook Green site (1894) and signing the contract (between the Governors of St Paul's School and the Holloway Brothers) to build St Paul's Girls' School. The deliberate pace of these developments was not the fault of the Mercers' Company. It was the Charity Commissioners who generated delays. First, in August 1895, they

30

insisted that the proposed site in Brook Green was (at £12,500) too expensive. The Mercers obediently negotiated the price near to the £10,000 set by the Commissioners. The Commissioners then took some persuading that the cost of the building was acceptable, especially as the estimates kept drifting upwards. Indeed, the tender received from Holloway Brothers of Victoria Wharf, Westminster, was the lowest of the ten taken (£54,750). Eventually, but not until July 1900, the Commissioners approved expenditure up to £80,000 and the final estimate came within that, at £77,900 (including a generous £10,000 for 'furnishing' and Horsley's well-deserved fee of £3,700). Then, in February 1901, a curious blip was provided by the High Master, Frederick Walker. He had discovered that a 'syndicate of Jews' was proposing to open a theatre in Hammersmith Road. Such a theatre, wrote Walker to the Mercers, would make the Brook Green site 'no longer fit' for a girls' school and 'the Charity Commissioners should be told so'. What Walker's motives were one can only speculate. At any rate, the Charity Commissioners were told. Their response was quite insouciant. Nonetheless, the matter fizzled on until April, when word arrived at Mercers' Hall that a licence for a theatre had been, for the moment, refused. Horsley was given immediate permission to send his specifications to the builders (15 April 1901).

Building meant demolition. The Ordnance Survey Map of 1894–96 shows that there was already a dense network of terraced housing along and off

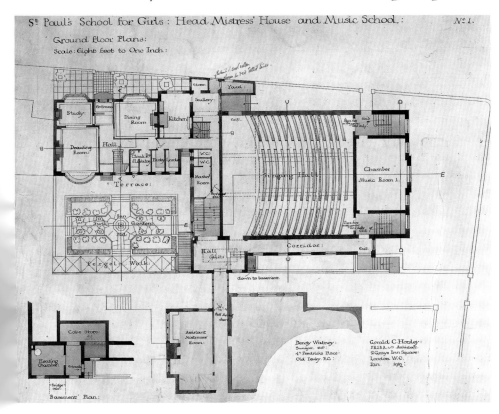

High Mistress's House and Music School, ground floor plan, with garden, by Gerald C. Horsley, January 1912 (Mercers' Company Archives SPGS Roll 26.6). Reproduced by courtesy of the Mercers' Company.

An early gymnastics class.

Brook Green. On the chosen site were three houses, the largest known as 'the Grange' and home to the actor and impresario Henry Irving, from 1881 to 1889. (Richard Briers, the actor, whose daughter Lucy is a Paulina and an actress, unveiled, on 2 November 1988, a plaque on the school gates to commemorate Irving's residence.) That Irving had left the house because he found it too far from the West End and not fashionable for interesting guests suggests that, even in the 1880s, Brook Green was relatively quiet. An anonymous painting from the 1890s, held at St Paul's Girls' School, shows the Grange as an attractive red-brick residence. Preservation of such buildings was no concern at the turn of the century. In December 1895, the Grange was bought from the Hall family (for £4,495) and the adjoining End and Zion (or Franklyn) Houses were purchased (for £4,700). All were swept away, including two acres of flower gardens and an ancient apple orchard behind the Grange. Therefore, unlike several earlier girls' schools, St Paul's was wholly purpose-built and on an entirely clear site.

Romantic he may have been, but Horsley was also an architect adept at responding to precise and functional needs. The particular charm of his building lies in its combination of usefulness and beauty. In that, its architect was a true disciple of William Morris. Certain broad parameters were laid down by the Mercers. They wished the school to have a 'dignified and characteristic aspect'. It was to have an 'entrance hall' (by which they meant the Great Hall, not the Marble), a laboratory, lecture hall, museum, library and teachers' library, and the last three were 'to be handsome in appearance, as they will be much used for social purposes'. Moreover, it was 'proposed that it should be lighted with electricity'.

With imagination and precision, Horsley translated these sweeping requirements into meticulous architecture. His design embodies the school as an academic microcosm. The west wing was to accommodate and represent the Arts; the east wing, the Sciences. The Library and the 'teachers' library' were on the west side, reflecting the contemporary assumption that libraries were chiefly concerned with the humanities. Off the Library was the Museum, a nice touch which soon disappeared with the need for more shelving space. Within the east wing were two laboratories and the lecture theatre (transformed into the History room with the completion of the new Science Block in 1933 and then into the staff common rooms when the Theatre was completed in 1985). One of Horsley's friends, Henry Pegram RA, who shared the ideal of the artist-craftsman, sculpted swirling reliefs on the gables to symbolise the Arts and Sciences. In the centre, as Horsley wrote, was 'carved work representing the Trees of Life and Knowledge'. High above the entrance, the Maid of the Mercers testified to the historic origins of St Paul's Girls' School. One of Horsley's ideas for the façade fell by the wayside. He had intended the bust of Colet to go in the central niche and thereby complement the Mercers' Maid. It had been Frederick Walker who, in 1896, proposed that two copies be made of Torrigiano's bust of John Colet and that one replica be given to what was then envisaged as the humble 'Dean Colet's Girls' School'. This tribute to the origins of the school went, however, for an unexplained reason, to the mantelpiece of the Library. With the arrival in 1923 of Philip de Laszlo's fine portrait of Miss Gray (1922), the bust migrated to an end niche of the Marble, where it remains. A splendid turret clock, designed by J. W. Benson ('Manufacturers of Church, Turret, Railway and Station Clocks, Carillons, Sun and Wind Dials, Bells, etc.') was added in 1908 and enhanced the rear façade.

The rest of the design unfolded with the clarity which explains why the

Early life-drawing class.

original building is still the school's practical as well as symbolic centre. Off the entrance was the Head Mistress's study and reception room, mirrored by the porter's lodge and Music rooms. A grand corridor linked the Science and Arts Wings and provided space between the classrooms, and the laboratories and Library. Towards the Second World War, this corridor became known as 'the Marble'; the High Mistress was using the term in her correspondence with the Clerk by the late 1930s. Beyond the 'corridor' was the Central Hall, soon to be known as the Great Hall. Class and divisions rooms were arranged around the Hall.

A topmost floor accommodated a splendid studio in the mode then current, with a vast north-facing clerestory window to provide filtered light. To the east lay the Gymnasium. By the end of the 1990s, this seemed to be very dated and the PE department and Paulinas were delighted with the completion, in autumn 1999, of a new and splendid Sports Hall. In 1904, however, the gym was modern indeed. An early photograph shows us the ropes, climbing frames and support bars which implied gymnasticswas more energetic than the restrained callisthenics often then thought suitable for girls. Similarly, the kitchen was equipped in the latest fashion, with a gas range, just as there were Bunsen burners in the laboratory. The Gym gallery was used, at least initially, for a purpose that modern Paulinas would find surprising. Deputies to the International Art Congress of 1908, who were entertained at St Paul's Girls' School, observed that *la salle de Gymnastique a sa belle place . . . a la galérie qui la domine, le fauteuil de la diréctrice and deux chaises prouvent que les leçons sont suivies et dirigées par la direction.*

The corridor at the school, commonly known as 'The Marble'.

A lower ground floor absorbed the dining rooms, the 'covered playground' (which became the bomb shelter during the Second World War and then a dining room), kitchens and services. In order to light the basement properly, Horsley gave it a generous height. This has enabled the floor to be used for many other purposes since 1904. Originally, the playroom occupied one side of the space and the 'light' and 'dark' (inner) dining rooms the other. Miss Gray believed that children should dine substantially as well as elegantly. When at St Katharines in St Andrews, she had introduced a mid-morning break of gingerbread and milk. This was much appreciated. At St Paul's therefore, girls were given what Miss Gray called (in an eighteenth-century manner) a 'luncheon' of milk and biscuits at 11 a.m. Dinner, prefaced by Grace, was served formally between about 1 and 2 p.m. by maids in starched aprons. Silver cutlery was used, and Miss Gray ordered the first consignment from Mappin & Webb. Second helpings were readily available. A Mistress would either sit with Paulinas or (on off-duty days) join the high table with the Head, 'on the College plan'. But formal dining remained until the 1960s. 'Heaven forbid!' wrote Miss Osborn to the Clerk with uncharacteristic vehemence (20 October 1952) that the school should ever adopt 'a cafeteria system'. Her successor, however, was determined to adopt just that, and Mrs Alison Munro (High Mistress 1964–74) swept away the old dining

The new school.

arrangements in 1971. Despite some regret at the loss of a tradition, many staff were pleased, since formal dining had taken a significant portion of each busy day. During the development of the mid-1960s, the basement was also converted into the PE office and medical rooms. The original medical room was on the first floor, in what is the now the Classics department, and its entrance mosaic commemorates the school's first doctor, Helen Webb. In the 1980s, the former staff dining area became a seminar room and an adjoining room formed, from 1995, the Studio Theatre.

The delights of Horsley's building lie not only in its broad conception but in the details of its construction. 'Any carving or ornament of any description must be both well designed and well executed, otherwise it is better to have none,' Horsley told the *Girls' Realm* in 1904. To create a sense of warmth and brightness, he used strawberry-red bricks from Bracknell, Berkshire and Portland stone for the facings. Ground-floor casement windows, in wrought iron and with individual opening panes, picked up the Queen Anne theme. Austrian oak provided the panels of the Great Hall and the 'Corridor', which was paved with Devonshire marble (for the red squares) and Italian (for the green and white). An honours board in marble and mosaic (1909), with the

35

names of scholarship holders picked out in gold, completed the design for the 'Corridor'. By the 1970s, the gilt names were spreading on to the oak below. He assumed that the Hall would be used for dancing and therefore asked for small oaken joists to provide a 'spring and give' to the floor. In a famous instance of their high standards, he and Miss Gray had an entire consignment of floorboards returned to the suppliers because they saw that they were slightly warped. When the school opened, the oak panelling was light in colour and Horsley looked forward to the time when it should have acquired its patina. One elderly Paulina visited the school in 1995 and saw the Hall oak for the first time in sixty years: 'Oh, how dark it is!' she exclaimed. Floral designs and touches of gilding on the headwater pipes made those useful objects quite beautiful. Fan scallops finished the rear niches. Fine wrought-iron gates set off the façade and defined the school space from the street.

Within this graceful exterior, Horsley adopted the most recent technology. Two large shafts and electric fans were installed below the roof of the second floor to ventilate the whole building and to provide warm air. As early as 1907, the school had its own dark room; by 1909, forty 'synchronised electric clocks'. Behind the moulded oak shields on the Hall balcony was fireproof bakelite. Concrete fireproof floors were built extensively, even on the gallery of the Great Hall. Massive steel beams provided the structural support for the balcony and ceiling of the Hall. The fact that electricity was used everywhere, even in the kitchen and for the drying machines (in which, as the *Girls' Realm* put it rather oddly, 'wet garments and boots can be doctored with hot air'), attracted admiration from the press. Within the Hall, wrote the *Daily Paper* (21 January 1904) 'electric light, with which the whole school is lit, glows from the pendants of old brass'.

If Horsley had had his way, the Great Hall would be more ornate and more obviously within the Arts and Crafts tradition than it is. A pen and ink drawing he published in the *Builder* (31 May 1902) shows his original conception. Ornamented ceiling frames and roundels, and the great semicircle above the end gallery, were designed for paintings in fresco secco. Edwin Lambert, RA, produced sumptuous modellos for the frescoes, but the Governors took matters no further. Horsley also envisaged a circular window above the planned organ, adorned with a 'carved garland in oak' and with stained glass 'Della Robbia in character'. The Governors turned his proposals down on the grounds of cost. In the face of astringent criticism from Norman Shaw, Horsley did insist upon the retention of the 'musicians' gallery' at the north end of the Great Hall. Shaw urged John Watney to strike the gallery from the plans, arguing that it would be used only 'half a dozen times a year', that it would make the end of the Hall 'dismal and dark' and that the pillars 'would be seriously in the way – for purposes of drill, etc.'. What kind of school did Shaw have in mind? Fortunately, the gallery was retained, is in constant use and provides the best view of school concerts. But the fine red

The clock in the Main Hall, still in use today. Copyright Mrs V Irene Cockcroft, photography Mr David Cockcoft and published with the kind permission of Mr and Mrs Cockcroft.

Horsley's sketch of the Great Hall, published in The Builder, *31 May 1902.*

curtains of Utrecht velvet which were bought to hang under the gallery seem never to have been used. If the Hall's ceiling and upper walls had been painted with frescoes in High Victorian colours, if coloured light were diffused through the a large southern window and if deep-red curtains closed the entrance, it would have a distinctly different feel from its contemporary cool, filtered ambience.

One artefact was pure Arts and Crafts: the Great Hall clock. It was designed by Nelson Dawson, a noted enamellist and Quaker, who, with his wife Edith, ran Dawson Arts & Crafts from Swan House, Chiswick Mall. His daughters Rhoda and Mary came to St Paul's from this 'Quaker-artist family, very odd really' (according to Rhoda, Mrs Bickerdike, in 1986). Edith Dawson's influential study of *Enamels* (Methuen, 1906) is dedicated 'To my Jewels, R. and M.'. An example of Edith and Nelson's work may be seen in *The World of Antiques* (Spring, 1990): a belt-buckle, in which cobalt-blue flowers glow against a green enamel base and silver frame. Rhoda, who endowed the school's Mary Dawson Poetry Prize, also became a successful artist, especially in watercolours, and a keen traveller and conservationist. By 1908, when the Hall clock was made, Nelson Dawson was already famous

and Rhoda, writing in *Apollo* (November 1988), claimed that he was mentioned 'in the same breath as Steer, Sickert and Clausen'. She was, admittedly,
a partial witness, but her father had enjoyed some grand commissions, such
as the design for the entrance to Palace Gate House. Nevertheless, he treated
the commission for St Paul's as an honour and designed enthusiastically with
Horsley and Miss Gray. By spring 1909 a fine new clock, its green-enamelled
fruit and floral swags and laurels typical of Dawson's art, adorned the Hall.

From the outset, the Governors had intended that the Hall should have an
organ. 'No organ-maker', Maurice Forsyth-Grant wrote in *Twenty-One Years
of Organ-Building* (1987), 'could ask for a better acoustic than this hall.' As
soon as the clock was completed, they invited tenders, and accepted the contract offered by the celebrated firm of J. W. Walker & Sons. By summer 1910,
the humble harmonium had been replaced with the great organ. Its magnificent case, carved by Aumonier & Son, was to Horsley's design so that, as the
Chairman of the Governors ponderously remarked in his Speech Day address
of July 1910: 'the harmonious strains of the organ might not be disturbed by
a want of visual harmony'. Horsley combined the ornate frame with technical sophistication: the bellows and feeders were powered by an hydraulic
action, activated by mains pressure. The organist Sir Frederick Bridge, who
had played at Westminster Abbey for Queen Victoria's Jubilee and Edward
VII's coronation, christened the St Paul's organ with a recital and pronounced
it 'a most delightful instrument'. It was exciting for Paulinas to have their own
organ as well as the Broadwood grand piano in the Hall. 'The dull grey metal
pipes and the beautifully carved oak harmonise with the rest of the Hall',
wrote the editor of *Paulina* (July 1910), while the secretary of the Literary
Society was prompted to an appropriate metaphor: the 'young orator . . .
began her paper in a low quavering voice, faintly resembling the tremolo of
an organ, when controlled by unskilful hands' (November 1910).

For many years, the Walker organ produced beautiful music, but by the
late 1960s it was showing signs of wear. It is 'inadequate, and will in time
become disastrous', wrote one adviser firmly. After much discussion, the
Governors decided upon a new organ, but to be built within Horsley's existing case. J. W. Walker & Sons submitted an estimate for a fine instrument but
at a high cost (£12,560). Therefore, the Governors turned, for a cheaper alternative (at £9,500), to the smaller firm of Grant, Degens & Bradbeer. Walker &
Sons were, naturally, wounded at this decision, the more so since their service contract of sixty years' standing ended with it. One can hardly criticise the
Governors. They were assured by their expert, Cecil Clutton, that to have an
organ of this quality for about £9,000 was 'astonishing value for money'.
Grant, Degens & Bradbeer were attracting praise for 'fine craftsmanship and
innovative design' (Peter Hurford in his obituary of the organ's builder,
Maurice Forsyth-Grant, the *Independent*, 19 November 1992). At Imogen
Holst's instance, the ivory organ stops of the old Walker instrument, on
which Holst had played for so many years, were saved and sent to the

The original swimming pool had not changed, apart from the lighting, when this photograph was taken in 1952.

Cheltenham Holst Birthplace museum. Obviously, many Paulinas were sad to see the old instrument go, but most came to love the sound of the new one and would not quarrel with F. G. Hunter's judgement (*The Organ*, October 1967) that its makers were 'in the first league of British organ builders'. Its inaugural concert was held on 19 November 1971.

St Paul's was one of the first schools in England to build its own swimming pool or bath, to use the original term. In Sara Burstall's *Public Schools for Girls* (Longmans, 1911), it is the only girls' school mentioned as having 'a private swimming bath'. Hammersmith in the early twentieth century was less peaceful than one might assume: the files of pupils taken to the municipal baths were at first assaulted by 'street urchins who abounded in that neighbourhood' and had to be escorted by the police. The Governors, very concerned, ordered the construction of a swimming bath (on the site of the original brick bicycle shed). They also, declared the Master when he opened the new bath, 'recognised that swimming was a womanly art'. Designed by Horsley, built of white glazed brick, brightly lit from above with wide windows, roofed in Westmorland green slate, this was the last word in swimming bath construction. The pool, with a slide and diving board, was large enough for 'fifty girls [to] disport themselves at a time', and the water could be heated and purified. As a finishing touch, wet bathing costumes could be dropped into a chute, washed, dried and then returned to the form rooms. Before the invention of quick-drying synthetics, this service was a necessity rather than a luxury. Bathing costumes should be, as Miss Gray wrote to the parents, 'of alpaca or cotton twill . . . Turkey twill is recommended.' Joan Evans in *Not Bad for a Beginner* (1996) recalls the 'black shapeless costume' that was compulsory for swimming. In fact, navy was the colour authorised for competent swimmers and red for those learning to swim. The reds, 'clumsy and sometimes helpless' (*Paulina*, July 1917), aroused some mockery and it was the ambition of every non-swimmer to become a 'blue' as soon as possible. In a curious episode of Princess Mary's visit in 1921, the school's divers displayed their expertise before Her Royal Highness by plunging for a 'leaded quoit bound in the School colours' which she had tossed into the water.

The First World War had no effect on school swimming. The pool was emptied and refilled twice weekly and used by 300 girls a day in the summer. With the Second World War, however, the pool was taken over by the local authorities and kept filled for fire brigade use. Early in 1945, the bath was returned to St Paul's, but attempts to resume swimming were abandoned 'owing to flying bombs', the Governors minuted. With peace, the pool returned to its normal function. By the early 1970s, however, it was showing its age. Mrs Munro in 1971 launched the complicated process of finding the right location and the best designer for a new pool. Four years later, under her successor, a beautiful new swimming pool was opened at Bute. 'The Swimming Pool has been in use for exactly a year,' said Mrs Heather Brigstocke on Governors' Day on 13 July 1976, 'and we are still thrilled by it.'

THE LIBRARIES

Sketch of the Library by Margaret Sifton from the St Paul's Book *of 1925.*

Libraries to academic institutions are as souls to bodies. A great collection of books evokes the inspiring sense of minds sweeping across many fields of human endeavour. The old Library has had such a status in the history of the school. Only recently has the school's intranet created a vast and alternative body of information. With St Paul's Girls' School's access to the Internet, the old Library's holdings may seem modest. They are, nonetheless, all the more precious for that. It is easy to forget, in the generation of mass paperbacks, the immense dependence of children and students upon their school and public libraries. This reliance was keenly felt in the period during and just after the Second World War. The High Mistress told the Governors in February 1941 that 'no new books were bought during the past year'. Only three books were purchased in the succeeding year. For some time after the war, new publications were scarce and expensive. There was no difficulty staying within the library budget since the librarian could hardly find enough books to spend the money on. Indeed, wrote Miss Dorothy Patrick (History department, 1919–55) 'if a book appeared in a shop it was snapped up almost regardless, despite the terrible paper'.

As Horsley's ground plan shows, the Library was to dominate the 'Arts' side of the school. The chief room was beautifully proportioned and flooded with light from the great windows giving on to Rowan Road. Once the Music Wing was built between the west side of the school and Rowan Road, the Library was no longer suffused with natural light. Indeed, as the High

Mistress pointed out when the new Colet Library was opened, on 23 January 1997, it is now that room which enjoys an open aspect to the west. Next to the Library was the 'teachers' library', which rapidly became the staff room and, in 1985, the first Colet Library. When the school was officially opened in April 1904, the Library was still largely unfurnished, both with books and actual furniture. Indeed, items had to be borrowed from Maples to give the Library a suitable appearance for the royal visit. One wall only, the fireplace side, was shelved, as an original photograph shows. Miss Gray moved quickly on these matters. The Library was equipped with oak tables, and oak chairs 'cushioned in morocco'. Miss Patrick described the leather as a 'lovely warm red, almost a dull cherry red', which the school found impossible to replace exactly after the Second World War. By 1911, the two other walls were shelved. It took some time to fill the bookcases, if we are to judge from a sketch printed in the *St Paul's Girls' School Book* of 1925. Purchases and gifts rapidly expanded the school's holdings, however, and another pre-war picture, placed in Miss Gray's bound set of Paulina 1904–14, shows an impressive sweep of books. St Paul's first Inspectors, in 1920, praised 'the beautiful and (considering the youth of the school) very well-equipped library.' Many of the books were gifts. From the outset, St Paul's has benefited from the extraordinary generosity of Paulinas, parents and other friends of the school.

Successive editions of the early Paulinas give us some idea of acquisitions. In 1939 we find, amongst many others, Jowett on Plato, André Maurois on English history, Keith Feiling on the Tory Party, with a highly valuable seventeenth-century edition of Plutarch and Dostoevsky's *The Brothers Karamazov* joining the shelves. There does seem to have been a formidable leaning towards the humanities: of all the books given in that year, only two were clearly on science (one being J. C. Speakman, *Modern Atomic Theory* and donated by Rosalind Franklin). By 1955, rare books included a 1556 Spanish New Testament and a late Elizabethan edition of Chaucer and the glazed shelving was created in that year to protect the more valuable volumes. As late as 1965, an HMI Report noticed how slight the Mathematics and Science holdings were compared with the humanities. Mrs Munro acted on the comment of the Inspectors and by 1985, the school had such a good collection of science publications that it gained its own department when the staff room was converted that year into the Colet Library. The status of science and social science books was confirmed when they were housed within the grander Colet Library of 1997.

Miss Noakes, the first Mistress to be entitled 'Librarian' (1907), organised the books according to what she called 'modified Dewey'. Its modifications were, to some staff, 'baffling'. Miss Murray, on joining the Classics department in 1945, was also asked to assist Miss Patrick (a rôle known, irreverently, as 'library slave'). By that stage, Miss Patrick dominated the Library and treated 'modified Dewey' as sacrosanct. Anything which did not

The original Library Bookplate

fit obvious academic categories she threw into 'Sociology', which thereby became a very odd collection. When she retired, as her successor wrote in *Paulina*, 1956, 'senior Paulinas, like generations of their predecessors, could not imagine the Library without her'. It became an established tradition to dust the whole collection annually and to have the shelves polished by the porter and cleaners.

Throughout her period of office, Miss Gray kept a vigilant eye on the Library. She was determined that the Library should elevate its users. It was a matter of pride to her that Miss Noakes had established the rule of silence 'without written notices to that effect'. Some French deputies to the International Art Congress, who visited the school in Miss Noakes's first year as Librarian, were most impressed. *Ce qu'il y a de remarquable, c'est la grande independance respectée ici chez l'enfant. Pas de bibliothécaire [poor Miss Noakes, so efficient as to be unnoticed!]: l'enfant choisit son volume, en inscrit le titre, le nom de l'auteur, la date du prêt; et lorsqu'elle n'en a plus besoin, en le rapportant, met on regard, sur le même registre, la date du retour. Ici nul livre egaré: il est confié a la seule sauvegarde de l'élève, et est d'autant plus respecté.* The year 1997 records a wonderful instance of a Paulina respecting her library book. In July 1939 she borrowed a copy of a Sheridan, was evacuated over the summer and lost track of the book. Fifty-eight years later, she found the Sheridan amongst her late husband's many books, and returned it, 'somewhat later than she had intended'. To ensure the literary merit of new books, Miss Gray for some years sent her list of proposed purchases to Adolphus Ward, an editor of the *Cambridge Modern History* and of the *Cambridge History of English Literature*. Miss Strudwick, her successor, enjoyed discussing the termly book order with her colleagues. The Library is well-stocked with reference books, observed the *Graphic* (18 February 1922), and with 'only such fiction as can be termed classic'.

Many girls found the Library inspiring. Miss Murray tells the story of an entrance candidate who was asked what she thought of the Library: 'Horrible: nothing but books.' Miss Murray adds: 'That was not received Paulina opinion: the Library, the Marble and the Oak . . . were venerated almost as sacred objects.' This comment seems to have been true of Dodie Smith, who managed to have a mystical experience in the Library. This is recounted in her autobiography, *Look Back with Mixed Feelings* (1978), and in Valerie Grove's biography, *Dear Dodie* (1996), which quotes Dodie's journal. Sitting on the Library steps, reading an eighteenth-century book, she 'suddenly had the most queer feeling that all the ages were muddled and that then is now . . . I thought of all the girls who would sit and work in the library long after I am dead and imagined that I could almost see them. The library was quite empty and the late afternoon sun was shining right onto me so that I seemed to be in a golden haze.' 'I have always liked to remember myself', she wrote to Miss Murray (12 June 1978) 'sitting on top of the library ladder in the afternoon sunlight.'

The room's atmosphere on a studious day is well captured by the comment of *Paulina's* editor, Margery Hirschfeld (July 1930): 'The Library is now such an abode of silent concentration that one dares hardly turn the pages of the Lexicon for fear of breaking the deathlike stillness.' 'I was able to read voraciously', remembered Nicolete Gray, *née* Binyon, 'all Scott's historical novels, Lord Lytton, Miss Yonge, etc.'. An HMI Report of 1954 praised the 'diligence' of girls in using the Library, 'suitably furnished and admirably maintained', in or out of school hours. When it came to books, the bleak prose of the next HMI Report (1965) flickered into life: 'It is a pleasure to record that St Paul's is a school where girls read books avidly and with pleasure and that the reading habit runs vigorously through the whole school.' Another Paulina's poem evokes the sense of quiet elation bookish children feel in a grand library (*Paulina*, March 1920):

> The books have many autumn-tinted backs,
> Yellow, and gold, and red, and mauve, and blue;
> And I sit with wonder overawed,
> And scarcely dare to think my poor small thoughts.

Miss Gray's successor, Ethel Strudwick, launched a competition for a St Paul's Girls' School Library bookplate. The winner was Beatrice Langdon, a Paulina of 1911–16. Her design was cut by Emery Walker. To this author, the Arts and Crafts design has considerable charm, but not everybody liked it. At the time, Miss Hirschfeld (Classics) grumbled about the 'irregularities' of the print, which Emery Walker dismissed as 'trifling'. Miss Murray thought that the bookplate was a 'debased Art Nouveau thing' and neither she nor Miss Patrick was sorry when it was dropped in Jubilee year. A new design, published as the cover of *Paulina* for 1954, and embodying the Colet insignia, was approved by the Mercers and inspired in part by the Company's coat of arms.

Complementing the Library proper was a delightful room overlooking Brook Green and originally designated as the school's museum. Before long, St Paul's dispensed with such a luxury, though the gift of a fine display case by leaving Prefects in 1934 acknowledged the room's original use. For nine years, this room was used to supplement the music chambers. Singing classes often were diverted to the 'museum' and to what Miss Patrick called a 'desecration' of the Library's silence. With the new Music Wing (1913) there was no more singing in the museum. By then, it had become a History or reading room. So matters continued until 1939, when the main Library had become so crammed with books that the Governors decided to use the inner room as the 'Library extension'. Barely had the shelves and 'periodical fitments' in old English oak been delivered than the declaration of war on 3 September emptied the school of Paulinas. Many of the books followed them to Wycombe Abbey. For some months, remaining staff had the uncanny experience of staying in a school bereft both of pupils and much of its book collection.

St Paul's was lucky in that its Library survived the war with little damage. Some of its more valuable contents were removed. After months of agitation by the League and Miss Strudwick, de Laszlo's portrait was put in the safe, as were the finest books. On the night of Friday 15 November 1940, the feared bombing attack occurred. We are fortunate that Miss Winifred Pasmore's account has been preserved for us in Miss Etain Kabraji's *Looking Back*. Over twenty incendiary bombs landed on the school and its grounds. Some melted the leads (the flat roof, used for debating, off the western balcony of the Great Hall). One landed in the Gym and another crashed through the Library ceiling. Miss Pasmore and other staff ran over the grounds, picking up the incendiaries with the standard-issue 'long-handed scoops'. Eventually, with much reluctance, they went out to call for a fire brigade, clambering over the locked school gates, Miss Pasmore in her nightgown topped with 'a new and extremely warm overcoat'. It was the heroic efforts of Misses Pasmore, Dobrée, Wenham and others that saved St Paul's from a general conflagration. The firemen did arrive and their hoses damaged much of the stock, especially the Geography books, which were just below the bombed part of the ceiling. For some time, the 'Library smelt horribly of mould, damp and smoke', Miss Patrick wrote, and the ceiling was not properly repaired for some years. As late as October 1946 the High Mistress wrote to the Clerk, begging that the Governors should do something about the Library, 'a beautiful room which has been sadly disfigured by the incendiary bomb'. The ceiling, which had been patched up in 1941, was then fully restored.

Relative prosperity in the 1950s brought a constant expansion of the holdings. Miss Murray, a book lover and a great reader, took over as Librarian in 1955 and under her the institution continued to flourish. During the next decade, the Junior Library, which had at first been placed in the old lecture room, found a new home in the High Mistress's house. Mrs Alison Munro decided that the accommodation was too great for her needs. So she relinquished the ground floor. Part was handed over to Oxford and Cambridge candidates. To the Junior Library was given a 'very pleasant' room with an attractive collection that inspired 'vivacious and critical' book reviews (HMI Report, 1965). Here, Paulinas were trusted to read and work unsupervised. This decision seems to have caused no problems, recalls Mrs Munro. During the rearrangements of the 1970s, the Junior books, as the 'New Library', migrated to classrooms off the Great Hall. Finally, with the new Colet Library, the distinction between 'junior' and 'senior' libraries disappeared altogether.

An appealing addition was made to what was now the 'old' Library in 1986. Four years earlier, Sir Siegmund Warburg, president of the great bankers, S. G. Warburg & Co., had died. His widow wrote to the then High Mistress, Mrs Heather Brigstocke, offering the school his splendid collection of books on European history, politics and literature. A catalogue (1995) of

The High Mistress's house, 48 Rowan Road.

Sir Siegmund's books was later produced by the librarian, Mrs Jacqueline Childs. Lady Warburg was influenced by her daughter Anna, a Paulina. Anna (Mrs Biegun) wrote to the High Mistress on 16 February 1983, saying her father 'was always interested in the young and in exchanging ideas with them, and perhaps the books will continue to stimulate and provoke thinking and keep another dialogue going'. Lady Warburg's generous offer, which included the cost of transport and new shelving, was accepted with alacrity by the school. The Library extension thus became the Siegmund Warburg Memorial Library and was improved with new shelving, cunningly devised by Platonoff and Harris to suit the existing oak. A splendid opening of the Warburg Library on 23 September 1986 revealed an appropriate president: Lord Roll, an emigré, like Siegmund Warburg, from central Europe.

During the mid-century developments, the 'teachers' library' of Horsley's original conception (that is, the staff room until 1985) had been altered by the insertion of a mezzanine floor. Undeniably useful, this had marred the proportions of the room. When the Governors and Miss Janet Gough (High Mistress 1992–8) resolved upon an major refurbishment of the Colet, the opportunity was seized to restore something of the Library's original appearance. The Colet was therefore opened on 23 January 1997 as a wonderful complement to the old Library. Virtually the entire space is lined with shelves in American white oak. A spiral staircase gives access to an upper gallery, flooded with light from windows on three sides. The polished iron whorls of the staircase spindles and the use of solid oak avoid pastiche but provide continuity with the old Library. Part of the Colet area, named the Helen Wallis Centre in honour of St Paul's most distinguished geographer, is devoted to electronic communication with access to hundreds of compact discs and the Internet. By the Electronic Library is sometimes displayed Helen Wallis's stunning edition of *The Boke of Idrography*, presented by John Rotz to Henry VIII in 1542 and republished by the Roxburghe Club (1981). There could be no better illustration of a school's ability to respond to the new without losing the old.

The Music Wing

Responding to Miss Gray's proposal, the Governors in 1910 decided to build a Music Wing. Accompanying this, and not something for which Miss Gray had asked, was to be a house for the Head Mistress, who received the title 'High' in that year. Horsley, who remained the school's architect until his relatively early death in 1917, designed the Wing in the same style as the main school. This was an aesthetic and practical triumph: the 'Music Wing is a model conservatoire', as the *Graphic* wrote primly in February 1922. On the western façade, a central row of *oeils-de-boeuf* was balanced by a line of rectangular windows. Slightly pinker bricks betray the fact that the Music School

Holst's purpose-built, sound-proof room, now occupied by Dr Derek Bourgeois.

is ten years younger than the original edifice. A stone front, with classical swags, appears to invite an entrance, but in fact access to the Wing is through a corridor created from the 'teachers' library' which had adjoined the main Library. New rooms included a Singing Hall (a panelled auditorium), a 'retiring chamber' for the Director of Music and soundproof practice rooms. An intense concentration upon lectures and chamber music can be generated by the Singing Hall, with its immaculate acoustics and tiny, elevated windows, reminiscent of a Quaker meeting hall. Holst took immediately to his 'retiring chamber', known at once as Mr Holst's room, into which he could slip through a side-door off Rowan Road. It became his favourite place for work and it was here that he composed *The Planets* in its original version for two pianos. Imogen Holst in *Gustav Holst* (1938/1967) conveyed the emotional effect of this retreat upon her father:

> It had double windows, and two pianos, and a writing-desk that was wide enough for the fullest score, and a system of central heating that sent the thermometer shooting up to heights rivalling the deserts of Algeria.
> On week-days he would be teaching in it . . . but on Sundays . . . it would be all his own. And every August there would be thirty-one days of absolute quietness, and he was to be able to write . . . That room was to have a profound influence on his life . . . he would find it so easy to write that he used to speak of the 'spell' that his room held for him. The St Paul's Suite was the first thing he wrote there.

The original music chambers were inconveniently placed off the entrance and next to the Marble. Despite Horsley's efforts at soundproofing – by hanging felt curtains within hollow brick walls and by packing apertures with slag-wool – a lot of noise escaped. When rooms above the head's office were used too, matters grew worse. As Vally Lasker recalled in Paulina (1955): one 'music room is bad enough for anyone, but imagine two people, one playing in E flat and the other in F sharp above the High Mistress!' More rooms, below the Hall, were used for practice. Soundproofing was non-existent there: Misses Day and Lasker communicated with an agreed musical signal. The latter once astonished a pupil by saying that she would ask Miss Day a point of theory. She played the signal and then opened the door seconds later to her colleague standing there. Moreover, to have a singing class next to the main Library was calculated to create tension. Horsley was determined to silence the grumbles provoked by the noise of music teaching and practising. Here, again, he used contemporary technology, studying examples of soundproofing at the Royal Academy and the 'silence' chambers of the Marconi Company. Irene Bonnett (Mrs Swann) recalled being taken with Miss Gray and Holst to the Marconi centre: 'There I was shut up in a small room and told to make as much noise as possible on my violin.' Horsley then devised an ingenious system to baffle sound waves. Each of the music practice rooms was an insulated box. Its floor was composed of a cork carpet which lay on wooden sleepers. These in turn rested on Cabot's quilt, made of paper and cured eelgrass (a species of seaweed), supported by a wooden raft, itself lying on a material called mascolite. Below all was the ferrous-concrete floor. The walls were formed of plaster and slag on the inside, wooden battens in the middle and Cabot's quilt on the outside. This really was soundproofing; as far as music practice went, silence outside the rooms was the result. A complex system of ventilation ensured that the auditorium and practice chambers were properly aired.

The High Mistress's home was built to adjoin the Music Wing. This house has fine red brickwork, tall chimney stacks, steep gables, a drawing room that now runs the depth of the house, a sunken garden with pergola and sundial. It is a masterpiece of Queen Anne domestic architecture and Horsley's last contribution to St Paul's.

The Science Block,
the Rosalind Franklin Workshop,
the Mercers' Building and the Theatre

In 1904, St Paul's was one of the few girls' schools in Great Britain to pay serious attention to Science education. Most high schools had no laboratories and almost ignored the Sciences, though there were signal exceptions. The Governors seemed to take it for granted that St Paul's Girls' School should have laboratories and serious teaching in Science. Even so, Miss Gray's survey of the school in 1908 shows that Science was given much less weight than other academic subjects, with a slight allocation in the Junior School (taken, then, to be Fifth and below) and a correspondingly small staffing. Whereas there existed 'chief Mistresses' for Drawing, English Literature, Mathematics and Modern Languages, only one full Science Mistress was on the staff. (Sixty years later, there were five full-time Science teachers; in 1999, eleven.) So few lessons were given to junior Science that the original 'elementary' laboratory was soon used for senior Physics. Biology found an uncomfortable, but perhaps appropriate, home on the first floor in the original Cookery Room. Here Princess Mary, visiting St Paul's on 26 July 1921, 'was much interested in the stick insects and their eggs'. Miss Gray did, however, have the leader's art of making all disciplines feel valued. With that, the devotion of the teachers and the intrinsic interest of the subject matter, the Sciences flourished to the point where the Governors were ready (November 1931) to build a complete block for Biology, Chemistry and Physics.

On the former tennis courts, a simple, fine building was constructed, by Trollope and Colls, to the south at the school and at a cost of £22,495. An entrance, broken with the coat of arms, was the only concession to Horsley's Queen Anne classicism. With their usual thoroughness, the Governors commissioned four professors of Imperial College to give expert advice on the latest laboratory facilities needed. A mere eighteen months after the decision to build a Science Block, it was formally opened on 27 June 1933, by Princess Alice, Countess of Athlone, whose daughter May was a Paulina. Its seven laboratories, greenhouse and aquarium made the Science centre the most impressive amongst the London day schools of 1933. The *West London Observer*, (30 January 1933) described it as 'splendidly equipped with excellent lighting and ventilation'. Over twenty years later, the HMI called the Science facilities 'lavish', praising the department at the same time for its 'out-

The science room.

standing . . . sense of purpose'. Even in 1965, the Inspectorate praised the laboratories as 'excellent'.

By the 1980s, however, the technical provision for Science was becoming outdated and in 1990 the school committed itself to a formidable improvement of the laboratories. Some thought was given to building an entirely new block. Eventually, however, the Governors and High Mistress decided upon an adroit enlargement of the existing edifice. A complete floor, accommodated by a mansard roof, was inserted above the first storey and given state-of-the art laboratories. During 1997, the ground– and first-floor laboratories were modernised to the same level. Great care was taken by the architects, Green Lloyd, over the choice of bricks, stone and slate in order to blend the improvements with the original block and with the main school. A false balcony gave the façade a little post-modernist flourish. Concurrently, Trollope and Colls, sixty years after their Science Block, built a complete information-technology centre, in red brick, light stone and white-painted steel. The treads of the stairway are formed of green volcanic tuff, from Honister Quarry, Cumbria. With the refurbished Science Block, this was formally opened as the Mercers' Building on 18 January 1994.

Rosalind Franklin is St Paul's Girls' School's most celebrated scientific name. It was partly as a tribute to her that two Paulinas, Chatsuda Chierakul and Helen Goodridge, attempted, and succeeded, in devising a model of DNA's helical structure. In this they were helped by many people, including their teachers and Professor Sir Aaron Klug, of Cambridge's Laboratory of Molecular Biology, who won the Nobel Prize for Chemistry in 1982. This beautiful model is now on the top floor of the Science Block. Rosalind Franklin had already been commemorated in 1988. After the opening in 1975 of the new swimming pool, next to Bute House, the former swimming bath was rather cleverly rearranged as a theatre. Some Paulinas doubted whether this was an improvement on the Great Hall, but it did dispense with makeshift lighting arrangements. Lucy Briers said (on Shakespeare Day, 26 June 1997) that the old swimming bath was a good dramatic space. Not quite a proper theatre, it gave the actresses a sense of freedom: 'We could do anything there.' Once a new theatre had been built, the vacated space was brilliantly converted by Theo Crosby (the architect of the Globe Theatre and founder of Pentagram) into a design and technology centre and entitled the Rosalind Franklin Workshop. As the High Mistress said at the opening ceremony, on 4 February 1988: 'It was not an easy task to convert an old swimming pool built in 1908 into a 1988 high-tech workshop.' Many people came to remember Rosalind Franklin at the opening, including the guest of honour, the then Dr Klug, and Rosalind's sister, Mrs Jenifer Glynn.

The workshop was the last product of the Appeal, dazzlingly launched by Mrs Heather Brigstocke in early 1982 and with the Prime Minister as its patron, to finance an array of reconstruction. The previous summer, the Governors had approved the ambitious development, to include the work-

Rosalind Franklin, an outstanding scientist and major contributor to the discovery of the structure of DNA.

Facing page:
Top left and right: *Details of the reliefs on the façade symbolising the Sciences (left) and Arts (right).*
Top middle: *The School clock and bell tower.*
Bottom: *The Marble with the bust of John Colet visible in the niche on the far wall.*

shop and a theatre block with new History classrooms, a computer centre and a floor for the Bursary. A whirl of accompanying events created a sense of excitement over the next couple of years. The High Mistress visited New York in the autumn of 1983 to launch the 'American Friends of St Paul's Girls' School', an organisation which grew naturally out of the American exchanges she had established. A reception was held at 10 Downing St (1984), at which Paulinas performed. They had been warned to play softly so as not to drown conversation. 'So quiet?' said Mrs Thatcher as she approached. 'Do play up!' A private view in December 1983 of the Royal Academy's great Venetian exhibition was accompanied by a lecture by Charles Avery (whose triplets Charlotte, Susanna and Victoria, were Paulinas) on Venetian Art. Sunday 28 November 1982, witnessed an extraordinary Gala evening at the Aldwych theatre. Shortly after the launch of the Appeal, Dame Celia Johnson, the school's most distinguished theatrical Paulina, died (25 April 1982). Dame Celia's family gave the school permission to adopt the name the Celia Johnson Memorial Theatre and Queen Elizabeth, the Queen Mother, agreed to be patron of a fund-raising gala evening in Celia Johnson's honour. A glittering array of performers, gathered by enthusiastic parents and Paulinas, provided an evening of rare delights. Robert Tear sang 'Where e'er you walk' from Handel's *Semele*, Karen Jones, the flautist, played Debussy's *Syrinx*, a sequence of film clips reminded the audience of Celia Johnson's exquisite acting, Sir Ralph Richardson, Anthony Andrews and Jeremy Irons appeared, Cleo Laine sang to John Dankworth's saxophone, and Richard Briers teetered on the marble as a hopeful mother bracing herself for her daughter's stringent entrance exam and high fees.

On 14 February 1983, Mrs Brigstocke ceremonially cut the turf to begin the building of the theatre. Almost exactly two years later (23 February 1985) the Queen Mother opened the theatre to a John Mortimer play in miniature about Holst and a staged performance of Purcell's *Dido and Aeneas*. Paulinas at last had a theatre with gantries, professional lighting and movable seating. The theatre has doubled as an examination hall: sometimes it is used for play and sometimes in earnest, but can we always tell which is which? 'Miss Lord goes in for broad culture', says Samuel Barmby in Gissing's *In the Year of Jubilee*, 'that's quite a different thing from studying for examinations.' The theatre/examination hall reminds us that a good school can successfully do both.

Gala evening at the Aldwych Theatre with (top to bottom) Jeremy Irons, John Dankworth and Cleo Laine, and Richard Briers providing some of the entertainment.

3

BUTE HOUSE

Bute House had long been an object of desire to those who recognised that our playground shrank in size as the School grew.

FRANCES GRAY: *St Paul's Girls' School Book*, 1925

Bute holds a particular place in the affections of St Paul's Girls' School. Beyond the brick curtain wall on the western side of the playing field are the thundering highways of Shepherd's Bush Road and Hammersmith Broadway. Within the precinct, the rumble of traffic subsides to a hum on the borders of consciousness. Five acres in the heart of the borough include the playing field, the compact buildings of what is now Bute House Preparatory School, the swimming pool and the sports pavilion. Paulinas know the grounds well as their playing field for lacrosse and athletics. To most of the staff, it is the place of their annual pilgrimage to field Sports Day and of the unaccustomed supervision of javelin throwing or putting the shot. The great russet beech, from where the smaller girls look out at the larger girls with a mixture of interest and wariness, marks an undefined border between the Senior School and its sometime junior partner.

Before the Second World War, these five acres differed dramatically from their contemporary appearance. Bute House proper, a Georgian building with various Victorian additions, occupied the ground now taken up by the pavilion and the swimming pool. The *London Observer* (25 January 1935) described it as once 'the largest private residence in the borough'. Surviving photographs give us some sense of the interiors. Over one mantelpiece was mounted a pair of ancient Irish elk antlers, much treasured by Miss Janet Cunningham, Bute's first, and only, boarding House Mistress. These could be dated precisely, she was convinced, to 2000 BC. Josephine Turquet (Dr Munton) has dim childhood memories of a 'very dark dining room with a stag's head'. The surface of the original gravelled carriage drive remains

Girls enjoying the garden at Bute House, July 1931.

No. 57 Brook Green, the site of St Paul's Girls' School's first boarding house.

below the pavilion's forecourt and accounts for its good drainage on rainy days. By the time of the Great War, the grounds were a remnant of the former Bute estate, with orchards and a kitchen garden surrounded by crumbling stables, outbuildings and a couple of cottages. Wisteria trailed around the terrace and burr chestnuts lined the periphery.

Bute was to become the boarding house of St Paul's Girls' School, but not until 1922. It is curious that, just as the *Westminster Gazette* had reported the opening of St Paul's before it had taken place, so the *Girls' Realm*, in its Christmas number of 1905, described a boarding house before it was in existence. Sharpening her pen, in true house style, the editor of *Paulina* (December 1905) wrote caustically that the article in the *Girls' Realm* 'unfortunately contains many inaccuracies. The most flagrant is the announcement of the opening of a boarding house.' Such a house was, however, opened the next year at 57 Brook Green. Miss Gray had put forcibly to the Governors the need for boarding, declaring that she had received applications from parents living in Austria, India, Ireland and Spain. She described the accommodation at 57 Brook Green in glowing terms and was particularly pleased that living next door was 'Mr Frank Short, the artist, whose daughter is at the School'. But the Governors who looked at the place were not so readily impressed and found it to be ill-ventilated and gloomy. They were happy for two of the St Paul's staff to be licensed as boarding-house heads – Miss Rogers, the principal Classical Mistress, recommended by her Head Mistress as 'a person of extensive reading and considerable social gifts' and Miss Moore, who had worked for seven years with Miss Gray at St Katharines Preparatory School, St Andrews – but insisted on a rapid move (1909) to a better house in Gliddon Road. There the boarders stayed until after the Great War.

Old Bute house in the 1950s, seen from the rear.

By then, the Governors had bought (in 1916) the superb site of Bute, for the considerable sum of £34,000, from three freeholders (Anthony Bird Nunes, Herbert Bristow and Arthur Bingham). It was immediately used for games but also for gardening and the war effort. The inspiration behind the splendid kitchen garden and flower beds of Bute was Chrystabel Procter (St Paul's, 1908–12). She was the sister of Jane Procter, who was to become a distinguished zoologist. Chrystabel's own academic career had been disrupted by the onset, in her early teens, of deafness. Her father, though devoted to his daughters' education, accepted the contemporary medical advice that there was no point in sending Chrystabel to university. So she turned to horticulture, training at the Glynde College of Lady Gardeners in Sussex from 1915. Two years later, Miss Gray appointed Chrystabel as (surprisingly) 'Gardener's Boy'. She then sat examinations with the Royal Horticultural Society and in 1919 was granted the more appropriate title of 'Lady Gardener'. In retrospect, Chrystabel wrote that 'it was to Miss Gray and St Paul's that my sister and I owed our professional careers and much else besides'.

Celia Johnson in a wheelbarrow.

As Lady Gardener at Bute, Chrystabel was a triumph. She was an enthusiastic and warm-hearted teacher of the girls, publishing unofficial prize lists of the best gardeners in the school. The faded photographs of the garden in her time show Paulinas laughing and weeding, wearing floppy hats and overalls. Paulinas were allowed to keep rabbits at Bute and, if they lived near by, to bring their puppies. In one snapshot the young Celia Johnson is captured, unforgettably, enjoying a wheelbarrow ride. Chrystabel furnished the coach house as a study and classroom, with an anthracite stove to make it cosy in chilly weather. During term time, many came after school to learn advanced gardening from Miss Procter. Bute House girls still maintain their own flower pots and part of the grounds is kept as a 'weed garden' for botanical study.

When she arrived, the grounds were a disorderly array of weeds and overgrown beds, scattered with 'brickbats, pickle bottles and old boots'. Chrystabel immediately launched what she called 'the battle of Bute House' (*Paulina*, December 1917), 'child's play after the gruelling work at Glynde'. Whatever could be grown was tried. Foxgloves flourished in dark corners, asparagus, artichokes, parsnips, potatoes, strawberries and 'salads of all kinds' dotted the grounds. The Science department created a 'botanical garden' and the Mistresses maintained their own allotment: 'I have seen Miss Pantin gardening at dawn and again at dusk, and I have tasted her delicious early peas.' In time, Miss Procter grew more adventurous, and added stables, a poultry farm and a miniature piggery to the flora. The pigs were called Devonport and Rhondda, after the successive Ministers of Food and in honour of Bute's contribution to the war effort. On Sundays, Miss Gray would stroll across to Bute after Matins, see her pigs, scratch their backs with her umbrella and chat to the staff. But neighbours complained, both about the pigs and about Chrystabel's bonfires. One smothered fire broke into flames in the early morning, inciting a police complaint to the effect that Bute was being used for signals to the Germans. According to Chrystabel, Miss Gray told her to vary the place of her bonfires, 'so that it wouldn't always be the *same* neighbours that complained' and also persuaded the borough that the pigs were necessary for the war effort. With peace, Devonport and Rhondda lost their *raison d'être*, and had to go. With peace, too, came more flowers and fewer vegetables. Miss Gray solemnly asked the Governors' permission to spend the school's profit from the rabbit run and poultry farm on flower beds. 'The Mound' was turned into a 'sunshine garden' and some of the potato beds gave way to azaleas, lilies and delphiniums.

That Chrystabel's gardening triumphs at Bute coincided with the First World War shows how limited its impact upon the home front could be compared to the effects of the Second. At the height of the war in 1917, the grounds were used for a magnificent garden party, to welcome the Head Mistresses' Conference, in which 300, seated, enjoyed afternoon tea and an outdoor orchestra. Nor were the Governors ready to relinquish the grounds for other purposes. An appeal from the Borough in 1917 to use Bute, then vacant, for a Belgian refugee school, was at first briskly set aside. More remarkably, a request from none other than the Assistant Director of Recruiting for National Service to use the house as offices was firmly turned down. In the next war, the Governors would have no such option. In 1918 they relented over the Belgians, and their school briefly used Bute as its headquarters, leaving after a Christmas party in which the guests were delighted by the novelty of electric lights on the tree instead of candles: 'the effect was most fairy-like'.

To be fair, however, the Governors had to be vigilant to protect their pre-

The sitting room at old Bute House.

Gardening was encouraged at Bute and many girls were happy to get their hands dirty.

cious five acres in the heart of overcrowded Hammersmith. An extraordinary number of people seemed to be desperate to use these grounds. One company asked whether an hotel, so long as it were 'high-class' and 'non-licensed' could be built in part of the field. The Broadway Congregational Church wanted to hold their services at Bute. *Fulham Invicta* Football Club asked whether they could play their matches there. To each of these requests, the Governors replied that: 'This proposal be not entertained.' In Miss Osborn's time (January 1951), one of the neighbours was seen on several mornings taking five dogs in a stately procession along the perimeter of Bute. When questioned, she declared that she was exercising the dogs on behalf of 'the Central Social Department of the People's Dispensary for Sick Animals' and, as a personal friend of the High Mistress, has been granted special permission to take convalescent pets to Bute for exercise and fresh air. A startled Miss Osborn assured the Clerk that she knew nothing of the lady, her dogs or the People's Dispensary. There was some more serious discussion between the Mercers and the Borough over Bute and adjoining land to the west. In 1927, the Council sought a site for their planned new town hall. They offered the Governors not only £25,000 for one half-acre of Bute but the building, gratis, of a 'thoroughly up-to-date boarding house' on the patch of land between Bute and Phoenix Mansions. The Governors flickered – they had paid merely £16,000 for the entire site only eleven years previously – but did refuse. Fresh offers of land and a new boarding house across the Green failed to tempt them. After years of negotiation, and a threat of compulsory purchase, the Mercers in 1931 let the Borough have the land between Bute

*Miss Janet Cunningham,
who ran Bute House until
after the second World War.*

and Phoenix Mansions for the handsome sum already discussed: £25,000. Nonetheless, the Mercers came to regret this decision, afraid that the Council would build something considered undesirable next to Bute: a 'Remand Home, or such-like', or a cinema, or a even a church, where 'the ringing of bells . . . would have a most disturbing influence on Bute House' (as the Surveyor wrote to the Chairman, 10 February 1938). The Borough, hard up after the war, sold back the disputed patch in 1946 and the Mercers were able to use it, eventually, for a handsome housing development in 1984. Its subdued classicism, in materials of warm red bricks in Flemish bond with stone facings, was intended by the architect, John Melvin, to harmonise with St Paul's Girls' School.

With the Great War over, the Governors had the chance to exploit the site at Bute for a purpose other than games and gardening. Miss Gray, who had so enjoyed her boarding house at St Katharines in Fife, begged the Governors in 1919 to make Bute the boarding house of the school. The teachers who had been running the boarding house on Brook Green were more than ready to relinquish their duties to a full-time matron. Moreover, Miss Gray had a suitable replacement to hand. With a confidence that the post-war recession was soon to undermine, the Governors ordered the conversion of Bute to boarding purposes, at an expected cost of £3,000. Finances, as usual, proved to be a lurking predator. Unforeseen problems, like the collapse of the drawing-room ceiling and the rising price of materials lifted the final cost to £5,825 16s. 9d. It was not until February 1922 that the lease on Bute House was taken by Miss Janet La Touche Cunningham, from Dublin.

Miss Gray had offered her this post in the spring of 1918, so Miss Cunningham had waited nearly three years to take it up. Strictly speaking, the High Mistress did not appoint her: rather, Miss Cunningham simply rented Bute from the Mercers on the understanding that she would run it as a boarding house. She therefore took a twenty-one-year lease on the house, at a rent of £450 for the first year and £550 thereafter. The Scheme of 1879 and its successors did not empower the Governors directly to create a boarding house for St Paul's Girls' School. Janet Cunningham was an imperious and vivid personality, ready to develop a distinctive boarding house but anxious to please Miss Gray and to conform to the culture of St Paul's. For many years, she had served as housekeeper to the widowed Sir John Simon. Through him, she had met famous artists, politicians and writers and had formed some personal friendships amongst them, with Walter de la Mare in particular. 'She seemed to know everyone in London,' recalls Nancy Litt (St Paul's 1926–32; Mrs Dixon). Often Miss Cunningham went for weekends to the country, for she was a keen horsewoman. Mr L. T. Groves, who was groundsman between 1935 and 1958, was often distressed when Janet, wearing her elegant black habit, snowy cravat and riding boots, strode across the white lines of his cricket ground.

Miss Cunningham was determined that Bute House should be a haven of art and poetry within the prosaic setting of Hammersmith. Cultural entertainments became a feature of Bute: readings in the evening, or lectures on art, or Saturday outings to the National Gallery. Copies of masterpieces and some original paintings crowded the hessian-hung walls. 'Outside was the Broadway, where people shouted and the lights of the Citroen garage flashed in the sky,' recalled Meriel Tower (St Paul's, 1922–9), 'while inside we were hearing the voice of Walter de la Mare reading "dim, dank, dark, dismal and dreary-o" or Emile Cammaerts talking about the Van Eyck portrait of Arnolfini and his wife'. The annual House party and play were 'the highlight of the year for us'. While she boarded at Bute, the young Celia Johnson had a starring role in these plays. For dinner parties, writes Susan Wenham (1996), Miss Cunningham loved to place a great bowl of roses on the table, with goldfish swimming amongst the stalks. She always wore beautiful clothes. Angèle Maguire (St Paul's, 1916–22, Music Staff, 1945–80) remembered the flowing Chinese gowns she liked to wear in the evening. The drawing room overlooked the garden with its Tree of Heaven and a statue, bought by Chrystabel, of a boy gazing into a bird bath. Miss Cunningham's Siamese cat, Jayah, the Lord of Darkness, had free run of the rooms.

Her regime, though not lax, was liberal by boarding-school standards. 'No rules at Bute,' she would declare with pride. She believed in shopping as well as art, and often varied gallery visits with expeditions to High Street Kensington, where 'the height of pleasure', according to Susan Wenham, 'was a knickerbocker glory'. The older girls often went out alone on Saturday mornings but an evening expedition 'Cun' would lead herself, and sweep out into the Broadway traffic to hold two lanes to a halt while her charges crossed safely. Sunday meant Matins at St John's, Smith Square. Bute girls wore distinctive grey suits and hats in winter. In summer, they adopted the St Paul's straw hat, but were allowed to decorate it according to their taste. Meals were ample, though one favourite Sunday supper would perhaps be less popular now: boiled beef followed by blancmange or apples in suet pudding. A slightly risky tradition did develop of the younger boarders clambering up to the roof in order to perch behind the balustrades and survey the activity in the playing fields with lofty detachment. Miss Cunningham did not rigorously forbid the practice. This came to light when Miss Cunningham asked the Governors for a brand new balustrade, in order to provide proper support for the girls. The Clerk and Surveyor, clearly surprised, wondered what the girls were doing up there in the first place. Miss Cunningham, a little embarrassed, said that she had always sought to deter the girls from clambering up there by saying: 'What was the fun of doing what I even a quite old woman – could do without difficulty.' Moreover, she blamed Angela Brazil for inspiring such high jinks. This author, and others like her, had for years aroused the contempt of Miss Gray. In her assembly talks, the High Mistress had often been scathing about 'ripping yarns'. In 'Law and

Chrystabel Procter, Lady Gardner at Bute.

The statue in the garden of Bute.

Liberty' (28 October 1910) she declared: 'I should like you to make a pile of all the books that have been written about school, and a make a bonfire of them,' and in 'Friends' (16 November 1910) she characterised Angela Brazil's books as 'all bad, all vulgar, all trash'. Miss Cunningham had obviously absorbed the prevailing orthodoxy, since she told the Clerk that 'New girls who have not yet learnt our standards or brought up on Angela Brazil stories will occasionally think it an adventure to get on my roof.' The Surveyor and the Clerk responded pretty sharply by removing the entire balustrade and telling Miss Cunningham that on no account must girls be found on the roof.

As House Mistress, she was liked and admired. One of the Governors declared in 1934 that she 'has a wonderful capacity for making character out of what sometimes has seemed very poor stuff. I have this knowledge from both parents and girls'; not, one assumes, from the girls so changed. It is true that the boarders often shivered in the cold breezes that swept through open windows. Cold killed germs, said Miss Cunningham, and sitting on radiators could cause 'floating kidneys'. Open windows were par for the course in school boarding houses. Most memories of her are affectionate ones. Kate Fleming's biography of her mother, *Celia Johnson* (1991), tells us that 'Celia became very fond of Cunnie . . . Celia was never one to put much effort into keeping up with old friends, but she always remained in touch with Janet Cunningham, writing to her regularly in Ireland after her retirement.' Meriel Tower said that 'I would like to write in gratitude about many of the staff at St Paul's, but perhaps the one to whom I owe the most was Janet Cunningham.' Mary Valentine wrote that 'Miss Cunningham was interested in us as people rather than schoolgirls. '"Cun" introduced us to a wider life outside and expected us to behave as adults.'

Her relations with the Governors had their moments of tension. Some of these occurred partly because she was running, in effect, an independent business within the Mercers' property. For this reason, and through temperament, she therefore oscillated between consultation and sudden bursts of autonomous action. These caused the Surveyor and Clerk some anxieties. When she first took over the house, she embarked on improvements – buying ornamental urns, fine parquet flooring, York stone paving for the terrace – and then asked the Governors to strike the cost of all this off her rent. The Mercers were generous enough to do so but warned her not to rush into this kind of expenditure without prior permission. Then, pleased by the newly available electric goods, she bought a cooker, tea urns and toasters. To the consternation of the Surveyor in 1925, the overloaded power system was thereby destroyed and had to be completely replaced.

On the eve of the Second World War, the future of Bute did not seem to be in doubt. It is true that there were occasional worries over numbers. An original and strict rule was that Paulinas had either to live with their families or to board. Gradually, the Governors relaxed this regulation, so that some pupils were admitted to St Paul's while lodging with friends. This trend, in

Miss Cunningham's opinion, caused a falling roll-call in the early 1930s. It is more likely, however, that the Depression was to blame. Numbers fell from forty in 1928 to twenty-seven in 1933 and to twenty-five in 1934. In the next year, Miss Cunningham made a loss on the house. However, numbers seem to have moved upwards with the improving economy, and by 1937 Bute was back to its full complement of forty. In its heyday, the house did well for Miss Cunningham financially. From 1920 to 1930, her average annual net income from Bute was £389. In 1922, she drew £1,167, which was nearly as much as the £1,211 p.a. paid to the High Mistress in that year. We may compare these drawings with the £333 p.a. paid in 1929, for instance, to Miss Wenham, the Second Mistress. Accommodation, food and heating came free with the post of House Mistress. On the other hand, the average conceals wide swings in annual revenue, and Miss Cunningham bore the responsibility for those. In the opening year, she provided over £2,000 from her own capital to launch the venture, and in three years was faced with a net deficit. Nonetheless, the three years just before the war were good ones and the house was full. It was not quite accurate for Miss Cunningham to tell the Master, as she did, that Bute had not been profitable to her. The shock of war was therefore all the greater.

During the war scare of 1938, the Governors assumed that they could control school land just as they had done in the Great War. Under Home Office orders, the Borough dug trenches in the hockey field at Bute. Once the Munich Agreement of 29 September 1938 seemed to assure peace, the Surveyor wrote peremptorily to the Council, asking them to fill in the trenches: 'I have emphasised that . . . they have taken ground used for educational purposes, which is causing great inconvenience and limiting the

*Girls digging trenches for
victory in the hockey field
behind Bute.*

education and recreation of the School.' But the Council did not want to lose
the trenches: on the contrary, they wanted them ten feet deep and roofed in
concrete. The Mercers took the matter to the Home Office, which ruled that
the Borough did have to restore the grounds. The Town Clerk gave in, asking
with exaggerated courtesy what exactly was 'the thickness of top soil'
required before turfing.

Such traditional fencing between the Council and the Mercers was about
to be swept aside by the reality of war. Just before hostilities were declared
on the 3 September, the Balloon Barrage Corps asked permission to dig a
trench at Bute for their personnel. The Clerk consented, but told the Master
on 26 August 1939: 'I think I had better add that even if we had not given
them permission, they would have had to dig it just the same.' On 3
September itself, the Air Ministry formally requisitioned the grounds. Soon,
from massive concrete moorings, floated the great balloon of the barrage.
The boarding house was shut, and those Paulinas who remained on the roll
departed, 'in exile', as the High Mistress called it, for Wycombe Abbey. Next
year, the house proper was requisitioned. A bleak message of 21 July 1940,
from Staff Officer Col. C. C. Leveson-Gower reached the Mercers: 'I have to
find other offices for the Hd. Qrts. of F Zone London Defences and I shall be
obliged if you will kindly let me know where I can get the keys of Bute
House, Brook Green as it is about the size I want.'

In the midst of a global crisis, the Governors did not find it easy to deal
with Miss Cunningham. Barely had the Balloon Corps moved into the
grounds, than Janet fired off letters to the Clerk about their effrontery in
taking baths at Bute House. The evacuation from Brook Green she greeted
with asperity rather than distress. Moving to High Wycombe with the girls,
she immediately set up her own boarding arrangements, and that without
consulting the Governors. Towards the end of 1939, she had sixteen of her
boarders in one of the staff houses. Initially, Janet was buoyant: her little
establishment would be 'in the tradition of St Paul's'. Wycombe girls were,
she claimed cheerfully, 'irritated when my children rub in the superior
charms of Bute House!' She then cautioned the Governors that she was oper-
ating at a loss and would expect a subsidy. Repeatedly, the Governors
warned her that she was taking boarders without their permission and would
have to bear the losses herself.

Gradually, her spirits fell. With the Clerk, she shared her anxiety about her
precious furniture at Bute; with the Master, her worries about her bleak
future: 'there has not been much profit to me' from Bute, she wrote (27 May
1940), uneasily shifting between tenses, 'but that did not seem serious, when
there is always a workhouse to retire to, and when it was part of the great
scheme of St Paul's to help to bring . . . dignity and beauty and real values
to young things growing up to cope with a difficult world'. When it became
clear in summer 1940 that St Paul's would probably reopen at Brook Green,
she hoped that the boarding house would follow suit, otherwise some

Paulinas would drift into unsuitable lodgings. 'Two young things,' she told Sir Frank Watney in July 1940, 'have taken a flat to themselves!' Moreover, she did not want to give 'Hitler any point especially as big a one as the destruction of Bute House!' She did not seem to appreciate that the question of reopening was irrelevant while the entire site was requisitioned. The Clerk took matters in hand. Miss Cunningham was told firmly that if she continued to maintain a boarding house at Wycombe, she would do so on her own financial responsibility and that no boarding house would reopen at Bute for the duration of hostilities. As if to emphasise his point, a high explosive bomb later landed 20 yards from Bute (September 1940), shattering the windows on the western side. Miss Strudwick intervened uneasily, aware that she had complied with Miss Cunningham's boarding arrangements at Wycombe yet sensing that that an era had come to an end. She told the Governors that some of the parents with boarders had 'yielded to pressure from their daughters' and would be 'relieved' to know that there would be no St Paul's boarders during the war. The Governors, however, were generous: in the midst of wartime stringency, they granted Miss Cunningham an *ex gratia* payment of £150 p.a., though she had not been a member of the St Paul's staff. Mixing gratitude with a certain rebuke to the Master: 'I have never before administered so little money and shall have a new adventure spreading it carefully over the weeks so as to have only an occasional fireless day instead of a spell of icy existence at the end of the quarter!', she swept into what proved to be a sociable and cheerful retirement in a 'small house quite at the back of beyond – in Donegal'.

Wycombe Abbey where the school relocated to during the Second World War, taking residents of Bute with them.

The Balloon Barrage Corps occupied the playing field from 1940–1945.

St Paul's reopened on 17 September 1940, with 114 pupils in the extraordinary conditions of wartime. Where the playing field was not occupied by the Balloon Barrage Corps, it was used for growing potatoes. Many photographs show smiling Paulinas digging for victory. Since Colet Court, the prep school of St Paul's School, was requisitioned, the main building of St Paul's Girls' was, from the spring of 1941, invaded by Coletines who had some lessons and their school dinners there. When Miss Murray joined the Classics staff in 1945, she was bemused to see, above the balcony, the tops of little (boys') heads filing along the right-hand side of the Hall. 'I never saw them anywhere else,' she writes, 'so even the sex was not clear . . . I was told they were Colet (no explanation).' Opposite the school, in a pair of late Victorian houses (92–3 Brook Green) a small girls' prep school had been established in September 1932 by Miss Florence Wigg, a former Mathematics Mistress of St Paul's (November 1918 to May 1931). Her school and the Bute boarding house therefore ran concurrently for seven years. Though independent, this new school had close links with St Paul's: many of its pupils crossed Brook Green when they were 11, and Miss Wigg adopted the name 'Colet Girls' School'. By a curiously informal wartime arrangement, she allowed the Colet Court masters to use her building and in return was given classroom space at St Paul's for her pupils. In 1941, since the numbers were so low, there was plenty of space. Soon, as more Londoners were prepared to outface the Luftwaffe, the student roll rose, and St Paul's became rather cramped, with Bute under requisition, the old playroom a bomb shelter and Paulinas, Coletines and Colet girls all using the 'dark' dining room. The little ones, the editor of *Paulina* observed gravely (Spring 1946), were in constant danger from 'collision with heavy swing doors or older Paulinas, who are more often than not in a hurry'.

As early as the summer of 1943, Miss Strudwick and the Governors were discussing post-war arrangements. Miss Strudwick had been impressed with the ability of Miss Wigg's Colet Girls' School, though in the midst of war and displaced, to attract pupils. Before the war, Miss Wigg had a roll of 120; as the autumn term opened in 1939, she was left with ten. By summer 1943, however, the numbers had risen to sixty-six. It was obvious that peacetime would bring a rush of applicants. The High Mistress believed, however, that such a school was unlikely to be left alone; it would be drawn into the state system. Miss Strudwick had been studying the drive of the wartime coalition towards state control. She was also aware of the educational proposals which produced R. A. Butler's Education Act the next year. What she put to an 'Extraordinary Meeting' of the Governors on 28 August 1943, was that any school which received any government or local grant would, in the post-war world, be offering free education. Private schools, by which she meant institutions not supported by a public foundation like that of Colet, would go to the wall. Only the established public schools, like St Paul's, would survive. Therefore, to absorb Colet Girls' would be a pre-emptive move against a probable local authority takeover. Miss Strudwick's immediate motivation was to maintain a prep school which would provide 11-year-olds trained in the ways she approved: 'the assurance would be secured, in the appointment of Miss Wigg's successor, that the St Paul's tradition would be maintained and that the school would not pass into the hands of some . . . body of persons, whose aims and ideals might be very different'.

These arguments persuaded the Governors. They were convinced that, once the Butler Bill had passed, they would be in a far stronger position to maintain an existing prep school than to found a new one. At this meeting, therefore, they resolved to form a Junior School, but by absorbing the existing Colet Girls' into Bute. Old Bute, therefore, went partly by default: a prep school mattered more than boarding. To allow for a gradual takeover, Miss Wigg, on 24 June 1944, granted the Governors a seven-year lease of 92–3 Brook Green, which was her freehold. These premises had escaped the bombs, although the Brook Green studios in Dunsany Road, which the Coletines used as a Gym, had suffered some damage. She was appointed Head Mistress in that summer, but on the understanding that she would retire as soon as the new school was settled in. For goodwill, she received £1,000. Arrangements during the mid-1940s, therefore, became confusing, with the Coletines still at St Paul's Girls' School until Colet Court was derequisitioned, some Colet Girls at St Paul's and others moving into vacated rooms at Bute, others moving back to 92–3 Brook Green as the Colet staff departed. Mrs Joan Harbord, who as Miss Robinson taught physical education at St Paul's, declared that she had never worked so hard in her life, since timetables were packed and she could expect to teach boys and girls from all three institutions at any of the three sites. Elizabeth Reid (Mrs Dick, Colet Girls' 1944–7 and St Paul's, 1947–54) remembers scurrying from Brook Green to Bute and seeing Miss Wigg suddenly leap in the air as a doodle-bug exploded.

With the peace, all these problems disappeared. Despite post-war economic stringency and high tax rates, there was no lack of parents who wanted their children to enter St Paul's. By September 1945, the Junior School was full and had a waiting list. It 'could be filled twice over if we had room!' Miss Strudwick told the Clerk. Her plan was to retain 92–3 Brook Green until a wholly new Junior School could be built on the Bute site. By the autumn term of 1948, the Brook Green house had been relinquished entirely, to be converted into flats by the Aquis Property Company (the title a pun on the owner's name, Bywaters). Florence Wigg, who had served St Paul's so well by allowing it to absorb her fine prep school, retired with an *ex gratia* payment of £200, a substantial sum in May 1947. So at last she left the St Paul's scene, with one auspicing and one dropping eye: 'the work here has been a great joy to me and I give it up with much regret . . . my one desire now is to have a small house and garden in the country'. Her replacement, Miss M. Parry Okeden, was everything that parents could expect of a prep school head: Brian Lemesle Adams, the architect of the new Bute in the 1950s, describes her as 'terrific, very supportive, with a heart of gold . . . a remarkable intelligence . . . a wonderful way with children'.

Bute's educational and financial prosperity during the 1950s was at one with the optimism of that decade. It therefore startled parents and staff to hear, towards the end of 1955, that the Mercers had decided to shut the prep school. The Mercers' motives seem to have been entirely financial. They were facing an immense task: the move of St Paul's School and Colet Court across the river to Barnes. Initially, it appeared as if the girls' school might go with them. Amongst competing priorities, Bute House seemed to be dispensable. Moreover, the yield from the Foundation was collapsing in the post-war economy. The Mercers did insist that it was only with 'great reluctance' that they had resolved upon closure. Part of the problem was the dilapidation of the fabric. In the conservationist mood of the 1990s, a house like Bute would

The Hall at old Bute House

probably be saved. 1955 was different: social housing blocks were sweeping away Victorian terraces, country houses were disappearing, the South Bank had been transformed by the Festival of 1951 and the Festival Hall. Bute appeared to be an elderly and expensive house with nothing to recommend it. Indeed, some of the Governors had been wanting to demolish it for some time. Lady Evans in 1934 described it as 'labour-wasting with its large basement and long passages' and declared that any money spent on its reconstruction must 'ultimately be wasted'. Successive surveyors' reports confirmed the Governors' bleak view of the old house. With a certain relish, the Surveyor wrote in 1954 of a 'bulging rear wall', the collapsed dining room ceiling, a 'moving south main wall . . . dry rot and settlement throughout the whole fabric'. The governing body did not need to be persuaded that old Bute had come to the end of its useful life.

To move from that to closure of the whole school was, nevertheless, a move that caused surprise, not to say consternation, amongst the parents: Geoffrey Crowther told *The Times* (3 December 1955) that the decision was 'quite outrageous'. Miss Osborn appears to have raised no protest at all, even behind the scenes. The staff meeting minute book for 24 November 1955 simply records: 'Miss Osborn announced that the Junior School was to be closed in 1958.' She did, however, propose complicated arrangements for winding down the school, so that the staff could be dismissed by stages, the top three years could complete their education and the younger girls be given time to find alternative schools. This plan was based on the dubious premiss that, in a period of low unemployment (which stood at only 232,000 in 1955) and an acute shortage of teachers, good staff would be willing to remain for three years in a doomed school, with falling rolls and a dwindling common room.

In the event, a group of remarkable parents saved Bute House. A small committee, headed by Dr Pierre Turquet and including Mrs Clare Turquet, Brian Lemesle Adams, Boris Berkoff, Geoffrey Crowther, Lord and Lady Hailsham and Tony Race, were determined to raise the funds needed to build a new school and formed the St Paul's Girls' Preparatory School Company Limited to do so. The Chairman of the Governors, Commander E. W. Lane, was doubtful: if the Governors had decided that rebuilding was impossible, he said, then 'it may be that the parents might come to the same conclusion'. He was, however, happy to be proved wrong. Moreover, the Mercers were in the event extremely generous: they granted the new company a lease of the site at the peppercorn rent of £1 p.a., allowed it the use of Senior School facilities and the name 'St Paul's'. The opportunity cost incurred by the Mercers by giving Bute a free site was, and has continued to be, enormous. Armed with these assurances and a host of contacts, the new company raised capital from various sympathetic institutions and parents, especially through a system of loan notes, which allowed their 5 per cent interest to be set against school fees and therefore not liable to tax. Within two years, the company had the £45,000 needed. Brian Lemesle Adams, the architect, ingeniously fitted three storeys and an assembly hall on to a confined site: first-time visitors were surprised by what lay hidden off Luxemburg Gardens. With large windows, low ceilings and cosy classrooms, mostly facing the field and the great copper beech, his Bute House exemplified the new child-centred schools that were springing up in Scandinavia and the Netherlands. Mr Adam's watercolours of Bute House, for he is also a consummate artist, convey the sense of a protected environment.

Once the anxieties caused by the threatened closure had been allayed, many parents and staff came to feel that independence for Bute was preferable to dependence upon St Paul's. The new prep school, built swiftly in the first eight months of 1958, was formally opened on 24 October 1958, with plenty of press attention. This was (according to the *Times Educational Supplement*, 24 October 1958 and *The Times*, 20 October) the first new independent school in London since the war. Lord Hailsham, welcomed by Dr Turquet as Chairman of the new board of Governors, gave the address with a flourish: 'the little school which was condemned to death has risen like a phoenix from its ashes in less than a year. Here it is, confounding the Jeremiahs and challenging the Conformists.' Aware of his small daughter in the audience and of 'pert tots in blue checked overalls tumbling happily all over the buildings, swinging on bars, modelling clay', Lord Hailsham kept his speech very short.

Since 1958, Bute has flourished and sent many pupils to St Paul's, though through the same entrance examination as other Paulinas. The prep school

Brian Lemesle Adams's watercolour of the entrance court to new Bute House, reproduced with his kind permission.

has become known for an imaginative and liberal style of education, through 'the development of every child's natural gifts', as a journalist for *Harper's Bazaar* put it in 1968. She watched the 'junior-juniors' in their last half-hour of school: 'Some were drawing and painting . . . some were being read to . . . others were weighing things, splashing water in and out of measuring-cups.' Bute House has never had internal examinations or a scholarships board. Comments are preferred to marks. *Harpers and Queen* (November 1979) was therefore wide of the mark in warning its readers to 'Be prepared': Bute is the 'highly sought after hothouse for the intelligentsia'. Parents and staff could, however, feel gratified by the comment in the 1996 edition of Amanda Atha and Sarah Drummond's *The Good School Guide*: 'Currently the reigning London academic girls' prep school, a position which is well deserved.'

Towards the end of the millennium, Bute House completed a major building programme, with a new hall, classrooms, library, Science laboratory and Art, design and technology areas. Robert Adams, the son of Bute's architect in 1958, designed the development. A happy link with the original foundation remains: the Mercers' Company showed its confidence in the prep school's future by granting it a renewed lease for 125 years at a nominal rent.

Brian Lemesle Adams's watercolour of the new classrooms at Bute, reproduced with his kind permission.

4

HIGH MISTRESSES

Shall I not call her wise, who made me wise?

'What fear ye, brawlers? am not I your Head?
On me, me, me, the storm first breaks'

TENNYSON: *The Princess*

MISS F. R. GRAY, HEAD MISTRESS 1903–10 AND HIGH MISTRESS 1910–27

By the end of her career, Miss Frances Ralph Gray, the first High Mistress of St Paul's, had become an institution, and a rather intimidating one at that. Nicolete Binyon (the daughter of Laurence Binyon, the poet, and Keeper at the British Museum) recalled her as a 'rather remote, and magnificent figure, though small. She was commanding and had a grand manner.' Late in life, Alexandra Roudybush (*née* Brown, St Paul's 1926–9) wrote (1998) that 'Miss Gray was the only person who ever truly terrified me! She was really "awe-full" . . . I suppose it was due to her lovely, resonant voice, her beauty and her piercing, gimlet eyes.' Being sent to see Miss Gray, as many Paulinas of those days testified, was their greatest fear. Miss Gray's autobiography, *And Gladly wolde he learne and Gladly teche A Book About Learning and Teaching* (1931), written at the end of her life, enhanced her image as the remote and omniscient head. The book, though fascinating and humane, is curiously opaque on the details of her life and is peppered with sentiments about social arenas which Frances Gray rarely entered. If the ordinary English girl, wrote Miss Gray, 'is of a ducal house she is pretty certain to have been brought up very simply, to expect nothing in the way of per-

68

sonal attendance and to be ready to accept with a frank and hearty response any overtures made by the members of her form'. Almost no Paulinas were, in fact, of 'ducal' houses; perhaps Miss Gray was thinking of May, daughter of the Princess Alice and the Earl of Athlone. An anecdote with a hint of impropriety (about the mistranslation of a Greek sentence as 'It is good to love one another's brothers') in the manuscript of her book was omitted in the published version. Her memories of Plymouth High School include two accounts of her extraordinary general knowledge. On the first occasion, she was the only senior in her class to know the answer to the question, 'Who wrote *The Divine Comedy?*', which she felt compelled in honesty to give, though 'my heart beat wildly and . . . my ears burned painfully'. But: 'the Seniors were great creatures and forgave greatly'. On another occasion of 'worse luck for me', she was the only girl to know the answer to a question about Old Norse: 'After that my encyclopaedic knowledge was a firmly held Article of Belief in the Form.'

Portrait of Frances Ralph Gray by Philip de Laszlo.

Yet the image of a remote or priggish Miss Gray is one that is partial or misleading. She was in fact deeply engaged in the lives of others and was a warm and charming friend. She was also a powerful woman, significant not only to the history of this school but to the rise of professional women in England generally. If she was at once innovative and conventional, then in that she epitomised many of the pioneers of women's education and economic independence. The circumstances of her career illustrate the opportunities open to ambitious women during the late Victorian and Edwardian period. At the same time, a career usually demanded sacrifices, most obviously of the opportunity to marry. It was difficult to achieve economic independence within a family context. *Independent women*, to quote the title of Martha Vicinus's famous book (Virago, 1985) had to form female communities: university colleges, schools, sisterhoods, suffragist societies.

Frances Ralph, born 9 July 1861, was the youngest daughter of Sarah Meredith and James Gray, of Roscrea, County Tipperary. As Clerk to the Roscrea Boards of Guardians, he had a respectable salary. Frances and her father had, apparently, a happy relationship. In retirement, he joined his daughters Frances and Sarah when they took a flat in Hyde Park Mansions (not something a college lecturer and a medical student would be likely to afford now) and greatly enjoyed London life. After Frances's appointment to St Paul's, Mr Gray became a familiar figure in the school until his death in 1909, at the age of 91. The Castlecomer Latin Prize (1909) was his memorial. Her mother educated Frances at home until she was 17, when she entered Plymouth High School. For her two years there, we have to rely upon her own account in *Gladly, Gladly*, but she must have been perceived as impressive. The school supported her application to Newnham College, Cambridge. When she arrived at Newnham, it had only recently opened (1880). Frances recalled that her footsteps were left, literally, in the drying cement of the vestibule. Newnham was known for its familial atmosphere; students were known to form 'sewing bees'. Indeed, this was exactly Frances Gray's experience; barely had she set foot in college than she was asked to join a group hemming dusters. Many years later, she remarked to Elizabeth Macleod (St Paul's, 1911–14) that 'she found doing a little sewing in the evening very relaxing'. Immediately, she took to the environment: the combination of discreet freedom, hours of private study, the luxury of her own room, the friendships fostered by the celebrated cocoa-evenings. 'Later generations may smile', writes Helen Fowler in *Cambridge Women* (1996), 'at the famous evening cocoa parties, but they represented a social freedom from a possibly stifling home life.' She loved and admired A. (Anne) J. Clough, the college's first principal, and Eleanor Sidgwick, its second. To use her own expression, she was thrilled to meet famous people, such as Helen Gladstone, and to hear something of Mr Gladstone and the world of politics.

It is perhaps surprising to find that Frances's academic achievements were modest. She sat only Part I of the Classical Tripos and secured therein a Third Class. The MA later suffixed to her name was awarded as an honorary degree by Trinity College, Dublin. To be fair to Frances Gray, however, one must allow for the difficulties faced by the early generations of female Classics students at Oxford and Cambridge. Many of them had come late to Latin and Greek. Their male competitors had often had ten or more years of grammatical training at the public schools. Moreover, Newnham's philosophy at first set it apart from Girton. To Miss Emily Davies, the founder of Girton, examinations were all: women and men must enter the same arena. She therefore looked for men to teach her students. At Newnham, by contrast, Anne Clough and Eleanor Sidgwick encouraged an approach that some observers chose to call more ladylike: education for its own sake without an obsessive concern with examination performance. Much of the teaching at Newnham, therefore, was provided by the college tutors. It was by no means unusual for a Newnham undergraduate, like Frances, to take Part I only. Nonetheless, she found her deficiencies in formal training stressful enough. With intensive coaching, she gleaned enough Mathematics to struggle through the previous examination ('Little-Go') but found that the 'low cunning' of Algebra 'oppressed me with a sense of indignant helplessness'.

(Clockwise from left) Miss Maynard, Miss Gray and Miss Beloe in 1889 at Westfield College.

If late Victorian women endured many constraints upon their professional ambitions, they could also enjoy some pioneering opportunities. Even before Frances had left Newnham, she was appointed Classical Lecturer, Westfield College, University of London (October 1883). As a devout Anglican of evangelical leanings, she appealed to the Council of the college, newly founded on 'a scriptural basis, and conducted on distinctly religious principles', as Janet Sondheimer writes in *Castle Adamant*, her superb history of Westfield College. The photograph in Janet Sondheimer's book shows the grave and appealing face of Frances, then 22, standing behind her Principal, Constance Maynard of Girton. As the Dean of St Paul's said to the League on 14 December 1935, Frances Gray 'always seems to have been a pioneer . . . it is remarkable how she was always somehow in the beginning of things'. Frances entered Newnham as Sidgwick Hall opened, was the second appointee as Resident Lecturer at Westfield and was the first Head Mistress of St Katharines School, Fife. It is no coincidence that, in 1903, she was excited by the possibility of launching a new and great girls' public school.

Despite her title at Westfield, Frances Gray had to teach a variety of subjects. Some of the students, indeed, came to Westfield for no more than matriculation. Most, however, sought to benefit from the University of London's decision, in 1878, to open all of its degrees, except medicine, to women. Her expertise was still deemed to be Classics, and it was wounding to have her Latin grammar corrected on occasion by the Principal. The years that Ralph, as she was known to Constance, spent at Westfield were emotionally profound. A keen engagement in the life of her students was sustained by constant social contact: at luncheon, on outings, at dinner. The Maynard diaries (now in Queen Mary and Westfield College) show that she and Constance developed an intense friendship. Constance was both Frances Gray's intimate and instructress. She taught Frances German hymns, read her poetry while she worked, took her riding. On one occasion they went to copy a Della Robbia at the Victoria and Albert Museum. It was a stained-glass window, 'very Della Robbia', that Miss Gray hoped in 1920 to see installed at the organ end of the Great Hall at St Paul's. Constance was a little upset when Ralph chose to move out of college into her own flat, but consoled herself with frequent visits: 'a little of the new Tennyson, & then a fire, light talk, & prayers, & a little German, & to bed' (entry for 3 January 1886). Soon after Ralph's arrival at Westfield, Constance engraved nuts with their names. On All Hallow's Eve, 1884, they burned the nuts on Sarah Gray's fire: 'FRG & I blazed up beautifully, making one steady flame' (1 November 1884).

We might speculate that too much of such intimacy, especially with someone who was her senior in years and status, prompted Frances to look elsewhere. What is certain, however, is that Frances was excited by an opportunity to enter an institution almost at its creation. Her appointment as Head Mistress of St Katharines School, St Andrews, again shows that professional women enjoyed opportunities as well as facing restrictions. Miss Gray, as we should now call her, was able to move immediately to a headship, taking full responsibility for an age group that she had never taught. St Katharines was formed in October 1894 from the junior department at St Leonard's, a school already famous. Miss Gray was therefore the first head of a new school at a new site, though in an old house, 91 North Street. She was an instant success in her post. We can only be impressed by her readiness to switch from teaching adults and living in her own apartment, to taking charge of girls of 4 to 11 and acting as Senior House Mistress herself. A contemporary description (February 1894) in M. E. Bushnell's history of St Katharines conveys something of the Fife scenery enjoyed by the new Head: 'the gnarled laburnum trees in front promise a golden screen in summer . . .

St Katharines School's new building at North Street, St Andrews, where Frances Gray was Head Mistress in the 1890s.

Early Hockey team.

we find it difficult to tear ourselves away from the glorious view of the bay and snow-capped mountains seen from the back windows'.

On many occasions, Miss Gray expressed her conviction that the chief aim of education was to fit girls to be mothers and homemakers. 'I used to wish', she wrote in *Gladly, Gladly*, 'that I could preach a crusade with "Back to the Home!" as its motto so that no one to whom it was not absolutely necessary would earn the money of the State.' Her Presidential address to the League in summer 1922 echoed the sentiment: 'Every woman that is born into the world is given by God the duty of being a home maker . . . Those of you who are doing the adventurous things, as far as in you lies be home makers because in doing that you are doing the very best and highest and greatest thing that can be given to woman.' In retrospect, it seems ironic that such advice should have come from an ambitious teacher who was ready to move from one end of the country to another when a suitable pathway opened. *The Spectator's* advertisement in January 1903 for the headship of the planned St Paul's Girls' School caught her eye and prompted her application.

Miss Gray was the outstanding candidate amongst sixty-seven applicants for the post. From the sixty-seven, the Mercers chose a 'long list' of ten, all unmarried and one from St Leonard's itself. The short list of three consisted of Miss Gray and the heads of two secondary schools, Bradford High School and Durham High School. The Mercers had lofty aims from the start, for the post at St Paul's Girls' School was presented as a promotion from a high school headship. Miss Gray's appointment dated from 2 February 1903. Her stipend reflected the tradition of proprietary heads: £200 p.a. with capitation 'fees' of £3 for the first hundred pupils and £2 for the next hundred. This arrangement was to cause difficulties on her retirement and did not last beyond her term of office.

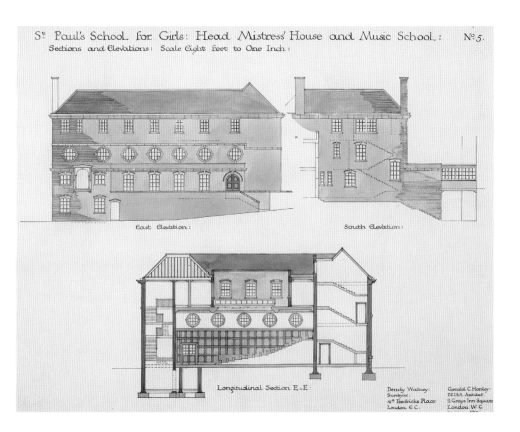

St. Paul's School for Girls: Head Mistress' House and Music School: Nº 5.
Sections and Elevations: Scale Eight feet to One Inch:

East Elevation:

South Elevation:

Longitudinal Section E-E:

Dendy Watney: Gerald C Horsley:
Surveyor: F.R.I.B.A. Architect:
4ᵗʰ Fredricks Place: 2 Grays Inn Square
London, E.C.   London W.C.

High Mistress's House and Music School, section and elevations, Gerald C. Horsley, January 1912 (Mercers' Company Archives SPGS Roll 26.8). Reproduced by courtesy of the Mercers' Company.

View of the School from Brook Green in the late 1990s.

Miss Diggory taking assembly in the Great Hall.

In early middle age, Miss Gray thus embarked upon what she saw as the great endeavour of her life, determined that 'our school cannot die . . . Nothing but a cataclysm which would lay all social order in ruins could bring us to an end.' Leaving behind her boarding house – its girls initially elated because they imagined that she could take them with her – Miss Gray moved back to London and to a house leased to her by the Mercers. For nearly a year she had the curious experience of preparing for a school which did not yet exist as a community and being obliged to meet prospective parents at the Grosvenor Hotel, whence she kept up an indefatigable correspondence with the first Chairman of the Governors, Mr John Williams Watson.

From St Katharines, Miss Gray brought three members of her staff, including Miss Hilda Wenham, the first deputy head of St Paul's Girls' School, who had not only taught at St Katharines but been a pupil of Miss Gray at Westfield, and Miss Ethel Moor, also a Westfield student and on the staff at St Katharines. Miss Gray also persuaded a pianist who had performed in St Andrews to join St Paul's as chief piano Mistress. This was Mrs Norman O'Neill, who remained in that post until 1936 and was, as *Paulina* recorded (Autumn 1947) 'with Mr Holst, the inspirer of the music of the School'. Such devotion testifies to the power and charm of Frances Gray's personality. Naturally, not all staff and students found her appealing. Between Miss Gray and Evelyn Sharp (St Paul's 1914–22, Permanent Secretary of the Ministry of Housing and Local Government 1955–66; created Baroness Sharp of Hornsey, 1966, the first woman to reach the rank of Permanent Secretary) developed a battle of wills. Evelyn, clever, ambitious and unsentimental, found Miss Gray's emotional and religious approach to education maddening. When Evelyn was called in for one her regular 'terrible wiggings', the High Mistress would hold up her arms and pray over her: she 'was that kind of showman'. To be fair to Miss Gray, Evelyn was outrageous. One Paulina recalled being egged on by her to scramble over the glass panes which roofed the swimming pool in order to fling missiles at the bathers. On one occasion, Miss Gray warned the girls about overwork and (entirely according to Evelyn) said that she had relaxed with a stroll in the fields the day before her finals (which, strictly speaking, Frances had not taken). 'I couldn't resist it – I said – "Yes *and* got a Third" out loud, so of course she heard.' Perhaps Evelyn lacked the instinct of deference. When he encountered her as a Permanent Secretary, Richard Crossman in his *Diaries* (22 October 1964) described her as 'to the Left in the sense of wanting improvement and social justice quite passionately and yet a tremendous patrician and utterly contemptuous and arrogant'. Another Paulina described Miss Gray as a 'wonderful Head Mistress but curiously fitful in likes and dislikes (the staff didn't like her at all. At least not those I knew and who talked about her after I left).'

Such critical comments are exceptional. If the surviving evidence is faithful to the reaction of her relevant contemporaries, many were her disciples

Miss Gray and Miss Wenham, who both came to St Paul's Girls' School from St Katharines.

The girls' kitchen at the school.

and most of them admired her and found her influence benign. Dodie Smith had an unhappy first year at the school, she was thought to be plain and dowdy and was mocked for her Lancashire accent. She was therefore ready to dislike Miss Gray too. On first encounter, she saw her as a 'short, sturdy woman in late middle age, with strong features . . . and white hair which suggested a barrister's wig . . . moving with such stateliness that she seemed liable to fall over backwards'. Gradually she was won over by the 'unheard of' privilege of a bathing each day, by Miss Gray's compliments over her essay writing and by her 'extreme graciousness'. In retrospect, Dodie Smith wrote that 'she again and again took trouble over me and, rebuffed by that too formidable façade, I was extremely unresponsive'. Many others needed little encouragement to be devoted to her. Katharine Sharp (Mrs Cornford) felt that she owed a lifelong debt to Miss Gray for her career advice. Inspired to try for a medical career by the memory of her father, who had been a doctor and died when she was a child of 9, Katharine found that she could not cope with Sciences at the level required. So Miss Gray guided her away from that course into an Arts degree at Westfield. Katharine spoke repeatedly of Miss Gray's 'kindness' and 'sweetness' during a difficult period in a young person's life. Similar impressions are left by the memories of Margaret Sweeten (St Paul's, 1918–28). Aged only 8, she was ushered into the High Mistress's study. The atmosphere was 'welcoming and informal' and Miss Gray was 'particularly gentle', perhaps because Margaret was a war orphan.

Chrystabel Procter, the Paulina who became a celebrated horticulturist, was another disciple. She lost her hearing in her mid-teens, when her mother was very ill and her sister Joan was rarely well. 'We were', wrote Chrystabel, 'powerfully helped through out family troubles by the Mistresses, especially Miss Gray.' Though the High Mistress was 'especially kind, helpful and understanding', she was also strict. 'School was for WORK!' Parties, plays and tennis matches were forbidden if they fell on schooldays. One observer referred to her 'wonderful aliveness', a quality difficult to recapture in memories. One Paulina (Janet Bevan, St Paul's 1911–12) wrote that 'I could never express how much I owe to her influence in my life' and another (Phoebe Coles, St Paul's 1927–34) that the 'shrine in my heart where her special memory dwells, has always been a very great inspiration to me'. Mary Huskisson, when Head Mistress of the County Girls' School, Harrow, wrote in 1926 that as a pupil she decided upon teaching and 'long cherished the hope that I might work as an Assistant under Miss Gray'. Examples of such feelings could be readily multiplied. To some Paulinas she was, of course, remote; it was difficult for a Head to be otherwise to some of her pupils. But many found her inspirational, enjoyed her reading of the scriptures and admired the snowy blouses and long silk dresses she invariably wore to school.

Though Frances Gray never set out her ideas on education in a systematic form, the lineaments of her career allow us to deduce her general views. Her reports to the Governors suggest a broad sympathy with all academic subjects and her support of games. There is little evidence that, in later life, she read poets and novelists who were then contemporary. Some of her beloved authors, though, such as Tennyson and Browning, would have seemed contemporary to someone approaching middle age by the turn of the century. As we should expect, she loved books and a touching photograph of her home in retirement shows the library given pride of place. Moreover, Janet Sondheimer, in *Castle Adamant* (1983), suggests that in her twenties, at any rate, Frances tried to encourage Westfield students to read some fashionable books, such as Matthew Arnold's *Culture and Anarchy*. Her interests lay with literature of high seriousness, classical in the original or the literary sense. This probably accounts for the extraordinary episode when she ordered a Paulina, given an Angela Brazil novel, to take the offending book with 'a pair of tongs' and place it in the kitchen stove. 'The Angela Brazil episode I well remember', wrote Daphne Inge to Mrs Brigstocke (27 February 1980), adding that it did not stop her from enjoying her cousin's books. Perhaps Angela Brazil was one of the authors whom Miss Gray attacked in a broadside that earned her more press attention than any other episode. In a speech to the Women Workers' Conference at the beginning of October 1913, she deplored 'a lack of moral fastidiousness' in literature generally available for girls and even in 'girls' clubs and Sunday schools'. Such books depicted an unreal life, their only subject was 'the love interest, and this love was a mere animal passion that should not be called love but lust'. To these lamentable novels she was ready to attribute the 'lawlessness' and 'self-gratification' of the age. Sadly, for the curious historian, she gave examples of neither names nor authors. This speech was reported in no fewer than eight national newspapers. *The Sheffield Telegraph* tried to create a stir with its headline: 'Perilous Novels . . . Protection for Girls' and added a rider to the effect that Miss F.

R. Gray, High Mistress of St Paul's Girls' School, 'demands unquestioning obedience from girls'.

Her commitment to education was profound. As a member and (from 1923 to 1925) President of the Association of Head Mistresses, she founded the Education Committee in which, wrote Ethel Strudwick in *Paulina* (December 1935), 'we have talked about Education and have been able to feel that, for an hour or so, at least, eight times a year, we could forget the restrictions that hampered our ideals, and think only of the ideals themselves'. A speech to the Association in July 1912, in which Miss Gray supported the training of teachers, reflects her concern with the status of the profession: 'There are many ways by which women now can earn their bread: let us not be afraid to bar the door of our profession against the unfit.' Although someone in her position could have been active on government committees, Miss Gray was not directly political. The nearest she seems to have come to political commitment was when she supported, with 222 co-signatories, the Association's suffragist petition of 1906 to Asquith, the Prime Minister. It is hardly significant that she was broadly Gladstonian and, said Dr Hermia Mills in 1980, 'being Irish . . . very pro-John Redmond'. When she did descend to details, the results were not very fruitful. An essay on the teaching of Classics in Sarah Burstall's *Public Schools for Girls* (1910), one of her few published items, is pedestrian. In 1909, at the Association, she proposed that a new sport for girls be devised on the grounds that hockey was too strenuous, deployed too few players, that cricket was dangerous, and that croquet would take by storm only 'curates and elderly ladies'. She appealed, therefore, for the invention of a new game which would demand moderate exertion, occupy many girls and a small space. The Association seemed to have been bemused by this proposal and especially by Miss Gray's insistence the game be 'absolutely dull as a spectacle'. Was the *Pall*

Gym class in 1904.

Mall Gazette (October 1909) quizzing her a little in reporting that her 'remarks were widely quoted, and attained considerable publicity, notwith-standing which the results up to date are entirely nil'? In passing, she did describe lacrosse as a game which, 'by reason of the free and graceful move-ments it requires, seems especially suited to the exercise of girls'.

Perhaps, as the years passed, her involvement in organisations outside the school diminished. Phyllis Seymour Holm (St Paul's, 1913–23; the close friend of Princess May) begged her to attend some meetings of the English Speaking Union and the Classical Association. Miss Gray wrote in reply, on 4 February 1922, that it was ten years since she had joined a meeting of the Classical Association and that it was impossible for her to attend some meet-ings of the ESU. It is not, she wrote, 'that I should not greatly enjoy the gatherings . . . but my own particular work must always come first'. We may assume, therefore, that her appointment to the OBE in 1926 was a general acknowledgement of her status as a leader and inspirer. There is no evidence that she contributed to precise educational policy.

The prefects in 1908, includ-ing the first Head Girl, Mary MacKenzie, standing second from right.

Where morals and behaviour were concerned she may have been, as Chrystabel Procter wrote, 'excessively modest in the Victorian sense'. It is easy to smile now at her story of Paulinas holding up each other's tunics to hide their serge knickers when they practised at the Gym bar. Miss Gray was, like many of her generation, obsessed with deportment and constantly scan-ning her pupils for signs of 'lateral curvature of the spine'. Nonetheless, she often displayed a liberality of temperament that helped to make St Paul's more progressive than many of its counterparts, if not as free as, say, a school like Bedales. She disliked the current practice of forcing children to eat food they did not like, and even encouraged a certain fussiness: 'we are not afraid to encourage the future caterers for future families to be . . . *un peu gourmet*'. Parties she loved, and Paulinas enjoyed a stream of lavish afternoon teas, dances (without men) in the Great Hall and fancy dress balls with staff and girls arrayed as figures from classical mythology and Shakespearian drama. Parties for the school's 'grandchildren', that is, for Paulinas and their offspring, were another Gray institution. Paulinas at the top of the school enjoyed something approaching indulgence. The Prefects (the whole of the then small Eighth Form) were allowed to play ping-pong in their room above the High Mistress's study, something of which she was, according to Agnes Ramsbotham (St Paul's, 1913–20; Dr Dunn), 'very toler-ant'. Agnes also found her an 'excellent and inspiring teacher . . . A splendid person indeed.'

With many, if not all, of her colleagues, she seems to have been far from remote. New appointees might find her intimidating. It is not difficult to sym-pathise with Miss Judith Bosch, who held a degree from Johannesburg and was offered in 1924 a post as a junior Mistress and who had been teaching for eight years. Miss Gray was gratified that she spoke English 'without a trace of a foreign or colonial accent' but said that she should not be placed

Miss Gray's study at Hindhead.

on the salary scale as if she had been teaching for the same time in good English schools. Miss Bosch, Miss Gray told the Governors, 'herself agrees with me': well she might! On the other hand, when Miss Bosch married two years later, her Head took the then radical step of allowing her to remain on the staff as Mrs Hobson. It did not take much to be on warm terms with the Head. Hilda Wenham, Second Mistress, went so far as to describe Miss Gray as 'racy', but, then, Miss Wenham was a quiet person. At a period when even close colleagues employed titles in addressing each other, Miss Gray readily used first names. Her correspondence with Miss Constance Flood Jones, the Art Mistress (who should, recorded a mock report of 1908, 'curtail her ardour for Woman suffrage') shows how affectionate and thoughtful Miss Gray could be to her staff. A rise in salary was accompanied by a note: 'My dear Art Mistress, I am glad to tell you that from now on your salary is to be £300 a year and long may you live to enjoy it!' Constance did occupy a special place for Frances Gray, since she played Dame Christian in the first performance of *The Masque.*

Christianity and her membership of the Church of England were fundamental to Frances Gray's mentality. This could lead her to an occasional austerity. In 1922, she was approached by a father seeking admission for his daughter. He refused to produce a birth certificate for the child because he did not, in principle, accept the legalisation of a marriage union. Miss Gray quoted a letter to her from the child's current Head Mistress, which recorded that 'We have never felt entirely happy about her . . . He is blindly conceited and rather aggressively agnostic.' The High Mistress therefore asked and gained the Governors' support in refusing the girl's application '*without* giving a reason'. When such concerns ceased to matter is not clear; perhaps they lapsed with Miss Gray. As far as accepting religious diversity went, she abided by the conscience clause of the original Scheme of 1879 which, in accordance with the Endowed Schools Act of 1869, allowed parents to remove their children from acts of worship and stated that the pupil should not thereby 'be deprived of any advantages or emoluments in either of the Schools'.

Therefore, freethinkers as well as non-Christians were welcome to attend the school and its cultural life was much enriched thereby. Nevertheless, Miss Gray clearly felt it her duty to propagate the gospel. With a hint of casuistry, she sought to distinguish between 'lifting a finger' to induce a girl from a non-religious home to attend prayers and appealing to the parents to allow her to do so. Analogy provided her argument: 'Would you put off teaching her any music until she is old enough to choose between all the instruments?' She claimed never to have made such an appeal in vain. Hermia Mills recorded otherwise. In the margin of her copy of *Gladly, Gladly*, which has been preserved by Mrs Irene Cockcroft, Hermia noted: 'She did to my Mother!' Hermia was one of Miss Gray's religious success stories, for Hermia's mother, a distinguished enamellist, was a leading member of the freethinking

Ethical Church. Miss Gray prevailed upon Hermia to accept Christianity and confirmation in the Church of England. 'I don't think', she wrote, 'anything I ever did upset my Mother more.' We catch a glimpse of Miss Gray as the fervent Anglican in her reaction to the news of Hermia's baptism and confirmation: 'I shall never forget the way she clasped me to her bosom, me being now over 20, saying "O my child, O my child".'

Retirement was not in Frances Gray's nature and her last years at the school show no sign of a slackening pace. She chose her own time (the end of the Easter term, 1927) to pass on the torch to her successor. It was natural to feel that she was irreplaceable. *The Yorkshire Post* of 22 October 1926, declared that it 'is almost impossible to imagine St Paul's Girls' School without its famous High Mistress' and to the editor of *Paulina* (March 1927) 'in one sense Miss Gray can have no successor'. Hundreds of letters flowed in from Paulinas, two issues of *Paulina* offered many tributes and the Governors passed a Resolution which was framed and sent to the High Mistress. It declared that 'The Governors desire to place on record their sincere appreciation of the eminent services which she has rendered to the cause of English education amongst women generally and to St Paul's Girls' School in particular . . . they wish to congratulate her on the brilliant achievement of her pupils and on her labours which have in so short a time placed the school in the front rank of the girls' schools in England.' Miss Gray found the Resolution 'charming' but declared that she did not deserve it and resolved to cover it with a curtain: 'and then I feel as I should like to begin all over again and do far better'. Nonetheless, she and her sister Sarah enjoyed their retirement at Churchside, Grayshott, near Hindhead. Many Paulinas came to see them, in their 'little cars' or 'in the very convenient motor bus from Haslemere station' (*Paulina*, December 1926). Miss Gray continued to attend League meetings, to correspond with Paulinas from afar, to supply reports of their activities to *Paulina*, to travel in France, Italy and elsewhere and to review books by Paulinas. Her death at home on 10 November 1935, came after a relatively brief illness. School was suspended for the day of her funeral (Wednesday 13 November 1935). At her memorial service, the order included 'St Patrick's Breastplate', which St Paul's had sung so often in her day that it was regarded as a second school hymn, Holst's setting of Cecil Spring Rice's 'I vow to thee my country' and the hymn she wrote for the attendants of the Spirit of Piety in *The Masque*: 'Oh! Let us render thanks to God above'. Thus the service paid tribute to her Irish origins, her patriotism, her faith and her long partnership with Gustav Holst, who had died the previous year.

> Dear Lady, you are weary, come within:
> The time grows near to sunset, and the air
> Grows chill for such as have not the strength to bear it.
>
> MARGARET TO DAME CHRISTIAN COLET: *The Masque*

Sketch of a Paulina of the late 1920s.

Portrait of Ethel Strudwick by James Gunn.

MISS ETHEL STRUDWICK, HIGH MISTRESS 1927–48

The second High Mistress of St Paul's had a stronger sense of humour than the first. 'I still retain a vivid picture of Miss Strudwick clinging to her seat in the Piccadilly Theatre from which gusts of uncontrollable laughter threatened to shake her', wrote Miss Margery Hirschfeld (the Head Girl of 1913 and on the Classics staff, 1918 to 1950). 'How Miss Strudwick loved to be amused, and when she was really amused her enjoyment was on an epic scale.' Visiting a Botany lesson, she 'burst out laughing' when Ursula Howells described what she was doing: 'We put the specimen under the microscope and then er – er – see what we can see.' Grisell Roy (St Paul's, 1929–37; Mrs Davies) was sent to the Head for writing with a shoe tag because she had forgotten a pen. Miss Strudwick turned her head away and said, sternly, 'Go'! But Grisell suspected later that she was dispatched quickly because Miss Strudwick was about to collapse with laughter. When the form of Miss Mollie Lehfeldt (Mathematics staff, 1930–61) wanted to have an afternoon off to see *Annie Get Your Gun*, 'she only laughed at our choice'. Recalling her Greek lessons with Miss Strudwick, Elizabeth Rawson, the classical scholar, wrote that 'my clearest memories are of her leaning back in her chair and throwing back her head to roar with laughter at our howlers'. Also uncharacteristic of Miss Gray was Ethel Strudwick's passion for the theatre. As a girl, she was a keen amateur actress. Many acquaintances later observed a theatrical element in her inflected pronunciation. The acting passed, but her passion for play-going remained. After Miss Strudwick's death, her old friend Elsa Forman picked up Ethel's 'Theatre Record', listing some 1,600 plays that she had attended.

Paulinas were inclined to think that Miss Strudwick was less engaging in appearance than Miss Gray. Certainly, the new High Mistress seemed to take little trouble over her clothes: Miss Gray's velvet shoes, silver buckles, lace fichu and full-length silk dresses gave way to shorter skirts and sensible footwear. The school adjusted and, after the first year or so, it hardly occurred to people to make sartorial comparisons. Nonetheless, Paulinas remained aware of her looks. Her colleagues sometimes called her 'striking', but the pupils could be less kind. In old age, Nicolete Gray (*née* Binyon) still remembered her as 'very plain'. Another Paulina recalls that when she and her friends arrived in their school they 'thought that she was ugly'. The girls were ready to believe that their High Mistress was unaware of her appearance, but they mistook diffidence for carelessness. In *Paulina* (1950), she wrote with wry humour of her sitting for the portrait by James Gunn: 'To be non-photogenic and at the same time acutely conscious of physical defects does not make for a good sitter. I am reminded of Bret Harte's wicked parody of *Jane Eyre*, in which he describes his heroine's one beauty, her temples, "which were like door knobs of purest porcelain" . . . a photograph catches the subject at an ineffaceable moment when she is looking her worst (passport photographs, from which I have suffered much, are an extreme case), while a portrait gives one a chance, at it were, to recover.' James Gunn had, in fact, fulfilled his commission with remarkable skill. Whereas de Laszlo's painting of Miss Gray was a romantic society portrait, Gunn's Strudwick adopts a more formal, classical mode. She gazes obliquely at the viewer. Her scholarship is suggested by a Renaissance pose, head resting pensively on her right arm, and her authority is conveyed by the fine chair and the subdued crimson of her robe.

Unlike her predecessor, Ethel came from an artistic and metropolitan background. She was born and brought up a Londoner, educated at a London school and college, and spent almost her entire her career in the capital. Her father was the artist John Melhuish Strudwick (1849–1937). Though not a household name, Strudwick was successful and his *Times* obituary described him as the 'last of the pre-Raphaelites'. 'A Golden Thread' is in the Tate Gallery, bought under the Chantry Bequest in 1885, the year it was exhibited. His 'Oh Swallow, Swallow', hung in the Royal Academy's Art Treasures of England, 1998, was commissioned by the shipping magnate George Holt. Public galleries in Cardiff, Liverpool, Manchester and Sydney hold Strudwicks. He knew some celebrated artists, especially Spencer Stanhope, with whom Studwick had his first assistantship, Burne-Jones, in whose studio he had his second assistantship, the tile designer William de Morgan and his wife Evelyn Pickering. Ethel, an only child, had a gentle but sophisticated upbringing, first in Edith Villas, Kensington and then in Bedford Park. Her school and college friend Edith Calkin remembered her as 'a quiet, dark-eyed child, with a serious expression. She nearly always wore smocked dresses, generally coloured green or terra-cotta. These colours seemed suitable, we all felt, for a painter's daughter.'

From the start, Ethel excelled academically. She attended Miss Mary Amelia Bennett's new Queen Elizabeth School in Kensington, an establishment which was, ironically, to be destroyed by the success of St Paul's. 'Our star pupils who positively never erred,' wrote M. V. Hughes in *A London Girl of the 1880s*, 'such as Ethel Strudwick and Edith Calkin, gave us so much trouble to praise sufficiently without sounding fulsome, that we were positively grateful to Violet Gask, another champion, of whom we could always say that her writing needed care'. From Queen Elizabeth's school, Ethel won the Reid scholarship (given for outstanding performance in the Oxford Senior Local Examinations) to Bedford College, where she took classical honours, second class. After a spell at the Laurels, a school in Rugby, she was invited back to Bedford. While on the staff as Assistant in Greek, she took the MA degree (1904), in which she was awarded a Special Distinction by the examiners. Then she moved through the ranks, as Assistant Lecturer in Greek, Lecturer in Latin and (1909–13) Head of Department. One wonders why she did not engage in original research and try to publish. Perhaps, as an aca-

City of London School for Girls, Carmelite Street, where Miss Strudwick taught from 1913 to 1927.

demic in a woman's college, she felt inhibited, though a similar appointment did not deter Kathleen Kenyon, the archaeologist, and someone of Miss Strudwick's generation, from publishing a great deal. Possibly Ethel preferred to concentrate on teaching. She was, indeed, a great success as a lecturer. 'Outstanding', wrote one of her pupils; 'enthralling', said another. Freya Stark, the travel writer, left a tribute in *Traveller's Prelude* (1950) to Miss Strudwick: 'I entered Bedford College as a day student . . . my formal, elaborate manner made me unpopular . . . I was much happier with my teachers, and particularly devoted to Miss Strudwick, who taught Latin in an inspired way so that the loveliness of the second book of the *Aeneid*, the silent ships moving out from Tenedos in the moonlight, are still woven about her memory.'

Commitment to teaching might explain her move, in 1913, to the City of London School for Girls, which had opened ten years before St Paul's. After a long and impressive tenure of that office, she applied for the post of High Mistress of St Paul's. The records of the Mercers' Company show how professionally the Governors set about the appointment. A first draft of the advertisement, which ran: 'ladies desiring of being candidates' was struck out by one Governor as too quaint and replaced with the single word 'candidates'. Miss Gray's offer to join the discussions and to give informal advice was firmly refused. During the selection process, the candidates' curricula vitae were properly printed as booklets for distribution. The Victorian system of basing the Head's salary on capitation, that is, so much per pupil, was abandoned. Frances Gray had accepted a basic salary of £200 p.a., with £3 for each entrant up to the hundredth and £2 for each one after that. She had, in fact, taken in pupils much more slowly than her financial interests dictated. In practice, her income by 1918 had settled at £1,200 p.a., and she received no inflationary increase between the end of the war and her retirement. The post was advertised in October 1926 at £1,000 to £1,200 p.a., Miss Strudwick being appointed on the latter figure and retiring on £1,450 p.a. To provide some comparison: her deputy received £500 and a full-time Mistress about £390. Ethel was chosen from a strong field of forty-six applicants, most of whom were already Head Mistresses. One candidate, however, seems to have mistaken the school, since her application dwelt on the 'Basket weaving, Raffia work and Canvas, also Cardboard modelling' that she had introduced as Head of her current institution. Ethel's references spoke of her 'power of management' and 'splendid spirit'.

'There are very few people one can picture at St Paul's,' wrote Beatrice Sparks of Cheltenham Ladies' College, 'but Miss Strudwick is one of them.' Miss Sparks's confidence in Ethel was justified. At St Paul's, she was an instant and enduring success. One of her former staff testifies that 'I have worked under six heads, and Miss Strudwick was, on all counts, far and away the best.' She continued to teach and took over half a timetable: eighteen or so periods a week. Indeed, she expressed surprise, on her retirement, to find that her successor wished to reduce her teaching to twelve periods. Perhaps

Swimming team.

Tennis team of 1932 with Miss Lewis.

the scholarship classes appreciated her more than the junior girls. A Paulina of the war years remembers Miss Strudwick's mode of Scripture teaching: to ask the Form to read, in alphabetical order, a verse each. Each sensible Paulina estimated the time it would take to reach her verse and busied herself with other work underneath the desk until the appropriate moment. Other memories are at variance with this. Elizabeth Rawson wrote that in 'her hands the Old Testament suddenly revealed itself as the history of a real race . . . I have continually to relearn my Greek irregular verbs; but I never shall forget Miss Strudwick'. Mary Corless, Head Girl and in the scholarship class, found her teaching of the *Iliad* 'wonderful' – and curiously associated with the rich, red pattern of the carpet in her office. Always the classicist, Miss Strudwick deplored the pronunciation of 'Eros' so that its first syllable rhymed with 'ear', and told the Governors in February 1938 that Miss Haydock unfortunately had broken her *tendo Achillis*.

She was also exceptionally thoughtful towards her subordinates. One Paulina, whose time crossed the Gray-Strudwick boundaries, said that she treated the Prefects (then the Eighth Form) as junior colleagues and believed that, whereas Miss Gray had a possessive nature, her successor 'never tried to possess anybody'. Mrs Stella Chapman, writing to Mrs Brigstocke on 4 October 1985, characterised her as this 'warm and radiant woman, so distinguished and yet caring about the smallest detail in other people's lives'. Uniquely amongst the St Paul's High Mistresses, she did not enter the staff room without warning; she would knock, put her head round the door and say: 'May I come in?' She may have been influenced by the tradition of a few boys' schools in which the Head Master visits the common room only by invitation. Perhaps she was following her innate awareness of other people's sensibilities. Her secretaries were devoted to her, despite the list of stringent requirements she read to the School Secretaries Conference of 1934 for the

Perfect Secretary: 'Allow for Artistic Temperament'; 'Able to produce small sums of money'; 'Possess a bracing quality, not too sympathetic to her Head.' When many of her colleagues were dismissed in 1940 because of the wartime collapse in school numbers, she was distressed. Indeed, she wrote formally, but privately, to the Governors to ask for a £200 reduction in her salary. When this request was refused, she told the Clerk (31 March 1941) that 'I will give it to the School in other ways; many will occur to me.' In her penultimate year she moved against tradition by appointing a married teacher as a junior Form Mistress, telling the Clerk (24 January 1947): 'She is, I am glad (though I ought perhaps to regret!) a married woman.'

Many of those who sat in her lessons or assemblies testify to her distinctive voice: rather deep and unusually modulated for the period. Perhaps she was influenced by the late Victorian and Edwardian actors, such as Forbes Robinson and Ellen Terry, whom she admired. Miss Murray writes perceptively: 'I never heard Miss Strudwick use the archaism "What think you of" (though her father had done) but compare its rhythm with "What do you think about" and you have a clue to the quality of the difference between hers and the run-of-mill way of speaking.' A report of the Classical Society in *Paulina*, March 1928, refers to her 'most beautiful reading' of some Latin lyrics. Professor Ruth Bowden recalled in 1995 her 'beautiful speaking voice. When she read the minor prophets or the imprecatory psalms, there was fire and brimstone.' By example, she sought to maintain a tradition of reading which, she declared at Speech Day, 29 July 1930, 'seems to be a lost art, and I venture to think that a very great pity. Many of the older generation owe their love of beautiful literature to the memory of it beautifully read to them when they were children.' Her voice carries across in her letters to the Governors, more emphatic than is usual in correspondence between a Head and her masters. When new light fittings were installed over the summer of 1938, she wrote to the Clerk, Captain Featherstone:

> I am bound to tell you that the new fittings are unanimously condemned as being in the opinion of all of us very ugly and disfiguring to the beauty of the school. The large white china balloons are neither beautiful nor impressive, and the effect of the fittings in the entrance hall is that of a number of pudding basins . . . I do feel that I might have been consulted on the subject of these fittings, and not left to look at them when they were up.

The Surveyor was pained: 'a little unkind', he responded.

Like her later successors Alison Munro and Heather Brigstocke, Ethel Strudwick took on an array of public commitments. Some reflected her academic ties: she was a member of the University of London Senate for thirty-one years and served on the Council of Westfield College for twenty. Other duties flowed from her position as head of a leading school. As she retired, she joined the Council of the Girls' Public Day School Trust. For two years, 1931–3, she was President of the Association of Head Mistresses and fought earnestly against any curtailment of educational grants. From 1933 to 1939 she chaired the Head Mistresses' Employment Committee, and she was first President of the British Federation of Business and Professional Women. After the war, she sat on the committee formed to consider the admission of women to the diplomatic service. For one so deeply a Londoner, it was gratifying to become, in 1934, a Trustee of the London Museum. Her Liberalism was both intellectual and practical, unswerving despite the party's collapse in the 1924 and successive General Elections. Ethel Strudwick saw English Liberalism as humane: it cared for society but gave scope to individual expression. For decades a stalwart of the Barnes Liberal Association, she replaced Lady Layton as President of the Women's Liberal Federation the year after retirement from St Paul's and worked until a few weeks of her death. Ethel Strudwick's public rôle was recognised by her appointment in 1936 to the OBE (raised in 1948 to the CBE), in the only honours list granted by Edward VIII in his brief reign.

Princess Alice, who opened the new science block in 1933.

Not given to public controversy, she did enter the lists with the BBC. This devotee of the living voice, in acting, reading or declamation, could not adjust to the art of the broadcast. Her concerns mirror a later generation's preoccupation with the effect of television upon patterns of learning. In *The Head Mistress Speaks*, published by Kegan Paul in 1937, she expressed her anxieties over homework done 'to the accompaniment of the wireless'. This habit, she argued, disrupted concentration and induced passivity. 'A world of listeners and watchers is not to my mind one which is likely to produce that informed, intelligent and active democracy on which the hope of the future depends.' Some years later, she wrote to the *Daily Telegraph* (22 January 1945) that 'the BBC has done a lot of harm to the family life of growing children'. For television, she felt only antipathy. Presumably it was with a repressed disapproval that she asked the Governors to authorise the purchase of the school's first gramophone in 1935 and its first wireless the year after.

Responsibilities within and without school did not inhibit her playgoing, or holidays abroad, especially in France, Italy and Holland. She was a keen walker and liked to cover 30 miles on a good day. Late in life, she decided to learn the piano. When some older girls began Hebrew with a visiting teacher, Miss Strudwick came to learn too. Her combination of artistic, political and intellectual interests helped to shape the culture of the school: liberal, curious and not obsessed with discipline. When Nicolete Binyon launched the avant-garde 'Group', which visited art galleries and saw modern plays, Miss Strudwick was completely supportive. After three years of her persuasion, the Governors agreed in 1938 to make 'Greek and country' dancing part of the formal curriculum. The High Mistress liked to say that she believed in three rules only: not to run in school, not to chatter in the streets and not to disturb others. It was natural for her to maintain a balance

Princess Alice (right) and her daughter May (left), who was a Paulina, in 1930.

between the Sciences and humanities, and the Science Block of 1933 was her achievement. As early as 1928, a year after her appointment, she asked the Governors to consider the building of a Science centre as 'our most urgent need'. This was fulfilled five years later, when the new building was opened (27 June 1933) by HRH Princess Alice, a granddaughter of Queen Victoria and mother of May, the only member of the royal family to have attended St Paul's.

By the time the Governors had absorbed the cost of the Science building (£23,000) and were ready to consider other plans, Miss Strudwick was facing the greatest challenge of her career: guiding the school through the Second World War. Well before the outbreak of hostilities, the Governors were contemplating options. The Czechoslovakian crisis of September 1938 had alarmed parents to such a degree that only five, instead of the usual sixty or seventy, sat the October entrance examination. Miss Strudwick put her views to the Governors. The school had, she wrote, 'a place among the girls' public schools of England which may, without exaggeration, be described as outstanding'. To close for the duration of a war would be disastrous, not merely for St Paul's as an institution but because closure would mean surrender to 'the doctrine that in a time of emergency education must be among the first casualties'. What she really wanted was for the whole school to move to the country. In this aim, she was fiercely supported by Lady Balfour, who confided to Miss Strudwick (6 February 1939) that she 'was astonished to learn that the Governors had not made arrangements to transfer the school as a whole, complete with staff'. Other parents urged the Master to adopt this policy: the Governors held, wrote one, 'the sacred trust of carrying on the ideals and work of the school whether in peace or war'. When the Governors stated that an independent move was not possible, Miss Strudwick prepared for a compromise by contacting the Heads of various schools, including the Godolphin School, Salisbury, Sherborne Girls', St Catherine's, Bramley and Wycombe Abbey to ascertain the possibility of accommodation there. It was with the last that the final arrangements were made. The Governors broadly endorsed this policy, while maintaining a brave show of confidence in the future: deciding upon the Library extension and a new 'Tasmanian oak' floor for the Gymnasium.

Britain and France declared war on Germany on 3 September 1939. Those on the diminished school roll were evacuated to High Wycombe. Of the 183 girls there, eighty-one were in the Abbey school proper, others in Miss Cunningham's temporary boarding house and the rest in various billets of the town. Miss Strudwick and the Governors were grateful to Wycombe for its hospitality. The ensuing months were, nonetheless, very difficult for her, as 'a shepherd without her flock', as one friend put it. Junior girls joined the Wycombe classes, and some of the St Paul's staff taught Wycombe and St Paul's girls together. Senior girls formed classes separate from the Wycombe girls.

The High Mistress oversaw the complicated arrangements. Every evening of term time, including the winter nights of 1939–40, saw Miss Strudwick walking down the slopes to the town, conducting the girls to their host billets, and then tramping back up the hill to the school. Meanwhile, the Governors seemed to be facing a sheer wall financially. Simultaneously, they were paying all the staff salaries, handing over the tuition fees of the fee-paying girls to Wycombe, supplying the tuition fees of the Foundation Scholars and maintaining the Brook Green site, all on a reduced roll of some 180.

Parental opinion was divided not only on the question of a return to Brook Green but on keeping Paulinas in Britain altogether. One mother wrote to a fellow parent on 28 May 1940: 'I am not a defeatist by any means, but we have to face facts. As things now stand, an invasion of England is no longer outside the range of possibility. . . I suggest that the parents should take direct action. They should withdraw their girls, engage some responsible teachers to take them out to Canada.' Her correspondent, Professor Finch of Imperial College, entirely opposed her views, arguing that 'the issue is now joined for every man, woman and child in Britain, and . . . the only proper thing to do is for us all – without any privileged exceptions whatever – to stand by our country and face it out'. Parental views on the issue of reopening were formally canvassed by the High Mistress and provided a majority (155:44) in favour of a return to Brook Green. With that, and driven by financial need, the Governors ordered the school to be opened on 1 May 1940 but with a much reduced staff. The playroom downstairs was turned into a high-quality bomb shelter, with air-conditioning, bunks and a first-aid room. When the autumn term began, only sixty-five Paulinas gathered in the Great Hall. Numbers did rapidly glide upwards, as Paulinas returned from Wycombe as elsewhere. On 17 September 1941, 114 girls were on the roll; about 300 by 1943. So the returning school caught the 'big Blitz' of September 1940 to May 1941, the 'little Blitz' of 1944 and the innumerable raids between. The swimming baths and Bute were requisitioned and the Science Block was closed for the first two years. There were no Speech Days between 1939 and 1943.

Within these extraordinary conditions, Miss Strudwick preserved the routines of teaching and learning. After the fire-bombing of 15 November 1940, parts of the building were flooded and much of the roof was under tarpaulin. The school gates and railings disappeared in February 1942, leaving the grounds 'terribly exposed to marauders', as Miss Strudwick told the Surveyor (9 June 1944). The High Mistress almost never left the site, joining fire-watching, teaching in the shelters. To relieve the pressure on her staff, she begged the Mercers for some help with fire-watching, but nobody could be spared. During the winters the shelter could become very cold: 'difficult to teach in such an atmosphere,' was her understatement in a freezing mid-January to the Mercers. Our General and Higher School Examinations, as she calmly

Bomb damage in Blythe Road, Hammersmith, 1944.

Portrait of Margaret Osborn by Ruskin Spear.

The Tennis team, winners of the Middlesex Schools' Championship in 1959.

said at Speech Day, on 19 December 1944, 'written under the constant rumblings of flying-bombs, were quite satisfactory in their results'. She even invited the Ministry of Education to carry out an inspection of the school. By 1945, the anxious tone of her letters had given way to a justifiable note of triumph. As soon as peace seemed imminent, both the planned Junior School and St Paul's developed long waiting lists. 'Not a day passes,' she wrote to the Governors on 30 May 1945, 'without letters begging for admission for their daughters.' 'For the wartime generation of Paulinas,' wrote Elspeth Harris, the Head Girl of 1941–2, 'Miss Strudwick stands as a bulwark against all that was uncertain, hazardous and fearful, and few of us will forget her voice ringing out again in the Great Hall at Morning Prayers when we returned, a tiny band, to Brook Green.'

MISS MARGARET OSBORN, HIGH MISTRESS 1948–63

Once she had guided St Paul's into the post-war years, Miss Strudwick left for a happy and busy, if brief, retirement. The wheel had turned, and it was considered as difficult to replace her as it had been to find an appropriate successor to Miss Gray. Advertisements, placed in September 1947, attracted a rather light response: only twenty-two applicants. Even the High Mistressship of St Paul's seemed to be affected by the post-war shortage of professionals. Moreover, two of the candidates appear to have misjudged their referees. The testimonial of one stated that 'she is not in the slightest suitable for the post of High Mistress at St Paul's'. The other attracted the comment that she is 'not of the calibre to be a worthy successor to Miss Gray or Miss Strudwick'. Four were married, and it was not clear that the Governors were yet ready to appoint a married woman. In the event, the Governors chose someone with unimpeachable academic and professional credentials.

Miss Margaret Osborn was aged 42 when she became High Mistress (the same age as Frances Gray on her appointment): slim, elegant and poised. A clergyman's daughter and a Scot, she had attended St Katharines, the prep school where Miss Gray had been head, and the adjoining St Leonard's, the grand public school of St Andrews. After reading Greats at St Hugh's College, Oxford (1925–9), where her friend Marjorie Reeves remembered her as 'very scholarly and thoughtful', she had been awarded the Henry Pelham Studentship. This allowed her to study at the British School at Rome for nearly a year. Returning to England, she attended the Cambridge Training College for Women, a preparation for teaching her predecessors had not considered necessary. Her career marked the stages of professional advancement with textbook precision: two years at St Mary and St Anne, Abbot's Bromley, ten years at the King Edward VI High School for Girls, Birmingham, five years as Head of St George's School for Girls, Edinburgh, then (May 1948) to

St Paul's. In a remarkable comment on the relative stability of prices since the 1920s, the salary range of £1,000 to £1,300 was similar to that offered in 1926. Four Heads who applied were, however, on lower salaries than that and without houses. Moreover, the salary laid down by the 1945 Burnham Scale for a Head Mistress of a school with over 500 pupils was £620.

In personality, Margaret Osborn was quite different from Miss Strudwick. The new High Mistress was reticent in manner. Some people found her diffident, even shy, though to Paulinas she was formidable enough. She had a good circle of friends, and could write from her retirement cottage in Chipping Campden that 'Letters and news take first place in the day, and I welcome many visitors here.' Conversation with her was not, however, always easy. Some teachers, especially the younger ones, found it an ordeal to sit next to her at what was then the formal luncheon. 'Miss Osborn was often distraite,' says one of her staff, 'she might scarcely seem to be listening and then suddenly offer a surprising interrogation, such as "Do you like the sea?"' She did not maintain Ethel Strudwick's range of contacts in public life. Not everyone found her clearly audible in the Great Hall, where microphones were not installed until 1989. Public speaking was something of an ordeal to her, if not a grave one. When asked to be the school's birthday speaker in 1969, she refused immediately: 'Honestly I cannot face it.' Two years later, she was invited again, but resisted Mrs Munro's plea: 'Do say "yes".' When she retired, Miss Osborn wrote to Mrs Munro on 29 May 1967: 'I found that I was giving up public speaking without regret, for it never really came easily to me, not even in the service of the school.'

When Miss Osborn arrived in Brook Green, her elderly parents came with her. For Margaret's entire term of office, her mother was a presence in the school, for she was to reach her centenary in 1969. Mrs Osborn wrote so long and elaborate a letter of thanks to the Queen in response to the formal congratulations upon her centenary that the Duke of Edinburgh replied in person. Whereas Miss Osborn was tall ('long and thin', to some rather impolite entrance candidates) her mother was diminutive, with snowy hair and rosy cheeks. 'All Paulinas were lambs to her', said Margaret, and Mrs Osborn became a familiar figure at school, often attending concerts and sometimes coming to Prayers. They had a happy relationship, though someone who knew Miss Osborn well believes that she was emotionally dominated by her mother and would have been more adventurous if the two had not lived in propinquity. Because she believed that she ought to spend holidays with her parents, Miss Osborn had travelled little since her visit to Rome. It was her need to look after Mrs Osborn which the High Mistress gave to the staff as the chief reason for her early retirement (though she also told the Governors that she 'wished to make way for someone younger'). To care for an aged parent was to Miss Osborn a duty she took for granted. A devout Christian, she was deeply concerned with the St Paul's charities in Stepney, of which more in the next chapter.

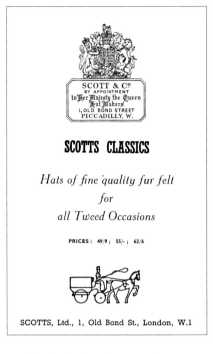

*Typical advertisement in
Paulina, 1957.*

The school's gates were requisitioned during the War and were temporarily replaced by these rather unattractive ones, later removed at the request of Miss Osborn.

As High Mistress, she was dedication itself. Her correspondence with the Mercers and her Bursar shows her to have been an adept in routine administration. Two complicated matters – the introduction of assisted places and the change of staff pensions from the St Paul's to the state scheme – generated a vast body of paperwork which she controlled perfectly. In all this, she paid little attention to her own pension arrangements. 'I always say that the girls' school runs on oiled wheels,' wrote one Chairman of the Governors. Parents and staff appreciated her unvarying courtesy. As a writer, she had a light and pleasant touch; her Governors' Day speeches read easily. 'The years which the locust have eaten,' she said at her first Speech Day, 'press heavily upon our national economy. Never was a time when the flowers of scholarship, and a gracious way of life, needed to be more strenuously cherished.' Her script was habitually neat and, in her markbooks, almost copperplate.

Whether she should have been more vigorous or had a precise programme of school development is a matter of opinion. Certainly, she could be unassertive to the point of meekness. When she began as High Mistress, Governors and parents often wrote to her as 'Miss Osborne'. Never were they corrected. Fifteen years later, she was still receiving some letters from Mercers' Hall addressed to 'Miss Osborne'. More significantly, she seemed to have no independent opinion on two matters of great moment to St Paul's: the proposal that the girls' school should accompany St Paul's to Barnes and the closure of Bute House. At the least, one would have expected her to have argued the merits of the Brook Green site and its splendid buildings. To be fair, perhaps she sensed that to move the girls' school was not being seriously considered and took the view that there was no point taking a hammer to an idea floated for discussion.

Though without Ethel Strudwick's commitment to party politics, Miss Osborn was ready to support certain broad political developments. In 1952, some Governors objected to Paulina participation in the Council for Education in World Citizenship, which had been founded by Professor Gilbert Murray and came under the aegis of the United Nations. When Miss Osborn asked whether St Paul's could host the next conference, the Chairman of the Governors told her he could not give his consent. It was claimed that the Council was being infiltrated by 'Bevanite MPs' and that questioners at some meetings (not Paulinas) were 'socialist and communist inspired'. Aneurin Bevan, who had resigned as Minister of Labour the previous year, was then turning the left wing of the party against Hugh Gaitskell. One of the conference speakers was to be Kingsley Martin, editor of the mildly left-wing *New Statesman*. Miss Osborn did protest. At such conferences, she argued, some left-wing views were bound to be heard. They should not be 'driven underground'. 'An effective Chairman and balanced speakers are the only remedy,' she wrote on 19 March 1952 (betraying her own political position by the last word), 'it seems to me almost impossible in the kind of world we live in nowadays for young people not to burn their fingers in politics.' The Chairman seems to have been appeased. Although the High Mistress thought it wise to abandon the plan to hold the conference at St Paul's (so that, as the *Evening Standard* gleefully reported on 28 February 1952, 'after accusations of left-wing bias the Governors decided the conference must meet elsewhere'), Paulinas remained active members of the CEWC. Successive editions of the school magazine carried reports of their activities, educational and charitable beyond reproach: supporting a refugee family in Germany, attending conferences on the Colombo Plan, visiting UN sites in Italy and Yugoslavia. There was even a dance on a Thames river boat. Whether Bevanite MPs were present too, history does not record.

On the issue of direct-grant status, Miss Osborn adopted a position which was almost radical. Under the 1944 Education Act and linked legislation, approved schools could receive funding direct from the Ministry of Education (£45 per pupil in London in 1957) so long as they abided by certain conditions, the chief of which was that 25 per cent of the places each year should be offered to pupils who had previously been attending a state school. In an adroit memorandum (30 January 1957), the High Mistress recommended direct-grant status for St Paul's. Her arguments were threefold. First, she pointed out that Local Education Authorities of Middlesex and Surrey were warning independent schools (a term just becoming current) that assisted places were too expensive to maintain. Once the baby boom of the post-war decade had passed, and once more state school buildings had gone up, assisted places would disappear. Second, she welcomed an increased intake from primary schools, because St Paul's reputation and competition from several Education Authorities would ensure a high calibre of candidates. Third, the economic pressure to increase fees would damage the school's 'broad base of scholarship' and thereby mean that St Paul's would 'lose more real independence from the educational point of view than by accepting a limited degree of control from the centre'. These worries were largely unfounded: LEA places did continue until taken over by the new assisted places scheme of the 1980s. The economic profile of St Paul's parents was not transformed by changing fee levels. Nevertheless, it is intriguing to see a High Mistress of the 1950s advising her Governors to abandon the independent status of St Paul's. She was confident that the school would retain, as she wrote to Mrs Brigstocke on 6 September 1974, 'an inner dynamic of its own, which would always make for both change and stability as required'.

As far as the school's development is concerned, she had been a Head Mistress during the war, and was schooled to expected strict economy. The year 1947, when she applied for the St Paul's headship, was that of the big freeze, the big thaw and national anxiety about overspending. Soon after her arrival, she asked for a fence to protect her front garden. Shocked to discover this was to cost £48, she abandoned her request. Contemporary Governors might smile to find Miss Osborn being chided, on one occasion, for being 'too careful' in expenditure. Nevertheless, as one can gather from the bursar-

The School's Jubilee celebration banquet at the Connaught Rooms.

Sketch of a Paulina in 1912 from the St Paul's Book *of 1925.*

Susan Mock (Mrs Shilling) with Anne Pasmore and Caroline Fleming performaing Everyman, *1956.*

ial correspondence and records of the Governors' meetings, more happened than appeared on the surface. Because of the war and post-war rationing, maintenance had been reduced to a minimum, and everything demanded attention: elderly boilers, peeling paintwork, the roof, window frames, the restoration of the swimming bath, the reinstatement of the flag pole. Not until 1956 did she ask for the High Mistress's house to be redecorated. Sometimes, she could be firm enough. For decades, senior Paulinas had used 'the Studio leads', the flat roof just beyond what are now the Classics rooms, for debating and public meeting. When it leaked (1955), the Surveyor asked the High Mistress to put the leads out of bounds. Miss Osborn urged him to order its immediate repair, since 'the use of this flat roof in the summer is a much valued privilege'. It was she who took the initiative over the replacement of the school gates. After their requisition, the school had been protected by an unpleasant mesh fencing. As part of the Jubilee commemorations, and helped by Miss Osborn, a group of Paulinas raised some £500 towards the total cost of £2,900. The Governors generously supplied the rest. From 1956, the school's appearance was restored by splendid new gates and railings in traditional wrought iron.

Within Miss Osborn's term of office fell the school's Jubilee, 1954. Various celebrations, from which post-war austerity seemed at last to be fading, were beautifully organised by Miss Osborn and her inexhaustible team. A volume of short essays on St Paul's past and present was edited by Miss Hirschfeld. This was a fine volume, but economically produced compared with the large and handsome *St Paul's Book* of 1925, bound in paper vellum. Unfortunately, one Paulina, Eileen Roberston (Mrs Foster) did take against its illustrations: 'I was one of the original 53, and can assure you that no one . . . looked anything like so dreadful as we are depicted. No one ever wore their knickers below their knees, except when the elastic broke! Also we had not all got elephantiasis . . . [sic].' Miss Osborn's closing words to the 1954 collection show her felicitous turn of phrase. 'An Epilogue of this kind', she wrote, 'contains a prologue to the future. Unlike the individual, a school greets advancing years with triumph, and makes haste to wear the mantle of antiquity . . . It was our flying start which was remarkable, whose impetus is with us yet.' On the Saturday before the school's official birthday on 19 January, a service at St Paul's, attended by a congregation of over 2,000, was followed by a banquet in the Connaught Rooms. In an extraordinary reunion, some 800 Paulinas were there. Miss Strudwick, in what must have been one of her last attendances at a school occasion, proposed the toast to the League. With luncheon, guests were offered not only white burgundy but, this being the 1950s, 'of course, cigarettes'. Nine coaches were needed to take the guests from the West End to the school for an evening entertainment, courtesy of some leading musical names amongst Paulinas and of Celia Johnson, who gave a recital. In the afternoon of 19 January, school was suspended for a great party and a staff revue, in which Miss Osborn appeared in an unlikely

guise as Landseer's Monarch of the Glen. 'I shall always remember that day, if only by the sore throat I got by cheering so much,' Vivette Luttrell told *Paulina*. 'I was not born when the School was founded, but I hope to see its hundredth anniversary, especially if it is as good as the fiftieth.' Caroline Crawley wrote to the High Mistress that 'the revue was marvellous. Long life to St Paul's and its Monarch of the Glen!' And for Jane Chaloner: 'If all future Jubilees are going to be like this one, I shall try to be present, even if only as a ghost.'

Throughout the preparations for the school's third royal visit, and on the day proper, 18 March 1954, Miss Osborn was calmness itself. The Queen Mother visited lessons, the Art rooms and the swimming pool ('that is a wonderful thing to have,' she said). Paulinas and teachers did their best to carry on normally as they kept a covert eye on the door about to open for Her Majesty. But the warmth of her personality dispelled nervousness. She had already told Miss Osborn that 'the chief wish of Her Majesty will be to be able to talk to the staff and the girls, and in these circumstances formalities should be reduced to a minimum'. Time was spared for a visit to the netball courts, where, as Miss Osborn said on Speech Day, the ball tumbled out from amongst the curtseying team and 'dismally and somewhat disrespectfully in the momentary silence trundled its leathery person towards the object of our regard'. After dropping in on the kitchen staff, a moment wonderfully caught on camera, the Queen Mother went to the Great Hall for a performance of *The Masque* music. The High Mistress had told the girls that when the Queen Mother entered the Hall, they should be silent 'but smile!' They did not have to be encouraged to do that. The music over, the Queen Mother followed

Pauline tradition and called upon Bishop Woodward, officiating, to grant a remedy, a holiday. As fifty years earlier, the assent to this was greeted with 'tumultuous applause'. In the send-off, Paulinas lined Brook Green, armed with cameras, for Captain Oliver Dawnay, Her Majesty's Private Secretary, had written that she 'will be delighted if the girls like to take their own photographs, with their Brownies, and there need be no restrictions'.

After nearly sixteen years in office, Miss Osborn retired to Roseglen Cottage in Chipping Campden. Here, avoiding public commitments, she looked after her garden, supported her parish church and enjoyed the Cotswolds: 'I have been rediscovering the beauties of one of the loveliest parts of rural England,' she wrote to Paulina in 1964. 'It is wonderful how much unspoiled upland and woodland there is to be found by way of the narrow lanes that lead off the motorways, and the stillness is startling.' She did, however, assiduously attend meetings of the League and of the Stepney charity. Towards the end of her life, she moved to a home near Woodstock in Oxfordshire. A treasured possession that remained with her until the end was the album of school photographs compiled for her by the staff and girls in 1963. 'I am really the one in debt to St Paul's and the outstanding teaching staff we had', she told Mrs Brigstocke in 1984. 'They were strenuously happy years for me, and the school keeps its lustre, as ever.' After her death, the staff of 1985 learned that she had left a substantial sum to them for the decoration and furnishing of the new common room.

MRS ALISON MUNRO, HIGH MISTRESS 1964–74

However much appreciated Miss Osborn may have been for her dedication to the school, the Governors seized the opportunity of her retirement to choose a different type of High Mistress. When considering Mrs Munro's application, one of the Mercers said that St Paul's was in danger of becoming 'an academically distinguished museum'. This comment may have been rather unfair to the energetic staff and their lively pupils, but was true to the opinions of some Governors and parents. Moreover, British culture had changed dramatically since 1948. Post-war austerity had faded and real incomes were rising quite rapidly. The Governors were now confident that the fall in the Foundation's income could be replenished by fee income. They were ready for a High Mistress wanting to launch significant changes and were prepared to fund them.

Dame Alison Munro is unique amongst St Paul's High Mistresses in being a Paulina. Her arrival as a school pupil was by an unusual route and shows that, even as a teenager, she had an extraordinary energy and tenacity of purpose. When Alison Donald was 11, her father, a doctor, had taken his family to South Africa. There, she attended Wynberg Girls' High School, where she remembers winning first prize in the annual national competition in 'the

Mrs Alison Munro, the School's fourth High Mistress, who attended St Paul's Girls' School as a pupil.

Knowledge of History' and where she became Head Girl. Resolved to go to Oxford, she was encouraged to consider St Paul's by a sister of Miss Ralph, who was a niece of Miss Gray and had been on the Classics staff at the school until her appointment in 1928 as Head Mistress of Guildford High. Alison was persuaded that St Paul's would give her the teaching needed for the Oxford Entrance Examination. Of her own volition, therefore, for she had lost both parents two years after her family's arrival in South Africa, she went to St Paul's and presented herself for admission. Miss Strudwick, 'astounded', refused to accept her. Alison planted herself in the outer office until the High Mistress gave in. Then next problem was matriculation: Miss Strudwick would not allow her to enter the Seventh Form, on line for Oxford Entrance in the Eighth. So Alison entered herself as an external student of London University, gained her matriculation. On return to school, she found herself still placed in the Sixth. 'I stormed into Miss Strudwick's room brandishing my First Class London University Matriculation certificate', Dame Alison writes in *Looking Back*. 'She smiled and quietly said I could skip the Lower Seventh and go immediately into the Upper Seventh.'

Although Alison flourished in the upper school, she did have to adapt quickly to her new environment. It was a shock moving from her position as Head Girl of Wynberg to one of the many: 'at first, I was nothing'. Moreover, in South Africa, she had perfected the art of learning by heart and reproducing large amounts of information on demand: the need to think and ponder, especially over the Oxford Entrance questions, required a painful adjustment. She was greatly helped by a 'tremendous' Mathematics department to win her place at St Hilda's College, Oxford. The culture of the school was also initially bewildering: she found it odd to have few rules and no penalties. With her ability and personality, she rapidly made her mark, both academically and in drama. Alison directed *A Midsummer Night's Dream* and *The Tempest*. Miss Strudwick and she clashed over Alison's decision to dress her Ariel, 'an elphin eleven-year-old', in a silver body suit. The High Mistress was outraged, declaring the suit 'a most indecent thing' and so Ariel was obliged to appear in silver pyjamas.

Career expectations for Paulinas, according to Dame Alison, were high even in the 1930s. After Oxford, however, she was uncertain over what course to pursue. To provide time for thought, she enrolled in a secretarial college. This she found 'intensely boring' and left after three months. Within six, 'I had my own secretary', at the Imperial College, Kensington. War brought personal tragedy: her husband, Alan Lamont Munro, was killed on active service as an RAF pilot in 1941, a year when two other Paulinas lost husbands in action. Mrs Munro was left carrying her future son. Twelve months later, employment was imperative. Impressed with Mrs Munro's work at Imperial, Sir Robert Watson-Watt, the developer of radar, invited her in 1942 to work with him in the Ministry of Aircraft Production. He took her on all his trips, including visits to the United States and to Canada. She excelled

95

Portrait of Dame Alison Munro by Norman Blamey, RA.

at turning his memoranda, written in a 'convoluted style', into lucid and concise documents suitable for circulation within government. Eventually, she joined the Cabinet Secretariat. At the end of the war, Mrs Munro was asked to compete for one of the fifty 'Mandarin' posts in the administrative level of the civil service and in 1945 was appointed Principal in the Ministry of Civil Aviation. From there, she reached the heights: Assistant Secretary in 1949, Under-Secretary of the Ministry of Transport and Civil Aviation in 1958. Only Evelyn Sharp amongst Paulinas could rival this achievement to date.

Within this context, her appointment as High Mistress was surprising. But the Governors were ready for a break with tradition. 'A High Mistress with a dress sense', Viscount Montgomery wrote with characteristic vigour to the Master, 'would be a novelty at St Paul's and anything that can be done to improve the rather dreary appearance of the average Paulina would be a step in the right direction.' Mrs Munro was prepared to leave the civil service. She had become restless with her prospects in Civil Aviation, which was about to merge with Military Aviation. It seemed plain to her that the Defence Chiefs would not accept a woman under-secretary. A fortuitous encounter opened a window of opportunity. At a British Embassy dinner in Berne, where she was negotiating an air traffic agreement with the Swiss government, Mrs Munro met a member of the Mercers' Company. 'We are looking for a new High Mistress,' he said, 'someone who will let the daylight in.' Initially, her response was light-hearted: 'You need someone like me', she told him. When her interest in the post was reciprocated by the Governors' interest in her, things became serious. Moreover, the field was limited. There were only nine applications in response to the advertisement of November 1962, for three of the twelve candidates had been asked to apply. The line adopted by the Mercers, in the statement issued to all the major newspapers, was simply that they required someone with a 'strong personality, a good presence, and considerable stature as a person, as well as intellectual quality and with considerable administrative ability'. Their appointee was the only candidate who fulfilled these needs. Montgomery added his own rider: 'Must be a lady. Must be young, in the thirties. Must have a sense of humour. Must have a good degree. Must have a "dress sense".' Mrs Munro scored on four out of five. When offered the post, she told the Governors that she wished to stay ten years only: 'more would be bad for you and not good for me'. On this she kept her word.

A flurry of controversy greeted the announcement in July 1963 of her new post, especially as another civil servant (Margaret Hampshire) had just been appointed Principal of the Cheltenham Ladies' College. According to the *Daily Express* (9 July 1963) Mrs Munro declared: 'I rather admire the Governors . . . they have been very brave.' Commenting on the Heads of other schools, Mrs Munro told the *Evening Standard* (17 May 1973) that they 'were all very civilised but I think there must have been a little resentment'. Press comment was divided. 'A shrewd and spectacular choice', said the

Daily Mail (13 July 1963). The *Guardian Journal* (29 July 1963) annoyed not a few teachers by declaring that 'It is obviously not teaching that the Governors of these schools are seeking . . . Teaching academic subjects is child's play compared with training girls able to play their right part as women in a world still in a state of flux.' According to the *Observer*, such appointments were necessary because women were entering wider career fields and that those who remained in teaching did not, 'unlike men . . . hanker for increased responsibility'. In the *Daily Herald* (11 July 1963) Jon Akass wrote rudely about Heads with 'chalkdust deep in their underclothes' and welcomed the news.

In contrast, the *Methodist Recorder* (8 August 1963) confided to its modest readership that 'It is all very puzzling . . . it seems unfortunate that such "plums" of promotion should be snatched from women who have laboured long and lovingly in the arena since college days.' One *Times* correspondent (26 July 1963) expressed dismay at the 'contempt' for teaching expressed by this appointment and at the growth of administration as a profession, 'irrespective, it seems, of who or what is being "administered"'. The *Sunday Telegraph* (28 July 1963) was kind enough to wish Mrs Munro 'good luck' but insisted that running a school demanded first-hand experience of the classroom: 'preserve us from a scramble of school Governors competing to establish a new trend in "top" appointments'. If such a trend was created, it was short-lived, and when she retired from St Paul's Mrs Munro advised the Governors to look for her replacement amongst 'the profession', as Miss Gray called it. A hostile *Telegraph* correspondent (12 July 1963) shared his paper's feelings: 'Is administration entirely divorced from the thing to be administered?' Still magisterial in 1963, *The Times* avoided supporting either side and merely wrote (11 December) of 'the delicate tremor that ran round staff rooms this year'. An editorial in the *Times Educational Supplement* (2 August 1963) was devoted to the matter, but spent most of its column space pondering the rarity of outstanding talent in all professions. It left the question open: 'whether those responsible for the recent appointments have fastened on pure gold can be discovered only in the next few years'. The *Women's Own* (7 September 1963) joined in: do you think your career is over, or has never begun, when you are 49?, it asked its readers. Of course not! Emulate Mrs Munro, try to become a head Mistress too: 'For inside every woman, whatever her age, there is a young, unquenchable spirit that whispers in her ear: "Life is starting now!"'

The tumult died away, and Mrs Munro duly took over in January 1964, at a lower salary (£2,500 p.a.) than she had been earning as under-secretary. A brief interregnum between headships had been covered by Miss Geraldine Noyes as acting High Mistress. Miss Noyes, on the History staff from 1946 to 1971 and Second Mistress for the last eleven years of her time at St Paul's, was an outstanding and much-loved teacher and administrator. 'I have a personal debt to her', wrote Mrs Munro, 'as it was she who, in my early years in

Left to right: Alexandra Clarke (Head Girl), Carol Thatcher and Margaret Thatcher at the opening of the new 7th and 8th form common room and the art rooms.

the school, guided me through unfamiliar territory.' With the new High Mistress, change became the watchword. According to the *Daily Telegraph* (31 August 1985), she said 'When I arrived and said I hadn't been in the place for thirty years, people told me I'd find nothing much had changed. I hope they couldn't say that ten years later when I left.' Instead of proposing a single major project, however, she tackled the difficult task of improving school facilities in almost every part of the existing building. Little persuasion was needed to win the Governors' approval of her plans. To hand, she had the HMI Report of 1965. Although full of compliments for an able staff and enthusiastic pupils, impressed by the laboratories and other facilities, the Inspectors urged modernisation in some areas. The kitchens were 'rambling', the staff rooms 'small and inconvenient', the 'dark' dining room was 'unattractive'.

So, in 1971, 'the Development' was launched: a common room for the Senior School, a better staff room, new Art studios, a new wing for Geography, a language laboratory, another dining room, a host of minor works and, most ambitiously, a new and splendid pool. The old swimming bath was nearing the end of its life. To refurbish it properly would have been too expensive, and 'the alternative of dropping swimming from the curriculum', as Mrs Munro wrote in the publicity brochure for the Development, 'is unthinkable'. So a splendid pool was built at Bute, and the old building became a theatre. On the stairs leading to the new Geography Wing now hangs the fine portrait of Dame Alison Munro by Norman Blamey, RA. Little of Horsley's architecture was sacrificed to these changes, though the mansard roof which provided the new Art rooms and common room would probably not be allowed now by English Heritage. Modernity led the way. Traditional dining, as we have observed in Chapter 2, gave way to a cafeteria system. Along the western side of the roof was built a new common room for the Seventh and Eighth Forms, intended to be a 'civilised setting for relaxation and informal discussion'. This and the Art rooms were opened in 1973 by the then Secretary of State for Education and Science, Mrs Margaret Thatcher, and Alexandra Clarke's diary entry as Head Girl evokes the mood of the time: 'We felt as if we were moving into an airport lounge, all pristine and open plan.' Teaching staff gained private work stations (hardly desks) rather than sharing large tables. All this ran to a cost of over half a million pounds, with a fifth and more being provided by generous parents and Paulinas. Most of the complicated work was finished by the time Mrs Munro left, though the swimming pool was completed and opened by her successor, Mrs Brigstocke.

Despite all these changes, Mrs Munro's High Mistress-ship was in harmony with the traditions of St Paul's. *The Times* (24 June 1974) relayed a story, perhaps apocryphal, which catches the tone of that tradition. On a parents' evening, a father complimented Mrs Munro on the quality of her pupils' home-baked cakes. 'We do not teach cookery; we teach chemistry', she is supposed to have replied. This article also quoted her thus: 'Don't send your daughter to St Paul's if you want her to be a deb.' More seriously, she had a profound respect for the academic expertise of her staff. As a good civil servant, she set clear strategic objectives and invited free discussion of the best means to achieve them. 'There was a genuine meeting of minds', says one former head of department. Determined to communicate with the young, she set herself to know the name of every pupil in the school. Concentration, a retentive memory and photographs above her desk of all the girls enabled the High Mistress to say goodbye by name to every Paulina in the school at the end of her first summer term.

Like Miss Strudwick, and rather more so, Mrs Munro remained a public figure. A retreat into the school was not for her. A year after becoming High Mistress, she helped to set up the Truman and Knightley Educational Trust Ltd and became one of its Council of Governors. This charity sought to provide bursaries for children to be educated at independent schools. Her link with aviation was preserved when she accepted in 1966 an invitation from Roy Jenkins, then Minister of Aviation, to become the first woman on the board of the British European Airways Corporation: 'High Mistress of the Air', in the *Daily Telegraph's* phrase (22 January 1972). Leaving St Paul's, she assumed a new rôle as Chairman of Merton, Sutton and Wandsworth Area Health Authority. Because her father had been a doctor and her brother, Professor Ian Donald, was pioneering ultrasonic-wave monitoring of the womb, Mrs Munro was well placed to join medical administration.

The Munro decade was a sparkling one, socially and academically. 'Oxford and Cambridge have been magnificently served, but the claims of other universities . . . have been firmly accorded their proper place,' wrote Marjorie Reeves in her farewell to the High Mistress (*Paulina*, 1974). Amidst warm tributes, Mrs Munro moved on to her next career. It was a proud moment for the school when she was created a DBE in 1985.

MRS HEATHER BRIGSTOCKE, HIGH MISTRESS 1974–89

With Mrs Munro, the Governors had become used to an innovative Head with a touch of iconoclasm. They were ready to appoint another Head prepared for change. Nonetheless, the Mercers were not inclined to provoke comment by looking for a candidate outside the profession. Their new Head was, indeed, a career teacher. But she had moved through the hierarchy with a speed and freedom which bore out her own assertion in *True Humanism* (1984) that school life and 'independence and individuality' were not incompatible. To the rôle of High Mistress Heather Brigstocke brought a sense of excitement, of worlds to be explored. The press gave her frequent attention: a 'continual hum of comment', as the *Observer* put it (25 September 1983), though Mrs Munro too had elicited her fair share of journalism.

Scots self-reliance was exemplified in Mrs Brigstocke's family and early

Heather Brigstocke, photographed by Terence Donovan. Reproduced with the kind permission of Mrs Diana Donovan and the Terence Donovan Archive.

life. Her paternal grandfather was a saddler and her father, John Renwick Brown, one of fourteen children. He left school in his early teens, worked briefly in the collieries west of Glasgow and then escaped the mines by enlisting in the Royal Flying Corps. Military aviation became his love as well as his career, and those who could fly planes secured his highest esteem. As Squadron-Leader J. R. Brown he was, to his daughters, 'very dashing'. During the First World War, he won, for reconnaissance, the Distinguished Flying Cross. In the 1930s, he taught the airforce in China, where Heather lived briefly as a child. During the Second World War, he served as a flying instructor in New Zealand. Mary Jane Calder Campbell, her mother, won a scholarship to the Glasgow School of Art, soon after its completion (1909) by Charles Rennie Mackintosh. Instead of taking up this award, however, she attended the University of Glasgow and graduated in 1913 with the degree of MA from that university, one of the first women to do so. Lady Brigstocke now slightly regrets that she did not, as a teenager, use more of her mother's familiarity with design to develop her own artistic instincts. Both parents powerfully shaped her education and attitudes. Her mother always supervised the homework of Heather and her sister Marie, bringing them their supper on trays to ensure that they did not waste a minute. Heather's father treated her rather like a boy; taking her up in his aeroplane, for instance, when she was only 5 years old. From him she acquired an acute sense of self-determination: 'he absolutely instilled in me a feeling that I could never rely upon anyone else and had to rely on myself; "you have got to be independent", he used to say'.

Most of Heather's years at the Abbey School, Reading (1940–7), coincided with the Second World War. Indeed, as she vividly remembers, her expected birthday celebrations on 2 September had been obliterated by the imminent declaration of war upon Germany. At the Abbey, she really was happy: 'I loved being with my friends, and cycling and most subjects, but hated games.' Unfortunately, she did lose her Prefect's badge for an inadvertent misdemeanour. The entire school was to go to see T. S. Eliot's *Murder in the Cathedral*. Heather invited her friends home for coffee and her mother's chocolate cake. She failed to notice how swiftly time was passing and made not only her party but the entire school miss the train and 'so lost my prefect's badge for talking too much'. The Head Mistress never quite appreciated her. In 1965 the two met for the first time since the Abbey School days in the Royal Festival Hall for a conference of the Association of Head Mistresses. 'Heather, what are you doing here?' was her startled comment. Heather had to confess that she had just been appointed Head Mistress of Francis Holland School, Clarence Gate.

As a teenager, and like other girls, Heather considered leaving school early and becoming, perhaps, a model – or a bank clerk. Fortunately, her Head Mistress brushed these notions aside. Embarking upon the Higher Certificate, Heather began with French, English and Mathematics. She was

Girton College at the time that Heather was a student there.

then switched to Latin and Greek in order to generate some teaching in Classics. Heather was not consulted; Heads were authoritarian then. In this fashion, she came under a formative influence: Mrs Annie Ure, a Classics teacher and married to Professor Percy Ure of Reading University. As Heather was taught alone for Greek and with one other girl for Latin, Mrs Ure shaped every aspect of her classical studies. To the weekly list of preps and study to be done Mrs Ure would add a 'treat': looking at Greek vases, or reading about Greek architecture. Professor Ure became involved and set Heather, who was doing Greek from a standing start, extravagantly difficult reading, such as Pindar's Odes. Mrs Ure directed her reading outside the Classics, took Heather to her first cathedral (Salisbury) and proposed her application to Girton College, Cambridge. 'I knew nothing about such things,' says Lady Brigstocke, 'but I would have lain down under a bus if she had asked me to do so.' She recalls Annie Ure's home-spun suits in ankle-length grey and brown worsted, 'which would be terribly fashionable nowadays', and her silk blouses, made from the material of pre-war dresses. The last two years at the Abbey she thinks of as a lovely time: 'I was, almost, becoming the school swot!'

At Girton, Heather found herself one of eight classicists, seven of whom were from Cheltenham Ladies' College. They had been taking Greek and Latin from the age of 12 or so. That was one reason why she switched to Archaeology and Anthropology for Part II of the degree. Another motive was to give herself more time for acting, which had become a governing passion. At school, she had only one significant part, as the elder brother in Milton's *Comus* (from which she still quotes with delight: ''Tis chastity, my brother, chastity, She that has that, is clad in complete steel'). Barely had she arrived in Cambridge, however, than Heather was asked to join the ADC, the Amateur Dramatic Club. Over the next three years, she played many rôles. A touring production to Sweden of *You Never Can Tell* provided the first chance to go abroad since her time in China as a child. She acted with John Barton and Julian Slade and was one of the first two women in the Cambridge Greek play, performing as Antigone in Sophocles' *Oedipus Coloneus*. Much of an entire term was spent in the King's audit room rehearsing: 'It was such an experience.' By the time of graduation and after she had won Cambridge University's Winchester Reading Prize, the first woman to do so, Heather was determined to become an actress. But her father's disapproval of this ambition and her own need for an income turned her away from the stage and, for eight months, to a traineeship at Selfridges. From that it seemed natural to go into teaching: it was her mother's profession and 'I had actually been teaching for years, coaching several of the children of my parents' friends.'

There followed her marriage to Geoffrey Brigstocke, a civil servant, children and teaching at Francis Holland School, Chelsea, and the Godolphin and Latymer School, Hammersmith. In her obituary of Dame Joyce Bishop

The 1975 opening of the new swimming pool.

Mrs Brigstocke digging the first spadeful of soil for the new science building, in February 1983.

(Head Mistress of Godolphin and Latymer School, 1935–63, the *Sunday Telegraph*, 13 August 1978), Lady Brigstocke mentions her former Head's 'strong commitment to the recruitment of young married women teachers'. This comment was true to her own experience. Miss Bishop appointed her when Heather's first child was 8 months old. When she became pregnant with her second child, she went to Miss Bishop 'in tears' to hand in her resignation. To Heather's surprise, her Head Mistress told her that, if she could find her own maternity cover, she could stay. That became the pattern: when she interrupted work to have another baby, she found her own replacement, organised the hand-over of classes and resumed teaching soon after the birth: 'in effect, I arranged my own maternity leave'. An exciting opportunity offered in the early 1960s when her husband was posted by the Ministry of Transport to serve as Shipping Attaché in the British Embassy, Washington DC. After three months on her own in London with her three children ('for it would not have occurred to me *not* to finish my examination classes'), she joined him in the USA. It was, Lady Brigstocke says, a 'thrilling' time to be in the American capital and to see the political formation of President Kennedy's 'New Frontier' at close quarters. Fortuitously, her daughter Persephone was invited to join the White House School, which was held in the private apartments and usually reserved for the children of senior White House staff. Kennedy was amongst the audience at school plays. Persephone was the only British child in the school. Arrangements for collecting the children caused some amusement, since the Brigstockes' red Ford Anglia contrasted oddly with the limousines clustering around the presidential residence. On one occasion, the *Washington Post* reported that a small red car had been seen waiting mysteriously by the Secret Service entrance; it was, of course, Heather picking up Persephone.

Her family's return from Washington imminent, Mrs Brigstocke was invited to apply for the headship of Francis Holland School, Clarence Gate, and was interviewed and appointed in a matter of days after her return, 'with twenty-five pieces of luggage'. According to a former pupil: 'she hit us like a thunderbolt. She made school exciting. Attendance at parents' meetings doubled. All the fathers started going' (the *Observer*, 25 September 1983). Eight years later, when the advertisement for the position of High Mistress was advertised (February 1973) she felt that she had achieved her aims at Francis Holland and was ready to move on. Though she was not familiar with St Paul's, she was intrigued by the way so many of her Cambridge contemporaries had spoken of their school and their then High Mistress, Miss Strudwick, with great affection. By the early 1970s, the fashion for choosing Heads from outside the teaching profession had receded. Indeed, Mrs Munro herself said in April 1974 that the Governors had taken some risk in appointing her direct from the civil service and that 'it would be quite wrong to repeat the process'. There was, moreover, simply no need to look further. The Governors had an outstanding candidate whose long teaching experi ence had been combined with successful years as Head of a major London school. It is a compliment to the appointment committee that they were prepared to see Mrs Brigstocke's family as an advantage rather than an obstacle: 'Mrs Brigstocke is remarkable,' they wrote, 'as she has a large family to bring up as well as run a school.' While looking forward to her arrival at St Paul's, Mrs Brigstocke then suffered a personal catastrophe. In April 1974, her husband Geoffrey, then under-secretary in the Department of Trade and Industry, was returning from Russia via Paris with a trade delegation. A luggage door left open in their Turkish DC10 caused the aeroplane to crash, five minutes after take-off from Orly airport. Mrs Brigstocke was left a widow at 44, with four children to care for and demanding new responsibilities to fulfil. She found the mental resources to do so, but was, she says, also 'fortunate to be able to throw myself into something'. The Paulinas were remarkably sensitive to the loss borne by their new High Mistress.

Fifteen years on, about to retire from St Paul's, Mrs Brigstocke reflected: 'I found it an impressive place and hope that I am leaving it one.' This was a modest self-assessment which conceals the fact that a great school is a changing community which requires constant vigilance to remain 'impressive'. As she once said to a young member of staff: 'This place really requires concentration.' Heather Brigstocke was a stylish High Mistress, but beneath the style there was formidable substance. As a leader of the young, one of her greatest strengths was to make school and the life outside to which it led seem exciting. When she took assembly (wearing, as was her custom, her academic gown), there was immediate silence and a sense of drama. 'I am so grateful,' she said in her farewell speech, 1989, 'to have been a member of this huge cast, which is St Paul's Girls' School.' Her voice, accustomed to projection, had no need of amplifiers to cope with the difficult acoustics of the Great Hall. On one occasion, she asked the entire staff to leave the Hall, since she wished to speak to her school alone. The teachers were not told why she wished to do so, and scarcely were inclined to ask. One new Middle Fourth girl left a vivid recollection of an assembly: 'Mrs Brigstocke came down the passage and swept on to the platform. It was then that the nicest thing of the whole day happened. She read a passage from the Sanskrit; one that I knew very well indeed, but I knew it as a poem. Anyway, I was thrilled to hear it in such an unexpected place. It seemed like a good omen and cheered me considerably' (*Paulina*, 1976).

In many ways, she took naturally to the liberal traditions of St Paul's and, if anything, extended them. With the help of the Education Council of the Marriage Research Centre (now One Plus One), she enhanced the sex education programme established by Mrs Munro (so that St Paul's anticipated by fourteen years the statutory requirement for such programmes in schools). As Lady Brigstocke said many years later in the Lords (11 June 1992): 'We ought to be asking how we can best teach the subject, not whether we should do so.' On arriving, she did find the atmosphere rather severe, and tried to

The Rosalind Franklin Workshop, opened by Aaron Klug in 1988.

soften it and to encourage more smiles in the corridors. During her first year, Mrs Brigstocke finally abolished the blue-grey school coat, which Paulinas had been required to wear to and from school. In part, she was trying to spare parental finances, since the coat was expensive. But she was concerned by the fact that 1974 was the year of the maxi, a long and trendy dress, which combined with the traditional St Paul's coat made Paulinas 'instantly recognisable' around Hammersmith. This innovation led to misleading press reports to the effect that she had abolished the 'school uniform'; properly speaking, St Paul's had no such thing. On sartorial matters, she was quite relaxed. Jeans, which swept the school in the last year of Mrs Munro's High Mistress-ship, were quietly accepted as 'the new school uniform', as *Paulina* put it (1976). Nonetheless, she did not like to see diluted versions of late 1970s punk in school and sleeveless tops were banned. The saying that *School is not a beach party* became proverbial.

The High Mistress may have appeared remote and, at times, alarming to many of her pupils; perhaps this is the fate of any successful Head Mistress. Those who worked directly with her, however, found support and generosity. She applauded achievement, of whatever kind. That was partly why she espoused drama so strongly, since it enabled girls to express their personalities in ways which academic subjects rarely allowed. The Creative Day of 1984, in which fifty workshops had Paulinas making jewellery, learning Caribbean dancing or playing in a medieval theatre, bore the Brigstocke touch.

Heather Brigstocke's term of office was marked by a host of innovations. She introduced the Duke of Edinburgh Scheme to the school and dispensed with 'Dalton Days' for the Senior School in favour of conferences or theme days. Because Mrs Munro had become a member of the British Library Board, St Paul's was the first secondary school in the country to be allowed (1979) to use the borrowing service of the national library. St Paul's was also an early venturer into computer programming, when a parent, Mr Mark Weinburg, gave the school in 1980 what was then called 'a small microcomputer which goes easily on a desk top'. The school gained a full-time librarian, and Economics was added to the A-level curriculum. Miss Sheila Hill became the school's first Surmistress (1983), Miss Janet Gough its first Director of Studies (1986). Weekly lectures, begun by Mrs Munro, became a permanent part of the senior curriculum. It would be invidious to choose many names from the hundreds of remarkable speakers who have given lectures at St Paul's over three decades, but a tradition that could provide Dame Ninette de Valois on ballet, Hugh Thomas on the Spanish Civil War, John Julius Norwich on Venice, Jessica Rawson on Chinese archaeology and Richard Dawkins on evolution is an achievement in itself.

Impressed by the co-operation between parents and staff at the Washington Cathedral School, where Mrs Brigstocke had taught part-time, she created the Parents' Guild in 1979. This drew together parents' work in the book room, fund raising, the library, the theatre and in providing the stunning flower displays which remain a daily delight of the Marble. Moreover, she formed in 1983 the American Friends of St Paul's, which preserved links between the school and the east coast cities and helped to raise funds. Her second Bursar, Mrs Pat Geater, remembers how she and her High Mistress celebrated the annual signing of accounts for the Friends: 'Now we will go to the Ritz for a sandwich and a glass of champagne!'

Another interesting innovation was the Dean Rusk Scholarship. Dr Helen Wallis, the greatest geographer amongst Paulinas, had close links with Davidson College, North Carolina (and was awarded, in 1985, an Hon. D.Litt by Davidson). She saw the opportunity for another transatlantic link. Dr Samuel Spencer, the President of Davidson, agreed to offer rooms and tuition to three Paulinas and three Paulines (from St Paul's School) for the spring quarter. These students were designated 'Dean Rusk Scholars' in honour of the former US Secretary of State, an alumnus of the college. This scheme flourished from 1977 until Mrs Brigstocke's retirement in 1989 and allowed thirty-six Paulinas to enjoy the extraordinary facilities of this 500-acre campus, to join college courses ('Women Writers', 'Theatre Arts' and even 'Edible Wild Plants'), to go canoeing on Davidson Lake or, like the Scholars of 1979, to offer their hosts 'an English tea party on St George's Day, complete with cucumber sandwiches, scones, a London red double-decker bus and a white Rolls-Royce'. Concurrently, the High Mistress launched staff exchanges with schools in New York: Nightingale Bamford and Brearley. The occasional exchange had occurred during the 1930s, but with Mrs Brigstocke exchanges became an established tradition. The first to go was Janet Gough, who began her report on Nighingale Bamford in characteristic mode: 'The joke about two countries separated by a common language is an old one: my vocabulary has certainly been considerably extended (semester, theme, k thru 12).' The next year, Miss Muriel Hall picked up the theme in her report on Brearley: 'I exchanged silence on the Marble for silence in the elevators, and instead of form rooms and timetables there were home rooms and schedules.'

Heather Brigstocke also directed her energies towards building. Once the last stages of 'Development' had been completed, including the opening of the new swimming pool, she devised an ambitious scheme: a new building to include a full professional theatre and a computing centre, and the transformation of the old swimming baths into an Engineering Workshop. She was determined that young women should feel that any profession of their choice lay open to them: 'This is not a girls' school,' she said when launching the scheme, 'this is a school the pupils of which happen to be female.' When the Mercers felt that the cost would be beyond the Governors' resources, Mrs Brigstocke launched an appeal with the target of one million pounds. Chapter 2 has described the dazzling array of fund-raising events, most memorably the Gala Evening in the Aldwych, in November 1982, which

Portrait of the Baroness Brigstocke by Paul Brason, RP. St Paul's Girls' School is grateful to the late Sir Emmanuel Kaye and Lady Kaye for their generous patronage of this painting.

helped the Appeal to exceed this amount. Even as she was preparing to leave, the High Mistress was planning to improve the Science Laboratories and install a new computer and technology suite. 'You should always have a building on the go,' she told her anxious Bursar, Mrs Pat Geater, 'like your knitting.'

Finally, the High Mistress maintained an extraordinary range of responsibilities outside St Paul's proper. To enumerate them all would turn this paragraph into a gazetteer. These commitments flowed partly from her natural zest and curiosity but were also a matter of deliberate policy: 'I always wanted to find out what was going on in the world,' she said, 'in order to know what we were training the girls <u>for</u>.' Some of her responsibilities reflected her interest in social reform: hence her membership of the Council of the Middlesex Hospital Medical School and her Presidency of the Bishop Creighton House Settlement. Other rôles, such as the Trusteeship of the National Gallery, Governorship of the Museum of London and membership of the Council of the Royal Society of Arts, allowed her to use her knowledge of art and archaeology. As an educationalist, she became involved in the City University, the London House for Overseas Graduates, the Royal Ballet School, the City Technology Colleges Trust, Forest School, the United World College of the Atlantic and served as President of the Girls' Schools Association (1980–1). The world of broadcasting and journalism also attracted her, so that she accepted an invitation to join London Weekend Television in 1983 as a non-executive director and to serve as a judge on the 1988 Whitbread Book of the Year Award.

Leaving St Paul's simply allowed Heather Brigstocke more time to pursue these paths. For few former Head Mistresses could the word 'retirement' be less appropriate. She followed her business instincts by joining Burberry's and becoming an independent director of *The Times*. Education has remained central. As Chairman of the English-Speaking Union (from 1993) and Chairman of the Board of Governors, Landau Forte College, Derby (1993–), she faced contrasting challenges: developing transatlantic and European links on the one hand and improving education in a single institution on the other. She has also launched English-Speaking Unions in China and Japan. It was, of course, a matter of pride to St Paul's that a former High Mistress was raised to the peerage, as Baroness Brigstocke (1990). For those who care about teaching as a profession, perhaps it mattered even more that a professional teacher should have joined the House of Lords. Since the passage of the Life Peerages Act (1958) many former permanent secretaries and businessmen have become members of the second chamber. Quite a few academics have done likewise. But it has been rare for a former Head Mistress do so. It was a striking testimony to what her own life had shown: that teachers do not need to be cloistered within the classroom and should look outwards rather than inwards.

Mrs Helen Williams, High Mistress 1989–92

When Mrs Helen Williams was appointed High Mistress, the popular assumption was that the Governors had deliberately chosen a contrast to her predecessor. Whereas Mrs Brigstocke was tall and dramatic, Mrs Williams was small and less demonstrative. One was a public figure with a host of commitments beyond St Paul's, whereas the other had preferred to concentrate her energies within her school, though she had joined, in 1988, the governing body of the School for Oriental and African Studies. As early as 3 May 1988, the *Evening Standard* chose to give its scoop of her appointment the misleading headline: 'New Head vows: I'll be different.' It is not clear, however, that this assumption was correct. Like all appointing bodies, the Governors' chief concern was to chose the best of the candidates available, and Mrs Williams seemed to be the right choice. She had excellent academic credentials. At Girton College, Cambridge, she read English and gained a first in Part I and a lower second in Part II. After achieving a distinction in her Postgraduate Certificate of Education, she taught for one year at St Paul's Girls' School and one year at St George's, Edinburgh and then was a lecturer during the next fourteen years at Edinburgh University. As an academic, she had one publication: a critical commentary on T. S. Eliot's *The Waste Land* for Edward Arnold (1968). Then she moved to Blackheath High School as Head Mistress and was in her tenth year when she became High Mistress elect. Indeed, it was the visit of some Governors to that school, after they had compared minutely the merits of the various applicants, that tipped the balance in Mrs Williams's favour. She appeared vivacious and determined, obviously in control of an exciting school.

St Paul's had a long wait for its new High Mistress. Applications were invited at the beginning of 1988 and Mrs Williams's appointment was announced officially on 4 May of that year. So expectations were high and had sixteen months to develop. Obviously, she was delighted to return to the school where, as she wrote in 1988, 'I remember still the intellectual excitement of my year's teaching.' It is a literary curiosity that A. S. Byatt had, in 1962, been set aside in favour of the then Miss Helen Thomas; the English department seems to have thought that Miss Byatt would prove too alarming for the younger girls. A first year of the new regime unfolded without major events. Many people in the school appreciated her pleasant, unassuming manner and enjoyed lunchtime conversations with her about films, plays and literature. 'A thoroughly good egg', Anna Pasternak described her in the *Evening Standard* (26 November 1990).

It was during the spring term of her second academic year that some controversy became public. In January 1991, the High Mistress called a special staff meeting at which she set out a new policy concerning the General Certificate of Education. It was her view that the new examination course for

Helen Williams in 1989.

14- to 16-year-olds stifled imagination and placed excessive burdens on pupils without offering commensurate intellectual rewards. So, her plan was to retain the public examination for the Sciences, Mathematics, English and a modern language and to allow other subjects – Art, Geography, History, Music and a second modern language – to be studied through school-based courses and validated by 'St Paul's Girls' School Certificates'. After some discussion, she added Latin to the list of GCSEs. The response to these radical proposals was divided. Some of the staff, especially those who had been in the school for some time, liked the idea because they remembered the tradition, common to quite a few independent schools, whereby History Ordinary level was omitted and the students moved directly into the Advanced Level. It was not until the mid-1980s that St Paul's had adopted History O level. Some shared the widespread doubts over the value of the early GCSE courses. Winchester College and Manchester Grammar also appeared to be contemplating a reduction in GCSEs. This was also the period when some leading historians campaigned against History GCSE and of various anomalies, such as the 100 per cent coursework assessment for English Literature, which were later removed. Moreover, the Governors were far from opposed to the scheme of reform and indeed welcomed any suggestion that would make the curriculum more flexible and rewarding. What they did want, however, was a clear strategy and reassurance that Mrs Williams was carrying the staff with her on the matter.

Others amongst staff and parents shared her scepticism over the value of GCSEs but were not sure that dropping them was the best way forward. Many arguments were put forward on behalf of retention. Some teachers were concerned that their employment prospects elsewhere might be damaged if they did not remain au courant with the new exam. Other questions were raised. Would the universities take proper account of the St Paul's certificate? Would Paulinas take the courses without a public examination as seriously as those with? Would Geography and History, already optional at 14, lose status within the school without a publicly awarded certificate at the end? Was it a good idea for schools, already sensitive to charges of élitism, to step aside from an examination course adopted by the rest of the nation? Nor did the relevant teachers accept that Geography and History in the middle school offered a 'desert' of teaching, if Lady Warnock's expression of Mrs Williams's views (in *The Times*, 24 August 1992) can be taken to be correct. Indeed, for many pupils and teachers, switching from O level to GCSE was a refreshing change.

Before long, the matter seemed to be rolling beyond Mrs Williams's control. Perhaps her greatest misjudgement in declaring that her priority would be to know Paulinas, as she put it, 'by name and by nature', was to underestimate the importance of the school's high social profile and, therefore, the inevitable interest of the press. The misquotations and distortions of press reporting played no small part in creating a public perception of crisis which was both exaggerated and almost impossible to control. 'Our children are too bright for the GCSE' was just the kind of headline the school did not want to see (the *Independent*, 2 May 1991). For some five terms, the school was buzzing with the GCSE issue. Some parents were sympathetic to the proposed change, others were worried. The exact timing of the new scheme remained unresolved as Mrs Williams's term of office moved into its third year. Meanwhile, the Governors' concerns were less with the GCSE reforms proper, which they supported 'in principle', than with the managerial problems that the planning of these reforms seemed to throw into relief. They observed that the High Mistress seemed to be losing the confidence of senior staff and not maintaining her authority over the girls. Throughout the years 1991–2 there were, accordingly, two concurrent developments: the debate over GCSEs and the Governors' concern over their High Mistress's administration of the school. At the end of a tense academic year (1991–2), a deeply unhappy time during which the senior staff were trying steer their ship of state through a whirlpool, Mrs Williams seemed to be on the point of resignation. Her final address on Governors' Day had a valedictory tone and was issued, almost as an apologia, to parents in advance of their formal assembly. Even more emphatically, her words in the common room on the last day of term seemed to be a farewell.

In the event, she resigned only well into the summer holidays, on 14 August 1992. The Hon. Henry Palmer, who had just taken over as Chairman of the Governors, had an extraordinary August and September, fielding hundreds of enquiries and expostulations from anxious parents and dealing with the details of Mrs Williams's resignation and compensation. What dominates the record of this time is the intense seriousness of his concern for the school in particular and the cause of education in general. He also resisted any response to the clamouring press, apart from writing a letter to *The Times* on Lady Warnock's article, 'Trampling on Teachers', published in that newspaper (24 August 1992). Some Paulinas, however, felt that a caricature of the school was being presented in the press and did respond in self-defence. 'Paulinas are fed up with the constant Paulina-bashing that has occurred in the media,' wrote one in the *Sunday Times* (30 August 1992). 'Charity has never been a case of "Daddy's chequebook" [this was a reference to the accusation in the *Sunday Times*, 23 August 1992, that Paulina charity work was achieved by 'asking daddy to sign'] and, being a Paulina, may I point out that mummy has a chequebook too.' One of the wisest comments on the whole affair came from Emma Wilkins, a Paulina of 1977–84, in *The Times* (27 August 1992): 'The "row" has been presented as two sides arguing over two choices', she wrote. 'In the red corner, Mrs Williams, insisting that examinations should be cut to a minimum in order to give the greatest possible breadth of education to her girls. In the blue corner, the parents . . . exam-fevered and determined to push the 15- and 16-year-olds through as many GCSE hoops as possible. But Paulinas have never accepted that things are so simple as a choice between one and the other.' Examination success and a broad education, she went on to insist, are not mutually incompatible: 'I remember being taught an extra book of the *Aeneid* because we wanted to find out how the story ended (it wasn't on the O-level syllabus, but we squeezed it in anyway).'

Indeed, much of the press coverage was far from helpful. GCSE students are taught to ask: for what is this source useful? The *Standard's* quotation (3 September 1991) of a supposed 15-year-old Paulina's comment on Mrs Williams's term of office: 'We're totally hassled. And she's started school 10 minutes earlier. It's a total nightmare', might be more useful as a source for metropolitan speech patterns than for what actually happened. As a matter of record, the story that her last Governors' Day speech was greeted with boos and hisses, as reported in the *Daily Express* (17 August 1992), the *Evening Standard* (9 July 1992), the *International Express* (1 September 1992), the *Independent on Sunday* (6 September 1992), the *Sunday Times* (16 August 1992) is incorrect. This anecdote seems to have been a distortion of a minor incident which occurred during assembly on the next day, when term ended.

Finally, though the journalists seemed to be convinced that the High Mistress had resigned because of the GCSE issue and because of 'parent power' (*The Times*, 31 August 1992), the Governors' position was quite otherwise. They were emphatic that they had not responded to parental pressure nor had they forced the resignation over the GCSE proposals, which the Governors had supported in principle throughout. Indeed, Mrs Williams's plans came to partial fruition, as St Paul's kept the GCSE examinations for Geography and History but adopted school-validated certificates for Art, Music and a second modern language. The Governors made it clear that the resignation had occurred because of a breakdown of relations between the Head and her Governors. Without the confidence of her governing body, no head could continue. The situation had became, as the Governors stated publicly, 'irretrievable'.

If not just the 'storm in a teacup' that Mrs Williams claimed for the crisis (*Sunday Times*, 23 August 1992), it did die away. One should also appreciate that the vast majority of the school's activities had continued as normal. Academic work was unaffected, and in the league tables of that year St Paul's had its best A-level results to date. For the former High Mistress, it was gratifying that she was able to re-establish her career. After holding a Trevelyan Fellowship at the University of Durham and teaching for a year at Brearley School, New York, she became the Principal of the Royal National Institute for the Blind, New College, Worcester.

MISS JANET GOUGH, HIGH MISTRESS 1992–8

If Alison Munro is the only High Mistress to have been a Paulina, then Janet Gough is the only one to have moved through the ranks as a teacher. Both arrived on the staff in the same month: January 1964. When the Governors chose Miss Gough to succeed Helen Williams, therefore, they hoped that her deep knowledge of the school would restore stability. Fortunately for St Paul's, their hopes were well founded. The new High Mistress ('acting' for the first year) combined a quirky sense of humour with a natural authority. During her first year of office, she restored calm and a sense of normality. Silence was re-established in assemblies. These Miss Gough took on Mondays, with a reading from the Authorised Version or, occasionally, from Tyndale's translation, and on Fridays, with a passage from some secular work. Like Miss Strudwick, her readings favoured the Old over the New Testament. According to *Harpers & Queen* in October 1994, 'Janet Gough, High Mistress of St Paul's, is doing a neat job of mixing the radical with old-school academic excellence.'

Janet Gough was born in Shropshire. She loves that county ('no proper countryside until you reach Shropshire,' she says), and, for her retirement, has settled in Ludlow. After attending the town's High School, she secured a place at Newnham College, Cambridge, where she read History and English. After graduation, she sent applications to a number of schools and went to St Paul's simply because it was the first to respond. At once, she took to the place. Its liberal traditions, the central position occupied by the library and by wide reading, the fascinating mix of cultures and languages amongst Paulinas and staff, the remarkable English department headed by Miss Rosamund Jenkinson, all appealed. 'When asked why I've stayed so long one answer always has been "I've enjoyed the company I've been able to keep",' she said at the end of her career at St Paul's. Nonetheless, after her first seven years there, a period she described to Muriel Hall (*Paulina*, 1998) as 'her apprenticeship', she left, wondering whether to turn from teaching to journalism or research. To teaching she did, however, quickly revert, and taught for a year in Manchester Grammar School and Worcester High School.

In 1973 she rejoined St Paul's and began to concentrate on upper school teaching, careers advice and university entrance. At the turn of the decade, she and Miss Muriel Hall were appointed Senior Tutors, the 'joint monarchy', in Mrs Brigstocke's phrase. As a Senior Tutor, then (1986) Director of Studies and (from 1988) Surmistress, she developed an extraordinary knowledge both of the university entrance system and of the needs of particular Paulinas. As a result, she was constantly sought after by the Seventh and Eighth Forms. 'Her diary has to be seen to be believed,' remarked a colleague. 'Individual interviews multiplied to the point where there seemed to be a permanent queue sitting on the steps outside her door,' writes Muriel Hall (*Paulina*, 1998). As Miss Gough was about to become High Mistress, one parent told the Governors that 'the seemingly endless trouble she took to arrange for interviews, cope with changes and seek out information made her', as an adviser, 'unparalleled'.

What was also remarkable was her calm. In the face of academic and

Portrait of Janet Gough by Paul Brason, RP. St Paul's Girls' School is grateful to the late Sir Emmanuel Kaye and Lady Kaye for their generous patronage of this painting. The book in the portrait is the Nonesuch Edition of Milton, open at Book Four of Paradise Lost, *at the point where Satan bewails the difficulty of expressing gratitude.*

The Sports Hall is today used for all sorts of activities, from gymnastics to fencing and basketball.

emotional stress she did seem to be unshakeable. For her challenges existed rather than problems, and no crisis was so grave that it would not admit of a solution. This attitude of mind was a strength to colleagues as well as students: 'a superb teacher of teachers,' as Heather Brigstocke said in her last Governors' Day speech. Very firm on occasion, she was nonetheless not easily shocked. A Paulina parent and journalist has confided to her public the difficulties she experienced with three teenage daughters (*Telegraph*, 3 October 1998). Whipped out of her boarding school by her mother, the eldest daughter shaved her head the weekend that she came home. The sequel can be left with the author:

> At my wits' end, I turned to the best and asked St Paul's Girls' School to take pity on us both. . . I knew there wasn't the faintest hope but when Rose turned up for interview with Mrs Brigstocke and Miss Gough (God bless them) at St Paul's, they turned not a hair. Rose, of course, had none to turn. (And is there a happy ending? Yes, yes. Straight As and on to King's College, Cambridge with loads of hair).

It is an article of faith with Janet Gough that young people must find their own pathways: what she often said was: 'set your own goals; we shall help you to achieve them'. As Blanche Girouard (Miss Gough's first Head Girl) noted in her diary for May 1993: 'This morning I asked Miss Gough what she thought SPGS offered students as far as the spiritual, ethical, moral nature was concerned. She said that she didn't like impositions on individuals, liked pupils finding their own voice.'

As the repository of arcane knowledge, Miss Gough was much admired. Those Paulinas who had seen her library blinked at its size and eclecticism. Like her predecessors, she added to the store of Paulina proverbs: 'What is freedom? Freedom is time to go to a library'; 'Once a Paulina, always a Paulina'; 'Gosh, it must have been Auden!'; 'Let us just stand and think about that' (after, perhaps, a particularly opaque passage from Simone Weil). Over the years, she developed the habit of applying to spoken language the care one might apply to written: 'What is remarkable', said Lady Brigstocke at Janet's farewell luncheon at the League, 'is that she speaks in paragraphs.' As a teacher, like the many other remarkable members of the St Paul's English department, she encouraged generation after generation of Paulinas to explore literature for themselves, to trust their own literary judgement. To Emily Wheeler-Bennett, 'Miss Gough . . . had a way of helping us to winkle out the meaning from the densest of texts, leaving her pupils with a gratifying sense of discovery.' Another Paulina treasures one of Miss Gough's comments on an essay: 'Weak conclusion, rather long-winded opening. Otherwise excellent.' She was, recalls Nicola Shulman (Lady Normanby) 'wholly independent in all her processes of thought. We saw in her scholarship without pedantry and wit without vulgarity . . . That she was also the person who treated us with the least condescension still seems to me a kind of miracle.' Tributes could be multiplied, but perhaps the most gratifying one is the remark of a young Paulina, that 'Miss Gough has been a key figure in my decision to become a teacher'.

As High Mistress, Janet Gough achieved a great deal within a relatively brief timespan. As recounted in the second chapter, she saw the new Information Technology block (the Mercers' Building) through to its formal opening in January 1994 and then proposed and completed the beautiful refurbishment of the Colet Library and the Helen Wallis multi-media room. To maintain and increase the contact between St Paul's and schools abroad was one of her cherished objectives. In 1998, for instance, there were exchanges with three schools in the States – the National Cathedral School, Washington, Nightingale Bamford, New York and St Paul's, Concord, New Hampshire – and with Ascham School, Sydney and Northlands School, Buenos Aires. Apart from these special exchanges, there were language visits to Barcelona, Bonn, Linz, Marseilles, Moscow, Munich and Paris. The planning of the Sports Hall, its construction finished in 1999, was begun during her last year. Symbolic innovations, maintained by her successor, included her standing on the Marble each morning to greet and talk to Paulinas and staff and opening her door to the school for several lunchtimes each week. Part of her time was devoted to developing links between current and Paulinas and she remains devoted to the St Paul's Girls' School League, of which she was elected Life Vice-President on her retirement.

The scheme dearest to Janet Gough's heart, the Scholarships Appeal of 1996–8, was a triumph. Initially, her aim was to raise £250,000 in order to fund two scholarships. In the event, the Appeal attracted so many contributions from Paulinas, parents and staff both past and current, that well over a million pounds was gathered. This has enabled the Scholarship Appeal Endowment to support eight scholarships (the Balli, Gatsby, Gough, Margaret Powell, Munro, Nina Pinto, Rowan Education Trust and Strudwick Scholarships). To celebrate this achievement, the school held a summer concert in July 1998, which closed with the first performance of Derek Bourgeois's *Opus 133*, a 'Song of Farewell to Janet Gough'. The cover of the programme bore a quotation from Miss Strudwick which nicely captures the spirit of the High Mistress who had spent longer within St Paul's than any other: 'Schools exist to show how many possibilities there are.'

Subjects such as Design and Technology provide Paulinas with a wide range of skills.

MISS ELIZABETH M. DIGGORY, HIGH MISTRESS SINCE 1998

As successor to Janet Gough, the governors chose the complete teaching professional. Miss Elizabeth Diggory had read History at Westfield, Miss Gray's alma mater and taken her Post-Graduate Certificate of Education at Hughes Hall, Cambridge. She then taught for many years as an outstanding history

Miss Elizabeth Diggory, the School's current High Mistress.

teacher (1968–73) and head of department (1973–82) at King Edward VI High School for Girls, before moving to headships at St Alban's High School for Girls (1983–94) and Manchester High (1994–98). As Elizabeth Diggory rose in the profession, her love of History (especially early modern European) was complemented by her growing interest in educational ideas and administration. She was a founder member of the Girls' Schools Association Professional Committee and served as the Association President in 1991–92. She has been part of the movement to promote a General Teaching Council for England and is also experienced as an Independent Schools Inspector. Tall, slim and always elegantly dressed, the High Mistress combines dignity and calm with a distinct energy. On the sartorial side, she favours long skirts and tailored jackets, occasionally a trouser suit. She will whip out of her study in an instant if she wants to see somebody quickly. She often walks to school. Paulinas were surprised to observe their head, soon after her appointment, surveying Hammersmith Broadway at four thirty in the afternoon: she wanted to see their typical going home conditions for herself. It is not surprising to find that she is a devoted hill walker. As a lover of music and the theatre, however, Elizabeth Diggory is well-suited by London and found her appointment to St Paul's something of a homecoming.

The accession of a new High Mistress has served only to maintain the pace of change within the school. Paulinas are enjoying the facilities of the grand Sports Hall, its planning well underway in Miss Gough's time and its construction brought to completion by her successor. A formal opening is planned for the end of June 2000, accompanied with a study day on the theme of 'Women of the Millennium'. During July 1999, while most of the school was relaxing into the first weeks of the summer holiday, nineteen seventh formers and two teachers (Amy Power and Alexandra Bailey) undertook St Paul's first World Challenge Expedition: four weeks of camping, trekking and charity work in Peru. In that summer, too, the first Paulinas entered McKinsey's on their new internship scheme. In September 1999, St Paul's began its partnership scheme with William Morris Academy in Hammersmith. As ever, the school enjoys a flow of exciting guests and speakers: the American ambassador to the Court of St James for a Friday lecture, the great pianist Howard Shelley for a master class, Harold Pinter for a performance of *A Kind of Alaska* and *One for the Road*. In millennium year, the High Mistress also faces the task of guiding the school safely into the new Advanced Levels. These, in their annual examinations and distinction between "advanced supplementary" (AS) and "advanced two" (A2) qualifications, mark a dramatic break with the tradition of two-year A-levels which has been with the nation since the 1950s. In 2004, St Paul's will have an opportunity to celebrate and reflect on its first centenary, a step, at least, towards the thousand-year history which Frances Gray wanted for her school.

5

PAULINAS AND STAFF

I have a little studied physic; but now
I'm all for music; save, in the forenoons,
An hour or two for painting. I would have
A lady, indeed, to have all letters and arts,
Be able to discourse, to write, to paint

LADY POLITIC WOULD-BE: *Volpone*

Since 1904, some 8,000 Paulinas have passed through St Paul's. No general observations on their experiences, manners, attitudes and expectations could hold true for all. Many have loved the school, some have been matter-of-fact about it, others have been unhappy here, either because of the institution or for personal reasons. Moreover, by the time a girl had spent seven years or so in the same school, usually she was more than ready to leave. 'It would have been unfeeling', wrote Diane Hopkinson (*née* Hubback, St Paul's 1925–31) in *The Incense Tree*, 'if I had not shed a tear at the singing of the school hymn at the last day of term, but at eighteen I was happy to escape. . . . After I had passed out of the school doors for the last time . . . I gave my school hat a last jaunty twist in the hope of making it look a little smarter. Then suddenly realising I should never need it again, I snatched it off and tossed it over the school railings.' Anne Scott-James, in *Sketches from a Life* (1993) writes that 'From the ages of ten to eighteen I went to St Paul's Girls' School, and I am going to put myself for ever among the philistines by saying how much I enjoyed it . . . Looking back, as we all do, on a chequered life, I remember St Paul's as one of the white squares.' Yet, even she concedes that, in her last year, a little 'boredom crept into my enjoyment of my school days'. Faced with an extraordinary range of experiences and achievements, the chronicler of St Paul's needs to tread carefully. To quote an old saying of the Royal Artillery: 'When in a minefield, don't get up and run.' Tracing each Paulina who has made her mark in a profession would be an enormous task and probably impossible to discharge. To present a selection would be invidious and arbitrary. Paulinas who appear in the following pages, therefore, do not speak for all nor do they necessarily represent the most distinguished. Rather, their experiences illustrate and focus the things that seem to have mattered to the school.

Yet, Paulinas do have a reputation and, as the seventh High Mistress observed to the *Sunday Telegraph* (19 October 1997) 'the most amazing network, and wherever I go there will be somebody saying, "Hi, Miss Gough!"' At the time of writing (1999), a Paulina is the Principal of Newnham College, Cambridge and a life peer; another is Warden of Merton College, Oxford, one is a High Court Judge, another is a Director of Condé Nast Publications, one is a leader writer on the *Financial Times*, one is the Property Correspondent of *The Times*, another is the editor of *Vogue*, a former Head Girl is Chief Executive of *The Economist*, another Paulina is deputy editor of the *Spectator*, and the Foreign Editor of *The Times* is a Paulina. One looks at the *Cambridge Italian Dictionary*: the General Editor is a Paulina (Barbara Reynolds). Blackwell's 'book of the month' for August 1999 was by a Paulina (Samantha Weinberg, *A Fish Caught in Time*, Fourth Estate). Many are actresses and familiar faces on screen or stage. There are hundreds of Paulinas in accountancy, business, journalism, law and medicine. They appear in surprising places. A Paulina who read English at Oxford became a circus ring mistress and, in the school tradition, wrote a book on her experiences (Nell Stroud, *Josser*, 1999).

To see the names of Paulinas in the national press is no recent phenomenon. With remarkable speed and apparent ease, the school established itself as a training ground for part of the nation's future élite. The original Head Girl, Mary Mackenzie, a medievalist, became the first woman to be appointed Royal Archivist at Windsor Castle. Mary Brinton, not quite an original Paulina, for she joined the school in October 1904, became a social reformer and writer in the mould of Beatrice Webb, and, unlike her friend and mentor, was happy to be raised to the peerage (as Baroness Stocks). A Paulina, Evelyn Sharp, was the first woman to become a Permanent Secretary. Celia Johnson was a household name for many years, Joan Cross, who created the rôle of Queen Elizabeth in Britten's *Gloriana*, was a soprano with a world reputation. From the first, the school has produced a stream of writers: Dodie Smith and Angela Thirkell (*née* Mackail) amongst best-selling pre-war novelists, Lesley Blanche (the 'baroque angel' of Anne Scott-James's recollection), Monica Dickens, Antonia White (*née* Botting), Marghanita Laski and Brigid Brophy for the middle years of the century. Joan Robinson, *née* Maurice, is one of the towering figures of twentieth-century economics. Kathleen Kenyon (St Paul's, 1919–25) and Beatrice De Cardi (St Paul's, 1924–31) occupy a similar place in the pantheon of modern archaeologists.

A fortuitous combination of circumstances enabled Paulinas to seize a sig-

Muriel Walmsley, one of the first pupils of the school

Princess Mary inspecting the Girl Guides, July 1921.

nificant rôle in English society. In the first place, timing helped. By 1904, the secondary and higher education of girls had become commonplace. London had thousands of parents who were ready to pay for their daughters' education. Great prestige accompanied the names of St Paul, John Colet and the Mercers' Company and it exercised a magnetic effect upon parents. Many were prepared to abandon high schools in favour of the girls' counterpart to St Paul's School. Of course, this initial impetus would be maintained only if St Paul's fulfilled expectations. As indeed it did so, the school was from 1903 onwards able to choose the cream of its applicants for places.

Secondly, an overwhelming advantage was derived from the Brook Green site, within the whirl of the metropolis but also able to draw on the huge reserves of London created during the late Victorian period. St Paul's benefited from parents who were ambitious and often highly educated themselves. Socially, they formed a cross-section of the middle and upper ranks of London society. We have seen, in Chapter 1, that Frances Gray imagined that a 'public school' would draw its pupils from a social stratum above those who were 'high school girls'. The social reality of the intake belied her expectations. There seems to have been no difference between the kind of parents who were prepared to send their daughters to St Paul's and those who sent them to the foundations of the Girls' Public Day School Trust. It is just conceivable that some children from affluent or landed households might have been diverted to St Paul's instead of proceeding, say, to the Ladies' College, Cheltenham. Even if this occurred, it was the case only infrequently, since few Paulinas came from the established gentry or aristocracy. Sometimes a link was established through marriage. Thus Mary Grenfell (St

117

Paul's, 1924–8), a gifted young historian who won a scholarship to Somerville, married Geoffrey Waldegrave, who succeeded his father as the twelfth Earl Waldegrave in 1936. Lady Waldegrave sent her daughters to St Paul's and became a Lady Governor (1950–70). Daughters of her son William are also Paulinas. Lady May Cambridge (St Paul's, 1921–3), daughter of Alice, daughter of Leopold, son of Queen Victoria, who attended school with her chaperone, was a talking point precisely because other members of the royal family were not attending St Paul's. The Countess of Huntingdon did send her daughters to St Paul's (Lady Harriet Hastings, Mrs Shackleton, 1957–63 and Lady Selina, the biographer, 1956–62). From 1904 onwards, however, the parents were predominantly professional: lawyers, academics, doctors, civil servants, journalists, some politicians, a few broadcasters, a sprinkling of actors, the occasional rock or jazz star (Pete Townshend, Cleo Laine and John Dankworth) to enliven the tapestry: 'a refined distillation of the chattering classes', according to the *Evening Standard* (9 July 1992).

Remarkable people do not have to come from exceptional family backgrounds. Nevertheless, many Paulina parents have had social and intellectual connections which have encouraged the creative intelligence of their children. Family links are also of some historical interest. Joan Robinson, for instance, described by Lord Kaldor as 'after Keynes . . . the most prominent name associated with the Cambridge School of Economics', was the great-granddaughter of F. D. Maurice, the Christian Socialist, the granddaughter of Major-General J. F. Maurice, a star of Victorian army reform and the daughter of Major-General Frederick Maurice of the notorious 'Maurice Debate' in 1918. A tradition of reform and the removal of proved injustice was the essence of the Maurice family. This did not dictate, of course, Joan's intellectual pathways. Nonetheless, she chose to read Economics because, as Professor G. C. Harcourt writes, 'she wanted to know why poverty and unemployment existed'. The family context of another great Paulina and classicist, Elizabeth Rawson, has been explored by Professor Peter Wiseman (*Proceedings of the British Academy*, 84: 1993). Her father Graham held a doctorate from the University of Jena, wrote historical dramas and translated German plays; her mother, 'an intellectual to the backbone' came from a Dutch Jewish family. Their relatives included the Gigliucci family of northern Italy, and over a period of twenty years Elizabeth Rawson regularly visited their mansions near Florence and Milan and absorbed there a profound sense of Roman history and Italian culture. When she came to St Paul's, she was already intellectually formidable. Professor Wiseman quotes a Paulina contemporary: 'She had read every book mentioned in English lessons, she knew more history than we were taught, her languages were excellent.' According to her brother John, she had read all Shakespeare by the age of 10. To take another instance: the novelist Angela Thirkell, *née* Mackail, was the granddaughter of Edward Burne-Jones; her father, John, was a civil servant but also a translator, biographer and was elected to the Chair of Poetry

at Oxford in 1905. Through her grandfather, Angela was drawn into the Wyndham, Tennant and Asquith families and later aspects of their lives and houses appear in her novels. Examples of Paulinas with comparable connections could be multiplied by the hundred. The status and social backgrounds of their parents did provide an intellectual charge.

Provision for scholarships was a third element in the high quality of the pupils. Though many of the St Paul's parents found the fees comfortably within their means, others needed financial help. The assumption that pre-war school fees were modest compared with their current levels hardly stands up to scrutiny. Initially, the tuition fee was £7 per term. As a rough guide to the real cost of fees in 1904, we can compare them with typical teaching salaries. In 1904, the median salary for St Paul's staff was approximately £150 p.a. This was probably rather above comparable salaries in grammar and high schools. Nigel Watson's history of Queenswood School (*In Hortis Reginae*, 1994) compares the recommended HMC scale of £105 to £150 with the average salary at Queenswood of £70 p.a. But if we take the St Paul's figure for comparison, then annual fees would have been 14 per cent of a £150 salary. The 1998–9 tuition fees at St Paul's were £7,377, accounting for 26.34 per cent of a median salary of, say, £28,000. Against this slightly higher proportion should be set, however, the original and formidable music fees, set in 1904 at £4.4s. a term, 60 per cent of the tuition fee. This was far higher in real terms than the 1998–9 figure of £130 per term for individual music lessons. Similarly, fees for lunch (or dinner, as it was called until the 1970s) were originally three guineas per term, nearly half the tuition fee. Moreover, yet more fees, of a guinea a term, were required for lessons in

Facing Page: *The organ in the Great Hall (main picture).*
Inset: *Orchestra with Dr Derek Bourgeois.*

deportment. So, although neat comparisons would be misleading, it would seem that, set beside their 1999 counterparts, the 1904 parents were paying more in real terms for fees if their daughters had music lessons and remained in school for the midday meal.

For many families, then, a system of scholarships was helpful or, in some cases, indispensable. Once committed to their public school for girls, the Mercers were determined to ensure that a generous provision of scholarships matched the splendid buildings. For many years, the Colet Foundation funded the awards and, indeed, much else. It was not until the 1970s that the school was running chiefly on fees. During the financial year ending 1909, for instance, the Colet Estate provided £10,000 and fees £6,361; twenty years later the figures were £10,000 and £18,968. For the year running September to September 1991–2, however, only £40,000 came from the Estate and almost £3 million from the fees. The real value of the scholarships (renamed 'First Year Awards' for the 11-year-olds in 1979–80) shadowed the fortunes of the Colet Foundation. Following the original 1879 Scheme of the Charity Commissioners, the school offered thirty-nine scholarships (increased in 1922 to fifty). These were awarded according to performance in scholarships examinations and they carried exemption from tuition fees. Since the criterion was academic merit, not need, the parents of some scholarships girls could have carried the fees easily, but, by the same token, others could not have sent their daughters to St Paul's without the scholarships. When, in 1921, some Governors proposed to dilute the principle of academic merit with some concern for financial need, Miss Gray replied firmly:

> If the Scholarships ever come to be looked upon as assistance given to Girls who . . . are not necessarily the best workers or the most able girls of the School, I think that Scholarships will lose a very great deal of their value, and they will not be sought for by many girls whose financial circumstances might justify them in holding them, simply because they will not choose to compete.

The Governors yielded to Miss Gray on this point, but, as a compromise, parents of scholarship girls were asked whether they wanted the financial benefit as well as the honour for their daughters. If parents were prepared to pay the fees after all, then the money was quietly transferred to girls in need. As the files at Mercers' Hall record, many generous parents inverted a common practice and, instead of having their fees waived, waived their fee remission.

From 1904 onwards, St Paul's has tried to find ways of opening its doors to able pupils whose parents could not afford the fees. The original system worked happily until the Second World War, when the yield from the Colet Foundation fell away drastically. Moreover, the Education Act of August 1944, which established the 'eleven-plus' examination in national consciousness, also permitted local authorities to pay fees for pupils at independent schools.

Basketball was a popular choice for early pupils of the school. Netball soon took over.

Miss Osborn responded enthusiatically and adroitly to both these challenges: the falling value of the Colet Foundation and the chance of securing bright pupils who were otherwise destined for the grammar schools. So, in 1952, the number of awards was increased to thirty scholarships and forty exhibitions, but they were to cover respectively only half and two-thirds of fees. Some 50 per cent of the awards were to go to candidates from outside the school. Moreover, the age at which the junior scholarships or exhibitions could be awarded was reduced to 11 (rather than 13), to divert some girls from grammar schools into St Paul's. Finally, Miss Osborn took some girls from primary schools whose fees were paid by the relevant local authorities. The Osborn system worked well into the late 1960s. By then, the Colet Foundation was nearly exhausted. The value of scholarships and exhibitions remained constant in absolute terms. After the inflationary decade of the 1970s, therefore, the awards were offering, apart from considerable prestige, little more than prize money. But by then the assisted places scheme of the successive Thatcher administrations allowed a number of girls to come free to the school. As assisted places were being phased out after the accession of Labour to power in 1997, the school responded by an ambitious expansion of its scholarship opportunities. Several awards have been established by former parents, some are funded directly by the Honourable Company of Mercers and others by the Scholarship Fund successfully launched by Janet Gough in her last two years as High Mistress.

If we were to identify a fourth reason for the fine intake of pupils, it could be the quality of the staff. Frances Gray deserves recognition for gathering a superb common room. She was determined that her staff should be able to live properly on teaching salaries, and was prepared to offer enough above the common rates to attract able and ambitious women. Before long, teachers in the area knew that St Paul's could serve as a springboard to swift promotion and often to headships. The loading on the salaries was not substantial but it was enough to matter. In 1904, the Deputy Head, Miss Hilda Wenham, was on £170 p.a. and most of the full-time staff on £130–50. This was only on the upper limit of the HMC recommendation of 1906, but over the next few years most of the staff moved towards £200. Moreover, many employers, especially of women teachers, paid less than the HMC-approved salaries. A respectable, if modest, income and the name of the school ensured that Miss Gray was inundated with applications. She was able to appoint some remarkable teachers to her first common room. The senior Maths Mistress, Miss E. T. Bullock, had not only taken a degree in that subject at Cambridge (Newnham) but had also gained First Class in the Modern Languages Tripos, Cambridge. The Second Mistress, Hilda Wenham, came with Miss Gray from St Katharines School, St Andrews. Although Miss Wenham had read Classics at Westfield College, London, she was a gifted Maths teacher. Miss Wenham was known as 'Madonna' because of her oval face, downcast eyes and gentle manner and, according to her niece Susan,

Hilda Wenham

Miss Hilda Wenham, Miss
Gray's Second Mistress.

Facing page: *Girls studying
in the light and spacious
Colet Library (main picture).*
Inset: *The original Library
with Frances Gray's portrait.*

'had a characteristic smooth walk which made the girls say that she went on along "on little wheels"'. 'Her work', the High Mistress told the Governors in 1914, 'has been beyond praise.' From St Andrews, too, came Miss Ethel Moor as senior Geography Mistress. Miss Gray cherished Miss Moor's subject and would claim, inexplicably, that the two most important subjects were 'Geography and Obedience'. Was she playing a variation on 'industry and obedience' in which Thackeray's amiable Miss Sedley had excelled at Miss Pinkerton's academy for young ladies? 'I used to go', said Miss Gray in bidding farewell to Miss Moor, 'and listen to her lessons for the sheer pleasure they gave me.' To the Inspectors of 1925, 'she has the power of infusing her own enthusiasm into the girls, with the result that Geography lessons are looked to with great eagerness'. Constance Flood-Jones, a member of the Royal Drawing Society, whose work had been praised as 'thoughtful and powerful' by *Vanity Fair* (November 1889) and for its 'freedom and intelligence' by *The Times* (15 October 1889), became 'Drawing and Painting' Mistress. Curiously, she was appointed, at £200 p.a., on a higher salary than the Second Mistress. She was Frances Gray's first Dame Christian of *The Masque*, she managed both to be a keen suffragist and a Dame of the Primrose League and, most importantly, made sure that Art really mattered in the curriculum. Of Miss Gray's exceptional Music department, more below.

Staff such as these, names taken from a long list of fine teachers, set standards, attracted parents and also made the common room a fascinating place in which to work. Its mood, at times a little satirical, is deliciously captured by D. M. Greenwood in *Holy Terrors* (1994). Some teachers are looking at a notice:

> The Upper School Lent Concert of Sacred Music will take place on Thursday 17 April at 7.45 p.m. Invitations to parents and Governors will go out by the end of seventh week. Heads of year please organise. The Senior School Orchestra will have the honour to be conducted by Sir Solomon Piatigorsky, the distinguished conductor. Staff will need to excuse girls from lessons for rehearsals from third week onwards. Mr Colt will arrange rehearsal times. Miss Brighouse will co-ordinate. I know the occasion will be a memorable one for us all. A.M.P.

> 'I wish she wouldn't tell us how distinguished everyone is', said Miss Troutbeck. A tall woman, she stood behind her colleagues and eyed the notice from a distance. 'And if you were in any doubt about the function of conductors, they conduct.'
> 'Piatigorsky's tempi at *Aida* last night were eccentric', said Miss Brighouse, whose interests were wide. She was on her way to gather books and gave it but a passing glance.
> 'I hope he's not going to be too ambitious with our girls' tempi', said Mrs Gulland, who never liked to be left behind in any conversation which combined social with intellectual snobbery.

'How does she know the occasion will be memorable before it's happened?' said Mr Colt in his Welsh innocence, pausing in his effort to move the cello towards the door.

'Can one use 'co-ordinate' as an intransitive?', Miss King enquired to no one in particular as the gong sounded for 9.15 a.m. school.

Dante Gabriel Cromwell, Head of Art, who was, on principle, late for all engagements, did not spare the notice so much as a glance as he strode through the staffroom to collect his mail.

Having, as it were, cut their teeth on the first Mistress's bone, they scattered in search of hymn books and Bibles, registers and markbooks, the paraphernalia of ordinary academic life without which even St Veep's could hardly function.

Joyce Field taking part in a League Tennis match on 20 July 1916.

For most Paulinas, the entrance examination was their first encounter with the school and for many it remained a vivid memory. Others, like Monica Dickens's heroine in *Mariana*, retained only a hazy sense of surprise that their performance had opened the great front doors. 'In spite of the fact that she paraphrased "Much have I travelled in the realms of gold" as "I have made several expeditions to the gold-mine district", and had to write a French essay on trees without knowing the word for leaf, Mary passed the entrance examination for St Martin's High School.' It is a now a full-blown range of interviews for all candidates and tests in English, Mathematics and comprehension which lies in wait for the St Paul's candidates at the end of the London senior entrance examinations. Things were less formal in the early days. The entrance test was usually conducted by Miss Gray in whatever way seemed to be appropriate to the candidate, like a miniature interview for a job. She apparently ignored the Scheme of 1879, which required that the admission examination take the following form: Reading; writing from dictation; the first four rules of Arithmetic; the Geography of England; and Plain Needlework. 'I took the Entrance Examination when I was little more than 8 years old', wrote Margaret Sweeten (*née* Barrie, St Paul's 1918–28) in *Paulina*, 1986. 'Miss Gray was sitting in a big, comfortable chair by a blazing fire. It was welcoming and informal; she smiled sweetly and asked me if I knew any poetry, so I set off at great speed with "The Pied Piper", planning to go the whole course but she started to laugh, stopped me and suggested that I tried some French. I pressed on, undaunted, until she told me to come and sit beside her. I was her slave from that moment.' Vera Woolcombe, an original Paulina, vaguely recalled on 19 January 1904 itself, the opening day, 'a sort of Entrance Exam., so that we would be sorted into Forms', taking place after morning assembly and between hockey and the distribution of school hats. Helen Franklin, whose niece would be Rosalind Franklin, found herself placed in what she described as 'a very low Form. This shocked me . . . So my first day at the school, I walked boldly into the room of Miss Gray. . . She was a charming Irish woman, with a keen sense of humour. Some found her alarming, but in these days I had not learnt to be frightened of people. When she asked me with, I imagine, some amusement, what I wanted, I explained that I wanted to be in the same Form as my friends.' So long as Helen promised 'to work hard and behave well', she was allowed to go up two Forms. For Alexandra Roudybush (*née* Brown, St Paul's 1926–9), 'Miss Gray, with her silky, snow-white hair piled on her head, her rustling black gown and her piercing blue eyes behind silver-rimmed glasses, was awe-inspiring indeed and her aura filled that tiny room' (the small office off the Marble). She then asked the well-nigh petrified child to read aloud, to do some arithmetic and Latin and to write an essay on the Pilgrim Fathers.

By the 1920s, the entrance exam had became more formal and included an English essay and arithmetic. Grisell Davies (*née* Roy, St Paul's 1929–37) was told (aged 10) that she had only to take 'a little examination', but her anxious mother warned her that 'the school had high standards' and 'Do try to remember that seven eights are fifty six!' By 1929, the examination had settled into the pattern it broadly retains: an essay, often in response to imagery, Mathematics and an interview. Grisell wrote on a picture from the *Illustrated London News* and told Miss Strudwick that her favourite subjects were 'Singing and Gym'. When Miss Kilroe asked her whether she had done vulgar fractions, Grisell replied 'with a shocked negative'. According to Diane Hopkinson (*née* Hubback, St Paul's 1925–31) in *The Incense Tree*, it was her essay on Walter de la Mare, 'Like Stars upon Some Gloomy Grove', that secured her place at St Paul's and, cunningly reworked, a junior scholarship the following year. 'No one spotted this bit of chicanery.' To be fair to Miss Gray, the scholarship papers were a different matter from the entrance examination and were formal and formidable from November 1903 onwards. Indeed, the very first one produced a disconcertingly high standard deviation; Ailsa Yoxall scored 88 per cent for Mathematics, astonishing for those days, but two sisters, both already at St Paul's, managed to score only 8 and 6 per cent respectively.

Successive High Mistresses have been right to dismiss the charge that St Paul's is a school controlled by examinations. Nevertheless, in a school that aspired to be highly academic, examination results could not but quickly assume a starring rôle. The Scheme of the Charity Commissioners (1879) required annual examinations to be sat – by the 'Scholars' according to the exact wording, but this technicality was bypassed. All Paulinas were set examinations. But Frances Gray looked to the school's reputation in the public sphere as well as the private. In this sense, she and some of her colleagues were pioneers. In 1908, for example, the Cambridge Board issued 1,079 certificates, the vast majority of which went to boys' schools. The presence of St Paul's Girls' was, however, already noticeable; it received eleven certificates while, to provide a comparison, Eton had twenty-five, South Hampstead Girls' one and Oxford High seven. Not all her counterparts

1919 Gymnastic team.

accepted that girls could compete equally with boys. In a popular collection of essays published in 1911, *Public Schools for Girls*, Miss Gadesden, the Head Mistress of Blackheath High School, wrote that examinations made girls 'run the risk of serious injury to brain and body'. It had been a commonplace of Victorian England that girls were by temperament unsuited for competitive examinations. Lord Lyttelton told the Court of the Mercers' Company (27 February 1874) that the proposed girls' school would be able to sit examinations only 'in a qualified or modified form'. By the turn of the century, however, this assumption was dissolving in the face of experience.

It did take a few years for St Paul's to adjust to the demands of the examination boards. Some glittering prizes were amongst the first cohort – twenty-five girls were entered for the Higher Local (Cambridge) Certificate in 1909 and of these nine gained first class and six were 'distinguished' in one or more subjects. Ailsa Yoxall won a three-year Cambridge Local scholarship, distinctions in Latin, Roman and Greek History and the Fletcher Prize for passing highest in Ancient Greek – as well as the Newnham Classical Scholarship. This was at a time when the examiners' report (for 1908) stated: 'The numbers of girls' schools who send candidates for this examination is markedly on the increase . . . [but] not many attempt Latin and Greek with success.' Early triumphs encouraged the High Mistress to put in a group for the Joint Oxford and Cambridge Board. To her disappointment, there were several failures. These occurred, she wrote, partly because some of the girls were 'much too young' but chiefly because of the unreasonable nature of the questions and because the relevant examiner was biased against girls' schools. Of one paper, to take an instance, she wrote: 'Number seven expects girls and boys to give an estimate of the part played in Greek History by any two of the following: Isagoras, Thrasybulus, Conon, Aeschines. Conon is all very well, but surely better known names should have been given instead of the other three.' (Only Aeschines gains an index reference in the 1998 edition of *The Oxford Companion to Classical Civilization*, a book one might take to be aimed at schools today.) The board accepted that such questions were unreasonably particular, but as for the accusation of bias: the Head Mistress of Putney High wrote to Frances Gray that the examiner in question 'had always found the girls' papers poor, and I gather that he intends to find them poor so long as he examines'.

Before long, however, a steady pattern of high performance emerged, for the Cambridge and the Joint boards and also for London matriculation. Twenty-five girls took the Higher (Cambridge) Local Examination in 1915: all eight entered for Languages achieved distinctions, nine of the eleven entered for History did likewise. Zoe Craies, dissolving the supposed 'snowline' between humanities and Science, won distinctions for both Mathematics and History. Academic successes were engraved on the honours board by Mr Green, with his 'unerring little hammer and his gold leaf' (Miss Osborn); by 1959 he had been the school's engraver for fifty-three years. St Paul's rapidly became celebrated for the number of Paulinas who won Oxford and Cambridge places, though from the 1960s, and largely because of Mrs Munro, there was growing sensitivity to an overplaying of the Oxbridge card. From 1980 Paulina began to publish university places gained as a simple alphabetical list, rather than isolating Oxford and Cambridge first in a position of honour. League tables have tended to reinforce the preoccupation with A-level results in general rather than with entrance to the ancient universities. Whatever one may think of the tables, they are apparently here to stay; parents study them and newspaper editors enjoy them. If the tables were not run semi-officially (with ISIS serving the data for independent schools to the press) then an enterprising publicist would certainly undertake their compilation. The *Daily Telegraph*, which bases its tables on the A/B percentage, plays the game with its 'Premier League' and 'First Division'. League tables have not, however, troubled St Paul's. The school has never been out of the *Daily Telegraph's* 'Premier League' of the top ten schools in England and Wales and has (up to 1999) twice headed the entire list. *The Times* from 1998 decided to base its results on average points per subject entry. By this criterion, St Paul's Girls' in that year came fifth (and also fifth by the *Daily Telegraph* measurement). In 1999 the school was fourth in *The Times* list. As for GCSE, the achievement is even more striking: St Paul's topped *The Times* and the *Daily Telegraph's* national tables for 1996, 1997, 1998 and 1999. *The Times*, 30 August 1997, carried the headline: 'GIRLS' SCHOOL SHATTERS GCSE RECORD' and continued: 'Some 95 per cent of St Paul's Girls' entries were awarded an A or A* grade. More than 60 per cent reached the coveted A*, compared with the national average of 3.6 per cent.' Forget Eton, ran the caption to the accompanying cartoon, put him down for St Paul's Girls [sic]'. The next year, 64 per cent reached the A*; in 1999, 67 per cent. The *Sunday Times*, 1 November 1998, gave a twirl to the figures by weighting A-level results (based on the A/B percentage) and GCSE results (based on the proportion of A/A* results). By this standard, St Paul's Girls' School was placed first in the national lists. The next year, in The *Sunday Times* for 14 November, it came second. For St Paul's, therefore, the league tables have served only to confirm its academic reputation. Amidst the whirl of statistics, however, it was reassuring to hear the High Mistress's comment to *The Times*, 5 September 1998: 'People do not think about league tables here . . . [Paulinas] are highly motivated, stable girls who benefit from excellent teaching. But we also put great store by Music, Sport and the other extracurricular activities that girls enjoy.'

Music is something the entire school has enjoyed from the first. 'It is of great importance', wrote Miss Gray to Sir John Watney on 5 May 1904, 'that the parents should understand . . . that we intend to make the music of the School of more than ordinary merit.' This modest aim was fulfilled with spectacular success. Our second chapter has shown how the Mercers equipped S

Paul's with the Walker organ and, in 1913, a genuine *conservatoire*. As far as staff were concerned, the school was exceptionally fortunate, but largely because of Frances Gray's unerring instinct for the right appointment. As the school opened, she managed to scoop Mrs Adine O'Neill, née Rückert, as chief piano Mistress. For concerts and in the prospectus, she was generally described as 'Mrs Norman O'Neill, Medallist of the Paris *Conservatoire*, pupil of Clara Schumann'. Of Swiss and French parentage, she had grown up and studied in Paris. Her husband was a composer who had been born in Kensington, had studied at the Frankfurt Conservatorium and for many years (1924–34) was Professor of Harmony and Composition at the Royal Academy of Music. During her thirty-three years at St Paul's, Adine O'Neill brought a touch of international excitement to its music. Not only was she a revered teacher, so that there were far more pupils who wished to study with her than she could take on, she played at the Proms and for the BBC, was famed as an interpreter of Scarlatti and Debussy and served for fifteen years as London critic of *Le Monde Musicale* and as President of the Society of Women Musicians from 1921 to 1923. Warm, fashionable and talkative, 'she mothered us all', wrote Vally Lasker in *Paulina* (Autumn 1947). 'We were told what concerts to go to, what societies to join, what clothes to wear and where to buy them . . . Her knowledge of the English language was not great and in moments of agitation she would burst into French and I into German and sometimes Mr O'Neill had to be called in to interpret.' Vally Lasker (1885–1978) herself was a famous piano teacher, who taught at St Paul's until her seventies and then worked, Imogen Holst remembered, until she was over 90 at the Royal College of Music, 'binding and repairing vocal scores in

Orchestral rehearsal with Hilary Davan Wetton.

Gustav Holst, probably St Paul's Girls' School's most famous teacher.

the opera department'. (Even she was exceeded, in longevity as a teacher, by Signorini Manzi, the Italian teacher, who retired in 1958 at the age of 82.) Before the war, Miss Murray writes, 'all the Mistresses were ladies and the Music staff grandes dames'.

It was Gustav Holst who gave the department a national reputation, however much he owed to the help, eloquently acknowledged, of others, 'the attendant satellites, who circled around him like planets' (Diana Hubback). In October 1905, Adine O'Neill told Miss Gray that Mr von Holst was a remarkable young composer. He was then 30. She interviewed him immediately. 'I have appointed Mr Gustav von Holst,' Miss Gray told the Governors in October 1905. 'He has made a special study of the care and development of girls' voices . . . I was guided . . . also by the fact that he is a musician who continues his own studies and is engaged in the production of original work. I am convinced that the best teachers of Music . . . are those who keep some time for their own study.' Thus was established the marvellous tradition of Directors of Music who have also been composers. The preposition *von* and Holst's ancestry – his great-grandfather Matthias had been harp teacher to the Russian imperial family – made him a trifle exotic. By 1905, however, the family was third-generation English, *von* had been adopted by his grandfather Gustavus Valentine only after settling in England, and Holst himself had no secure command of any European language apart from English. It is entirely appropriate that he was a leading composer of the twentieth-century renaissance of English music. Miss Gray and Holst became great friends; she loved the sense of a creative, original mind in her school and was happy to accommodate his manifold commitments, at James Allen Girls' School, Morley College, Wycombe Abbey, Thaxted and in the capital's concert halls. She had authority which his gentle, academic manner never challenged. 'Mr Holst asks my advice', Miss Gray told Nora Day, 'and then does something else. He told me it helped him to make up his mind.' Her powers of command were needed at first, since Holst had some trouble with discipline; one Paulina reported that a 'female dragon' (probably Vally Lasker) sat in his lessons to fix the girls with a glittering eye. Once he became famous, his reputation went before him. Joan Harris was astonished to hear that he was supposed to have had discipline problems, and also wrote (in *The Composer*, Summer 1974), that his 'manners were always courtly although he could be quite firm in showing his displeasure'.

Holst composed easily at St Paul's, especially when the new Music Wing was opened in 1913 and he acquired his beloved soundproof room from which, as Imogen Holst wrote, 'he could never be parted for very long'. For Holst, as Herbert Howells observed in 1951, 'the most desirable paths were those that led . . . to Brook Green . . . and to a quiet double-windowed room just along the corridor that flanks this Singing Hall'. Many of his pieces were either for Paulinas or composed in the context of the school. *The St Paul's Suite* (1913) was the first work composed in the new Music study and *The*

Brook Green Suite (1933) was one of the last. Much of *The Planets* was written in that room, with Vally Lasker and Nora Day, another stalwart of the Music department, acting as amanuenses and joint pianists to test the work in progress.Dorothy Ramsbotham (Mrs Otter) remembered turning the pages with her friend Nancy Gotch (Mrs Strode) for Misses Day and Lasker: 'We heard the most incredible, frightening sounds and had a glimpse of a new kind of conducting in 5/4 time. But mostly it was the task of reading the manuscript that absorbed us and the two pianists were also stretched. At the end Gussie bowed and said, "Well Nancy and Dorothy, you have been present at the performance of Mars." On another occasion, Nancy wrote in *The Conductors' Guild Bulletin* (Summer 1974), 'A friend and I peered through the double windows of Mr Holst's room and he, catching sight of us, called us in and said "What about not doing any harmony today – I've just finished a new piece, shall we play it?" It was Saturn, and it always remained my favourite of all *The Planets*.' It was exciting for the school to have a Director of Music who was gaining an international reputation. Virtually everyone was involved in the first performance of *The Planets*, a private occasion in the Queen's Hall, Sunday 29 September 1918, when it was received with a standing ovation. The news that his opera, *The Perfect Fool*, the story of a wizard whose attempts to win the princess are frustrated by the fool, was to be produced at Covent Garden (May 1923) provoked some awe at school. Unfortunately, unlike *The Planets*, this work attracted mixed notices and did not last. Although the *Daily News* (15 May 1923), welcomed it as 'brilliant . . . a work of first-rate interest', most reviews were in a different vein. To the *Sunday Times* it was a 'heavy and obscure musical joke'; to Truth, 'it is extremely dull even as an entertainment . . . the plot of the opera is simple but unintelligible'.

More satisfying was *The Masque*. This was composed to words by Frances Gray and first performed in 1909 to 'a fashionable and crowded audience' (*West London Observer*, 30 July). Dame Christian, mother of Dean Colet and mourning her son's death, falls asleep in her garden at Stebenhith (Stepney). She then has a dream or a vision in which she is visited by the Spirits of Learning, Piety, Patriotism and Poetry, who foretell the great achievements of St Paul's School. Attendants then dance, solemnly. Finally a child appears, representing St Paul's Girls' School, and to this child the four Spirits promise their help. *The Masque* mattered profoundly to Miss Gray. Once Constance Flood-Jones had played Colet's mother, Miss Gray liked to address her as 'Dear Dame Christian' and in her obituary of her senior Art Mistress Miss Gray wrote that 'perhaps the greatest service she performed for the School . . . was the presentation she gave of Dame Christian in *The Masque*'. The work poses some problems. Its music is beautiful – *The Times* (28 March 1935) wrote of 'its strong English tunes . . . and that mingling of purity and warmth which is Holst's most distinctive characteristic' – but it serves to conceal the artificial style of the libretto. Part of it is familiar to Paulinas now as

Holst in his specially-designed sound-proof room.

129

the *Hymn of Praise to God*, sung by the Attendants of the Spirit of Piety. In striving for solemnity, Miss Gray achieved an awkward text laden with falsely archaic language. This is the Child, speaking for St Paul's Girls' School:

> Sprung from thy lineage and co-heir with those
> That guard with filial zeal thy son's great name,
> Mother! I bring to thee a daughter's love,
> The offering of a daughter's tender care,
> Not all unworthy would I be of him:
> Not all unmeet to call myself thy child.

Nevertheless, taken in the right mood and as a period piece, *The Masque* can delight. A private recording of the music, made on 14 October 1973, seems to have been a lovely occasion: 'the Singing Hall was full of magic, warmth and excitement', recorded *Paulina*. Another and more famous piece has an intimate link with St Paul's. This is Gustav Holst's setting to music of *I vow to thee, my country*, by Sir Cecil Spring-Rice. The genesis of the hymn has been recounted by Eric James in *The Hymn Society: Bulletin* for January 1982. Spring-Rice had been replaced as ambassador to Washington by Lord Reading nine months after America's declaration of war on the German Empire, 3 April 1917. Spring-Rice, who loved the States and found his recall hard to bear, consoled himself, 'in some bitterness of soul' by writing the two stanzas of the poem. A month after leaving Washington, he died. His daughter Elizabeth, who had just become a Paulina, showed the words to Holst who found, to his astonishment, that they fitted the central melody of 'Jupiter' in *The Planets*. Thus was born one of the celebrated hymns of our age, often taken, and curiously in view of its origins, to be a tribute to Britain's imperial sunset.

Holst and his colleagues raised school Music to a standard which managed, almost, to move the educational inspectors. Singing, ran the University of London's Report of February 1920, 'is in the hands of a teacher who is not only reckoned amongst our most accomplished composers, but is also of great reputation as a conductor capable of exciting and maintaining the enthusiasm of any choir or orchestra under his control . . . The relations between master and pupils are obviously unusually happy'. The successors of Holst, who died in office on 25 May 1934, have maintained the great tradition: 'In its teaching of Music St Paul's has been', the Inspectors noted in May 1936, 'more than usually fortunate. That Music is not a luxury but a necessity has always been a guiding principle.' For a couple of years (1934–6), Ralph Vaughan Williams acted as the school's 'musical adviser', as he did not wish to become a permanent Director. It was at his urging, however, that Herbert Howells came to St Paul's. Christopher Palmer's *Herbert Howells – a Centenary Celebration* (1992) quotes Vaughan Williams's letter of 1936:

A performance of The Masque, *with words by Frances Gray and music by Holst, 1935.*

I do hope you will see your way to taking over SPGS. We all feel that some new blood is wanted and that there is a danger of the Gustav tradition becoming dry bones and also that Vally [Lasker] and Nora [Day] have no outside standard by which to judge their work . . . you are the only person who, because of your knowledge of the school and your love of Gustav, could at the same time work well with those who have been so nobly carrying on the great work of Gustav over the last two years. Do go soon to Miss Strudwick to talk it over.

Howells did so and became Director of Music for the next twenty-six years. He remained, however, part-time as he had a host of other commitments, not least at the Royal College of Music, where he was a professor from 1949. This 'tiny, immaculately neat man, silver white hair parted on one side, wearing a navy-blue Crombie', as Liane Aukin (St Paul's 1947–53) remembered him, combined inspirational teaching with formidably high standards. 'Dr Howells was held in awe', says Celia Hextall (Mrs Celia Rust, St Paul's 1946–51). He was also a shrewd organiser, and expanded the circle of distinguished peripatetic musicians who taught at the school. Winifred Roberts (St Paul's 1934–49; Mrs Geraint Jones), one of the school's finest musicians, has left a memorable judgement: 'Very few children have the luck to be in constant touch with a first-class practising musician, a man writing fine music and of the highest status in the profession . . . He made chords incredibly exciting, and his unfolding of the relationship of one note to another sent me spinning into a wild exploration of all sorts of music.'

Howells was succeeded by another composer, John Gardner (Director of

First page of the score for Brook Green Suite, *composed by Holst for the School.*

Music 1962–75). 'He was one to set the Thames on fire,' recalled Joan Harris, fondly. Like Howells, Gardner had an attractive physical presence and enormous energy. During the war he had been the master of the RAF Fighter Command Band and had flown as a navigator. Like Howells, too, Gardner combined his work at St Paul's with a myriad of other activities, including his Professorship of Composition and Harmony at the Royal Academy of Music (1956–86). It was Gardner who made the Christmas concert a special feature of St Paul's. 'On these occasions', wrote Joseph Horowitz, a fellow composer and a friend, 'he managed to make a large crowd of amateurs sing intricate contrapuntal structures within a few minutes by avoiding academic jargon, by imposing on us carefully chosen speeds which helped to sustain long notes, by adding piquant orchestral support when our melodic memory might have failed us.' Gardner's setting of 'Tomorrow shall be my Dancing Day', 'a tiny gem of a song' (Horowitz) has become a *sine qua non* of the Christmas concert. Gardner's successor was another Oxford musician: Nicola Le Fanu, Director of Music 1975–7, who had won the BBC Composers' Competition in 1971. When she left St Paul's to devote herself to university music and to composition, the High Mistress decided to make the post full-time. Her Director of Music from 1977 to 1993 was Hilary Davan Wetton. He is an exciting and gifted conductor with innumerable concerts and broadcasts and many recordings to his credit; few people can command such intense concentration from a choir of hundreds. Besides his post at St Paul's, he conducted the Milton Keynes City Orchestra and the Guildford Choral Society, the Holst Singers and other choirs. The appointment of Dr Derek Bourgeois (January 1994–) saw a return to the tradition of Director as composer as well as teacher; indeed, he studied composition with Herbert Howells at the Royal College. He has written seven symphonies, eight concertos and dozens of other instrumental and choral pieces as well as much music for television productions. But he is also a conductor and, as founder of the National Youth Chamber Orchestra (1988), deeply committed to musical education amongst the young. Admirers of Holst and his legacy can look with delight on the present and with optimism to the future.

As for the curriculum in general, St Paul's established powerful traditions in all the main academic subjects. Over the decades, the school day has gradually moved forward as has, more recently, the entire school year. Originally, the school day ran from 9.30 a.m., when Prayers were held, to 4.30 p.m., with twenty minutes for morning break, ninety minutes for the midday meal and the hours from 2.30 to 4.30 p.m. being devoted to games, prep, drawing, Gym and Music lessons. A 'luncheon' of milk and biscuits, in Miss Gray's phrase, was served at 11 a.m. This was something she seems to have carried over from St Katharines, where she had given the girls 'gingerbread with their eleven o'clock milk'. Paulinas were limited to two biscuits each, since the High Mistress had discovered, as she informed the school in 1912, that 'many girls were having what was practically their dinner by eating a great many biscuits'. Miss Gray felt strongly that her pupils should not be overtaxed, so the first prospectus stated that 'the younger girls take no lessons home'. In an address entitled 'Public Spirit' (31 November 1911) she declared: 'My dear girls, if the work is too much for you to do in the time allotted for it, it is only honourable and just to speak up and tell your Form Mistress.' She drove herself hard, however, so that her perception of a light load could well have been a Paulina's heavy burden. Certainly there was a culture of study, sometimes intense and girls were rarely mocked for wanting to put work first.

In *The Lost Traveller* (1950) Antonia White (*née* Botting) suggested that there were three main 'sets' during her time (1914–16): the Brainies or the effortlessly superior, the Hearties and the Swats. 'Nothing like the Swats had existed at Mount Hilary [her convent school]. They had minds like filing cabinets, and they worked with the nervous intensity of sheep feeding before a thunderstorm. To them Sophocles and Shakespeare were merely the raw material of "distinctions" and "alphas": they gazed down the long vistas of exams the goal of a post in some school exactly like St Mark's' (St Paul's, scarcely disguised).' Though autobiographical in inspiration, *The Lost Traveller* is fiction and Antonia White's taxonomy should be taken in the spirit in which it was composed.

Miss Gray did make some concessions to the less studious with the 'Special Seventh Form', created in 1907 as a nod in the direction of genteel education and finishing schools. It was, ran its rubric, unfinished comparison and all, 'intended for girls who are to complete their School Education by special preparation for home life . . . with a view to such instruction as will be found more useful in the management of a household'. Lessons were given in First Aid, Sewing, French and Literature, and in 1908 the Special Seventh had an exhibition of its 'Cookery and laundry work'. The Form still endured when Mrs Munro became High Mistress. She decided that the Special Seventh had had its day, especially as the Governors had recorded a rhetorical question in their minutes: 'Is the petty crime in the Special Seventh the result of frustration? Is the course too thin?'

Concessions like this apart, Miss Gray made academic prowess the *raison d'être* of her school. 'The school curriculum leads naturally to the university', observed the *Girls' Realm* of Christmas, 1905. It is possible that, until the Second World War, the school leaned towards the humanities rather than the Arts. This bias, however, was true of public school education in general rather than St Paul's in particular. Anne Scott-James, a Somerville scholar of 1931, reckoned in her *Sketches from a Life* (1993) that 'within the academic set, we were frightful snobs. We thought the only worthwhile subjects were Classics, Mathematics, History and possibly English.' Some teachers might have been complicit in that view: at a staff meeting of 8 March 1960, several of those present told Miss Osborn that Science was a 'fashion' at the moment 'but not needed for industry – except for mediocre posts'. During her last year at St Paul's, Mrs Munro did tell the Governors on 23 November 1973,

Head Girl Alexandra Clarke standing below the statue of Emmeline Pankhurst in 1973.

that 'our reputation [is] that we are a school that is strongly biased towards the Arts'. As High Mistress, however, she had energetically supported the Sciences. Just before her retirement, she made it mandatory for all Paulinas to take all three Sciences in the first three years.

Many other Paulinas do not recall a strong leaning one way or the other. When elected a Fellow of the Royal Society, Dr Sidnie Manton (Mrs Harding, St Paul's 1917–21) wrote to the Governors formally (5 June 1948) to express her 'gratitude to the school that set my feet on the way to a University career and for the leaving exhibition which, with other scholarships, enabled me to go to Girton in 1921'. Moreover, for the Governors to order laboratories for their new school in 1903 was advanced thinking indeed. Before long, the space and facilities provided became woefully inadequate, so that the University of London Inspectors of 1925 pitied the dedicated Science staff teaching under 'almost impossible conditions . . . owing to the inadequacy of the laboratories. These were built when the school first opened, and at a time when the importance of Science in the curriculum of a school was only just beginning to be realised.' Ten years later, after the completion of the Science Building, St Paul's could be complimented by the Inspectors on 'this magnificent block of buildings'. Even in the 1954 HMI Report the Science accommodation was characterised as 'lavish'. 'The outstanding feature of the department', the Inspectors also wrote, 'is its sense of purpose.' The laboratories were dramatically refurbished, as Chapter 2 has shown, in the 1990s.

Whatever the facilities, there has been no lack of gifted Science teachers within St Paul's and of famous scientists amongst Paulinas. Blanche Henrey (1906–83; St Paul's 1920–3), daughter of the Vicar of St George's, Brentford, whose church is now the site of a little music museum, was one of the earliest. Fascinated from childhood by botany, she published many exquisite books on British flowers, using photography to an extent hitherto unusual in horticulture. Because of her initial publication, *Flower Portraits* (1937), she became the first women to be elected a Fellow of the Royal Photographical Society. Her colossal *British Botanical and Horticultural Literature before 1800* (1975) was a bibliographical event of international importance; when she died, she had just completed a life of the eighteenth-century gardener Thomas Knowlton. A celebrated pair of scientific sisters were the Mantons (Sidnie, St Paul's 1917–21 and Irène, 1918–23), who both won scholarships to Girton College, Cambridge. Irène held the chair in Botany at the University of Leeds (1946–69) and, amongst many other achievements, pioneered the use of electron miscroscopy in the study of plants. In her time, she led the world in this field. Sidnie, a Reader at King's, London from 1949 to 1960, was one of 'the most distinguished invertebrate zoologists produced in Britain this century' (*The Times*, 16 September 1979). Between them they published a small library and gathered academic awards and honours across the world. They are the only sisters to have been elected to the Royal Society, but gained a more surprising distinction when a crater on Venus was named after

Zoology lesson in the science laboratory, with Miss Houliston, 1952.

them in 1992 by the United States Geological Survey. Remarkably, in a life which often, as her friend Gordon Leedale wrote in the *Independent* (13 June 1988), involved departmental work from nine to five and research from six in the evening till two in the morning, Irène was also an expert collector of Chinese and modern art and left a bequest of over 400 paintings, drawing and antiquities to the University Gallery, Leeds.

On the biological side, one of first Paulinas to win a national reputation was Dr Joan Beauchamp Procter, FZS (1897–1931; St Paul's 1908–16), after whom the Biology prize is named and the sister of Chrystabel (St Paul's, 1908–12), Lady Gardener at Bute (1916–25) and later (1933–45) Garden Steward at Girton College. From her childhood, Joan had an intense interest in reptiles: 'she preferred a large green Dalmatian lizard', wrote, E. W. MacBride, 'as a plaything to dolls'. It is interesting to note that her father and mother were amongst the more affluent of Paulina parents: he was from Buckinghamshire landed gentry while she was the daughter of a Manchester iron-master.

The school proved to be quite accommodating to Joan's enthusiasms, although Miss Dorothy Patrick (St Paul's 1911–14 and on the History staff, 1919–55), who perhaps had cause to be waspish about Joan, declared that she was 'very clever but not interested in anything but her subject'. According to a story told many times by Chrystabel and finally included in her autobiography, *Flora and Fauna*, kept amongst her papers at Girton, Joan developed the habit of bringing her reptiles to school. She did not do so to be a talking point, for she was a quiet, serious girl, but to ensure that they were properly cared for. Indeed, she had expert advice from Dr G. A. Boulenger of the British Museum on the care of amphibians and reptiles. Blizzard the lizard came first, wrapped up in a jersey, green to match his scales. Then, with the consent of her generous father, who tolerated the animals and plants with which his daughters were surrounded, Joan took to bringing her baby crocodile, Ramases, to school. At home, he generally lived in the bath until her father at last insisted that the crocodile be given a pond in the garden. Unfortunately, during a Maths lesson, the teacher (Miss M. Lynch) saw Joan playing with something and demanded, peremptorily, that she put it on the desk, but shrieked when she saw it was a crocodile. 'Miss Lynch', wrote Chrystabel, 'normally consficated objects played with during Geometry lessons, but, she daren't touch Ramases.' Joan was sent, in disgrace, to Miss Gray. She had enough imagination to realise that Joan was a professional herpetologist in the making and was therefore, to quote Chrystabel, 'very gentle and understanding about Ramases'. Nonetheless, Joan was told that she must not bring him to school again, 'because some people are afraid of little crocodiles'. There was yet another mishap before Joan left St Paul's for the Natural History Museum: during her talk with live exhibits to the Field Club, a sudden thunderstorm panicked her snake, which 'in its anguish swallowed the frog, which was meant to be displayed'.

Joan Procter and her infamous crocodile, Ramases.

135

As Joan was troubled with chronic illness, her family seems to have decided that she could not proceed to Cambridge. So she joined Dr Boulenger at the Natural History Museum in 1917, took over the collection of reptiles three years later and became Curator of Reptilia and Amphibia in 1923. She published readily, though in the form of scholarly articles, and accompanied her published researches with exquisite watercolours and sketches. Offprints of the papers, each inscribed 'with the author's love', landed on Miss Gray's desk. Visitors to South Kensington marvelled at Joan's extraordinary empathy with her charges: she was the curator who 'tamed dragons' because two great Komodo lizards would respond to her call. A friend lunched with her at the museum in 1922: 'Joan had a boa-constrictor there, and wound it round herself. She looked ill.' 'I have a study in the base-ment,' she told *Paulina* in November 1921, 'it is here that barrels of red snakes, violet tree-frogs and monstrous lizards are unpacked on the arrival from New Guinea.' Her early death deprived the Natural History Museum of 'one of the most brilliant naturalists in Great Britain' (E. W. MacBride wrote in the *Proceedings of the Linnean Society for 1931–2*), of 'a zoologist of genius' (*The Times*, 21 September 1931).

Despite her support for Joan, Miss Gray initially had not permitted the formal teaching of Zoology within school since, as Chrystabel wrote to Miss Etain Kabraji, 'Zoology would entail teaching about sex which was not suit-able for schoolgirls.' But by 1917 the High Mistress had discovered that the medical schools approved of Biology and since she was a keen supporter of woman doctors – her sister was in the profession – she appointed a Biology Mistress in 1917 and 'zoology was properly taught – sex and all!' (Chrystabel Procter).

For many years, Medicine has been one of the most attractive professions for Paulinas and for bright young women generally. By contrast, in the early years of the century, girls who wanted to be doctors felt like pioneers. It had been as recently as 1882 that the first two women qualified with medical degrees in the University of London. Many League members will remember Dr Grace Nicholls (St Paul's 1904–8) who was in the Great Hall on 19 January 1904, cut the school's birthday cake eighty years later and died shortly before her hundredth birthday. A similar figure is Professor Ruth Bowden (St Paul's 1928–34) who took the first MB at the London School of Medicine for Women. She has combined a long academic career (her several posts include her years as university professor and head of the Department of Anatomy at the Royal Free Hospital, 1959–80) with travelling across the world as adviser and examiner, to Egypt, Ghana, Jamaica, Malaysia, Russia and some twenty-five other countries. In supposed retirement, Professor Bowden has continued to research, to work for the World Health Organisation and to visit, for instance, medical centres and schools in Russia, Armenia (1985) and India.

Yet it was the young Ruth Bowden, determined from the age of 5 upon

The Library in the 1950s.

becoming a doctor, who had unforgettable English lessons with Miss M. A. Whiting: 'I used to live for those lessons . . . she seldom told us anything, but opened doors to exploration and imagination.' The English department quickly gained a reputation for its encouragement of wide and eclectic reading. This was cultivated from the start by Miss Gray and became a hallmark of the department. She told her Governors that the girls of whom she took charge in 1904 did not seem to realise that they were allowed to read freely and for pleasure, and she ensured that they felt liberated to do so. The Oxford and Cambridge Board noticed, in 1910, that there was 'no elaborate getting-up of textbooks on English Literature and painful committing to memory of facts and views without first-hand acquaintance of the writers' works'. Ten years later, University of London Inspectors observed that 'the girls have plenty of encouragement and opportunity to think for themselves . . . without having ready-made opinions forced upon them . . . In no part of the school are biographical notes and philological points allowed to usurp the place of better things.' The Inspectors of 1925 found that 'the treatment of Shakespeare is rapid, dramatic and quite delightful'. To jump two generations: Polly Vaizy told *Westside Magazine* in May 1988 that 'you could dine out on the books you'd read at school for the next twenty years'. Thousands of Paulinas, most of whom went into other fields, left the school with an enduring love of literature. 'She never seemed to look on us as recruits under orders,' one Paulina wrote of Miss Rosamund Jenkinson, who joined the

Anne Beguin as The Mother in Gloria Bax's production of Brecht's The Caucasian Chalk Circle, *1966.*

Thirty-three years on: Claire-Lise Honsinger as Grusha in Tessa Anslow and Catherine Price's production of The Caucasian Chalk Circle, *1999.*

English staff in 1938 and left, as head of department, in 1974, 'but rather as fellow-explorers joining with her in the same important quest.' Miss Etain Kabraji (Mrs Todds) was a figure of comparable stature: in the English department for thirty-one years (1958–89) and its head for twelve. A graceful and beautiful person, she wore clothes of fascinating colours and patterns in russet, ochre or green, hinting at the India of her childhood. We liked to think of her, said Emily Mortimer, as 'a bohemian academic'. A genius for friendship and her editorship of *Paulina* for twenty-three years enabled Etain Kabraji to develop a remarkable knowledge of the League and to compile her indispensable collection of reminiscences, *Looking Back*, which she printed privately to celebrate the ninetieth birthday of St Paul's. Her natural modesty ensured that *Looking Back* makes almost no reference to her own extraordinary contribution to the school. 'When I met Miss Kabraji I was a small unnoticeable grape', wrote one girl (*Paulina*, 1989), 'thanks to her I am now a bottle of champagne'. For another pupil: 'Thirty-one years of teaching English and she was still as enthusiastic and in love with literature as she must have been in her first years.'

Drama, the natural ally of the English department, was for many years directed through elocution classes and the John Colet Society. Founded in 1926 by Nicolete Binyon (Mrs Gray) this became in 1928 the school's chief society and a forum for the Arts generally. It arranged lectures, the first few reflecting Nicolete's left-wing leanings: Harold Laski came to talk on Communism. But the society also put on plays, often as staged readings rather than dramatic productions. During 1934–5, for instance, it invited Richard Pares to speak on 'Present-day Russia', Walter de la Mare on Lewis Carroll and it put on a forgotten play, Louis Parker's *Disraeli*. This pattern changed with the appointment of Miss Gladys Ellam, Paulina and a former actress on the lighter London stage, whose legacy founded the Ellam Rose Bowl Competition. She staged a production each year, while the John Colet play eventually became a preserve of the Seventh Form. The John Colet Society's various branches seceded to become societies in their own right. Miss Ellam's actresses were her own speech and drama pupils. Once Miss Gloria Bax joined the staff (1951–75: first as a teacher of elocution and then of Speech and Drama) school theatre became much more ambitious and involved a greater range of Paulinas. She was an exciting teacher, with the poise, bright eyes and beautiful enunciation characteristic of many drama teachers. Things were difficult at first, since Miss Bax was paid per capita and putting on plays required much rehearsal time and a Saturday dress rehearsal. Mrs Munro, however, put her on the salaried staff and allowed her pretty much a free hand to produce what she chose. So the girls were able to act in many modern as well as older classics and sometimes to play in the round on the floor of the Great Hall. Euripides' *Trojan Women* (1965), for instance, was followed with Bertold Brecht's *The Caucasian Chalk Circle* (1966) and Molière's *Malade Imaginaire* (1967) with the Capek brothers' *The*

Insect Play.

Gloria Bax developed a great friendship with Miss Winifred Pasmore, Head of Art (sister of the painter Victor Pasmore), a Paulina herself and on the staff for many years (1938–74). Art, blessed with the studios of the original building, has been integral to school life from 1904. Miss Pasmore was, says Gloria Bax, 'a wonderful character, with a great sense of humour, a wide knowledge of the Arts and theatre and able to inspire girls to study Art, pottery and weaving as well as painting'. The department preserved, according to the HMI Report of 1965 (at the height of the abstract movement), 'a more academic approach to the subject than is now normally adopted'. She was also a practising artist who often exhibited at the Royal Academy and elsewhere. Some of the Jubilee photographs of 1954 catch her in conversation with Queen Elizabeth, the Queen Mother. Winifred loved theatrical scenery and designed the sets for most of Gloria's plays. Miss Bax has kept a splendid book of Miss Pasmore's watercolours, year by year, of the set designs.

The Beggar's Opera, *directed by Nicholas Dakin; musical direction by Hilary Davan Wetton, performed in 1992.*

Languages and the humanities rapidly became formidable strengths of St Paul's. French and German (although German classes almost disappeared at the school during the Great War) were the central languages. These were supplemented by Italian from 1914 and later by Russian and Spanish. The school's first senior French Mistress was Miss Cecily R. Ash and therefore known as Crash (1904 to 1919, when she left to become Head Mistress of the Godolphin School). There was a tradition of innocent nicknames: Miss Robinson (Mrs Harbord) was Fuzzie Robinson on account of her frizzy hair, a soubriquet she rather cherished, Miss Patrick was Patty, Miss Rogers, the school's first senior Classics Mistress, was Podge and Holst was Gussie. Even Miss Strudwick was Strud or Struddy. Miss Gray had no nickname as such, apart from being called Ralph in her Westfield days, though her alter ego emerges as Miss Silver in Antonia White's *The Lost Traveller.* Miss Ash was an innovator in giving the spoken language equal weight with the written and helped to establish the tradition of using, during lessons, only the language being taught. She liked to communicate with *Paulina*, but only in French of course, and each week at dinner she presided over *une table francophone.* By definition, the language staff epitomises the exciting range of nationalities and origins within a metropolitan school. When St Paul's acquired a new Russian teacher in 1969, not many Paulinas realised that behind her English name, Mrs Wilsdon, lay Nina Brodiansky, a Paulina of 1929–38, daughter of Olga Yakhontova, actress, and of Michael Brodiansky, a supporter of the Provisional Government. She was in fact born in exile in Istanbul and had no nationality until, at the age of 21, she applied for British naturalisation. A brilliant student who won scholarships to both Cambridge and Oxford, she became Arthur Hugh Clough scholar at Newnham, 1941–2, lectured at the School of Slavonic Studies in the University of London, was for many years an examiner in Russian for the civil service commission and was a frequent contributor to the *Slavonic Review.*

The other major departments – Classics, Geography, History and Mathematics – have been strong from the start. The esteem in which Classics was held when the school opened said more about Edwardian society in general than the school in particular and it was not by chance that the first three High Mistresses were classicists. The department, however, won a high status on its own merits. 'We felt that it was very grand to be learning Greek at all', Elizabeth Rawson wrote, referring to the mid-1940s. In Mathematics, some outstanding teachers have served the school, such as Miss Mollie Lehfeldt (staff, 1930–61), Miss Sheila Hill (appointed in 1959 and retiring as Surmistress in 1988) or Miss Margaret Rudland, now Head Mistress of Goldolphin and Latymer School. In her obituary (1994) of Mollie Lehfeldt, Miss Hill praised 'the quality of her Mathematics, although it was rooted in a tradition then dying and now long past' and continued: 'I remember her astonishment at a departmental meeting when "the rest of Book V" had to be explained to me – Euclid, of course!' As for Miss Hill herself: one Paulina wrote of her 'ruthless logic' and 'acrobatic imagination'. Yet she cared for those for whom the subject was rather frightening as much as for the natural mathematicians. Of her fourth division in the Sixth Form one year she said, typically: 'I do love that class: we are all trying so hard!' and, indeed, their O-level results did not show that they had been a fourth division.

Miss Gray, as noticed above, had a particular affection for Geography. She went so far as to tell her Governors that 'our geographical work is recognised as the best that goes on from a Girls' School to the Universities'; whether her fellow-heads would readily have concurred with this assessment is another matter. Successive early inspectors were clearly surprised and impressed by the department's displays of minerals, posters, maps and its use of the magic lantern and stereoscopic views. If one were to choose a single Paulina to do credit to the Geography department that began her training, then it would be Helen Wallis (1924–95; St Paul's 1934–43), the first woman to be appointed Superintendent of the Map Room of the British Museum (1967). With the creation of the British Library, she became the nation's Map Librarian. Helen Wallis was a scholar and traveller of extraordinary energy who maintained hundreds of friendships across the globe. She was a warm friend to institutions as well as to people, and St Paul's has benefited greatly from her help over the years. It is in her honour that the multi-media room of the Colet Library is named, as it was built partly with her legacy of 1995. Sheila Fisher (Dr Cavanagh, St Paul's 1935–9) remembers her 'small neat face radiating energy, good humour and friendliness'; Brenda Hall, who became a lifelong friend, was surprised on meeting Helen 'that anyone so pretty and seemingly fragile should be so knowledgeable'. St Paul's suited Helen's roving intelligence: she was a Junior Foundation Scholar, a Senior Foundation Scholar, received a Leaving Exhibition (awarded by the school to two or three leaving Paulinas of the high academic calibre), took the Castlecomer Latin Prize and the Alice Lupton Senior Piano Prize and won the Mary Gray Allen Senior

Scholarship at St Hugh's College, Oxford. Yet someone less concerned with her own abilities can scarcely be supposed: her overwhelming interest was with human societies in the landscape, especially if remote and strange. After her early work on Pacific discovery, published as *The Exploration of the South Sea . . .* (1953) in three volumes, she moved on to study Drake's voyages, the exploration of north America, the Vinland map and scores of other topics. She wrote, published and travelled constantly; her Antipodean friends called her 'the honorary Australian'. 'She was often teased about her luggage,' wrote Brenda Hall in *The Globe my World: Tribute to Helen Wallis* (1995), 'even a weekend away would necessitate an enormous suitcase and at least one large bag of books and papers.' One collection of essays, which she edited with Sarah Tyacke, bore the apt title: *My Head is a Map*. An entire article of *The Map Collector* (1987), running to eight pages, was devoted to a bibliography of her publications. The work in which she seems to have had most delight was her edition of the stunning Rotz atlas, *The Boke of Idrography* (Roxburghe Club, 1981) and one of her treasured two copies was left to St Paul's in her will, the other going to St Hugh's. Another copy had been presented by the Queen and the Duke of Edinburgh to President Reagan in 1982. Valerie Scott, the editor of *The Map Collector*, recorded this compelling memory of Helen Wallis in *The Globe my World*:

Helen Wallis: The Globe My World.

> As an ambassador for the map world and for Britain she had no equal. Last summer I had a party for her 70th birthday at my house. It was not long after she had been told that she had cancer and the prognosis was uncertain. Despite this she sat in the sun under the apple tree laughing and chatting to her friends and showing immense courage in the face of the ultimate challenge. That's how I'll remember her.

The early History department was also praised, by successive Inspectors, for the profuse use of maps and illustrations, for the impersonation of historical characters by the girls, and for its emphasis on historical ideas: 'unimportant details and fruitless campaigns are set aside in favour of the deeper study of big movements and social changes' (1925 University of London Report). Did this approach account for a stern comment from the Oxford and Cambridge examiners of 1905 about the papers of some hapless pupils of the Lower Fifth?: 'The battle of Lewes, for example, was often confounded with that of Evesham and compurgation with ordeal.' From the 1920s to the mid-1950s, the department was dominated by the formidable personality of Miss Dorothy Patrick. She was, writes Miss Murray, 'a life-long enfant terrible and liked *épater les bourgeois*'. At intervals, 'she used to declare that Paulinas were no longer naughty, and lacked spirit. There may have been some element of truth in that statement, though it would be a rash child who tried being naughty within Miss Patrick's orbit.' *All eyes on me or your work*, was her firm class room rule. A Paulina of 1911 to 1914 – Joan Robinson (Mrs

141

Harbord) remembered her 'as a prefect, with her hair up and skirts to the floor, an impressive figure'. She won a leaving exhibition and, financed by this, took both parts of the Historical Tripos at Newnham College, Cambridge. In 1919 she was appointed to the staff and stayed at St Paul's until her retirement thirty-six years later. Katharine Graham (Mrs Ames-Lewis) remembers Miss Patrick standing in her tweed suit, thumbs in the pockets: 'you have got to get into the skin of the seventeenth century!' History with her was 'great fun', recalls Professor Ruth Bowden; 'Patty blew up and calmed down very quickly.' 'Woe betide the lazy or inattentive,' wrote Margaret Guthrie (of Miss Patrick in the 1920s), 'but this was hardly a problem, for attention was riveted by her own lively interest . . . Windows opened in all directions on seemingly boundless fields for exploration; painting, sculpture, architecture, literature, music, religion . . . I remember her one summer day, turning from the hall into the classroom rather too briskly even for her. Her feet went from under her and she skidded on her back, feet first towards the Mistress's desk. The horrified silence would not have been so profound had she been less popular and less respected. She picked herself up, dusted down the flowery linen dress and said, "You must be all dying to laugh – please do – it must have been the funniest sight"'. For Margaret Marker (St Paul's 1945–51 and writing in 1979 when Professor of Geography at Fort Hare, Ciskei, South Africa) 'Patty' was 'my most unforgettable character', the teacher who created History for her as a living experience and who laid the groundwork for her ability to 'think logically and write rational fluent prose for publication'.

Naturally, the individual pupil's experience of the curriculum varied enormously, according to inclination and aptitude of the Paulina or the skills and experience of the pedagogue. All teachers know that, whatever the pleasures of school for a good pupil, they are likely to be outweighed by the delight of leaving it. Many Paulinas spoke in glowing terms of Miss Wenham's lessons, but Nicolete Binyon said, devastatingly: 'Miss Wenham taught Mathematics – very slowly.' Suzanne Doyle (St Paul's 1935–41; Mrs Roland Oliver, Professor Miers), speaking of a period well after the Miss Ash era, said that French was usually taken by 'teachers with poor French accents, who took refuge at first in phonetics and later emphasised grammar'. As a fluent French speaker she was, however, judging her teachers by a high standard. Suzanne was also a little frustrated by Miss Patrick's History syllabus, which covered nothing later than the nineteenth century. It thus bypassed the First World War and was not related 'to the great questions of the day. We were never taught the philosophy of Marx or Hitler.' Indeed, the HMI Report of 1965, a decade after Miss Patrick's retirement, did urge the department to consider teaching some twentieth-century history. Helen Wallis went so far as to say that it was Miss Patrick's criticism of her prose style as too complex that tipped her towards Geography rather than History. Miss Patrick, said Helen crisply, 'favoured clear exposition over scholarship – like a journalist'.

On the other hand, Dr Wallis was, in a sense, as much a historian as a geographer and Professor Miers, a distinguished historian, says that Miss Patrick was 'a wonderfully inspiring teacher' and it was 'because of her that I loved History'. Another Paulina, Sonia Wheal (Mrs Tarlington, St Paul's 1939–42) has mentioned that Miss Patrick took American History lessons in the lunchtime, 'as she couldn't squeeze it into the curriculum. It was voluntary, of course, but well worth it.' Ruth Bowden, a child of the Plymouth Brethren, declares that she found the curriculum an 'enriching experience'. It is easy now to take the range of subjects offered by St Paul's in its early decades for granted. We need only to look at the curriculum of Milton Mount College in 1875, which comprised one lesson in Geography, five lessons in Arithmetic (no Mathematics), a little French, English History, Piano, Scripture and Zoology, all set against no fewer than eight weekly lessons in Drawing, to appreciate what St Paul's was ready to offer less than twenty years later.

Dalton Days were a tradition of St Paul's which tempered the academic steel of conventional lessons. American in origin, the Dalton Plan was a form of individual education in which pupils worked at their own pace through various assignments in a relaxed, child-centred environment. Miss Gray, although she insisted (in *Gladly, Gladly*) that no English school could adopt the Dalton Plan 'without any modification', thought that a Dalton Week would be an attractive idea. So was established a tradition whereby pupils were allowed to study according to their own inclination and their own pace for a week at the end of the spring or summer term. Many Paulinas had

Left to right: Ella Cave, Margery Hirschfield (Head Girl 1913–14) and Kathleen Osborn: older girls often wore their own dresses and blouses rather than the gym slip (right).

Facing page:
Top: Miss Diggory with three of the head girls from 1999––2000.
Bottom: The new up-to-date science laboratory.

happy memories of the Dalton Week, as did their teachers for perhaps their own reasons: 'School was a very peaceful place during those days', said Miss Strudwick, wistfully, in her Speech Day address of 1931. Suzanne Doyle, who found the curriculum rather narrow, said that her 'greatest joy was Dalton Week'. Josephine Turquet (Dr Munton, St Paul's 1961–7) feels that it was Dalton that awakened her interest in individual study and set her on the path to research. 'The pleasures of silent, private study were really tasted in a memorable way', said Katharine Ames-Lewis in an address to St Paul's on its birthday of 1996; 'tremendously enjoyable and a very good introduction to university', added Margaret Powell. Whether girls benefited from the time was perhaps dependent, however, on the degree to which they were already academically curious. Some were at a loss to fill four or five days fruitfully. *Paulina's* opinion poll in 1969 produced a variegated picture: all pupils in the first three years seemed to have enjoyed the Dalton Week but some of the Fifth expressed 'boredom and dissatisfaction with working conditions' and a considerable anxiety to go home once their projects were finished. The three top years used the time, in any case, for revision. Doubts about the value of Dalton Week began to permeate the staff during the next few years and it was whittled down to a couple of days by the early 1980s. Then, with the gradual introduction of coursework into many syllabuses, the time had come to let Dalton Days fade into the past.

If this tradition reflects a liberal aspect to St Paul's, the school's policy on uniform does likewise. St Paul's is now well known as a school without a uniform, except for games. Strictly speaking, it never has had a uniform, but this statement has to be hedged about with many qualifications. Frances Gray

declared that Paulinas should have no uniform, and enjoyed the compliments of *The Times* (12 May 1912) for the 'good sense' of her opinions. It does appear, however, that Miss Gray assumed that Paulinas would dress, depending on their age, as the best kind of girl or as young ladies. Many years later, Elizabeth Coxhead boldly claimed in the *Liverpool Daily Post*, (7 January 1954) that, at Somerville, 'Paulinas had considerably more dress sense than the rest of us' because Miss Gray's opposition to uniform had meant that her girls 'had become used to choosing their own clothes for school'. Early photographs show that many older Paulinas did dress as ladies and it is sometimes difficult to tell the Prefects or aediles, as Miss Gray rather preciously called their assistants, apart from the younger staff. Indeed, Miss Gray did not particularly care for sports clothes and told the annual conference of Head Mistresses in 1909 that she would like to find a sport which should require 'no special dress'. Picking up the mantle of Elijah, Miss Strudwick was pleased to maintain the tradition of non-uniforms. In 1945 she wrote a peremptory letter to Hope Brothers, one of the school's suppliers, which had provided three Paulinas with blazers bearing the St Paul's monogram: 'I must tell you that these are not school blazers and there is no regulation blazer.' Similarly, Miss Osborn wrote to the Clerk on 16 January 1953: 'We feel that rigid uniformity is undesirable as it does not lend itself to the development of good taste in dress which should be one of the hallmarks of the education which St Paul's provides.' On the same theme, she wrote to the parents in 1955: 'The variation indoors provides a happy result, provided that discretion is shown.'

Nevertheless, the pure concept of free dress was so diluted in operation that many Paulinas were and are convinced that they had a school uniform. It was understandable, though not entirely correct, for Avril Groom in the *Daily Telegraph* to claim that Mrs Munro was 'noted for abolishing uniforms'. From 1904 until the Second World War, Paulinas had to wear white dresses on Speech Days. Jewellery was firmly banned by Miss Gray, apart from gold sleepers and plain gold crucifixes, as 'it is not good form to wear jewellery in the day-time'. She was delighted to complete the academic year of 1905–6 without, as she told the parents, 'a single case of pearls around the neck'. A school coat, which varied from navy to brown and white check to blue-grey through the decades, had to be worn to and from school, with concessions (started by Miss Osborn in 1955) for 'very hot' weather. This rule lasted, at least in name, until the coat's final abolition by Mrs Brigstocke in 1974; it had already been dropped for the Seventh and Eighth Forms six years previously. Gloves likewise were to be worn. 'Your parents would agree with me', Miss Gray told the school in June 1913, 'that it is a mark of good breeding to wear gloves, so I want you to put on your gloves before you leave school and wear your gloves until you get to school.' For how long was this stipulation observed? In mock-heroic mode, *Paulina* of 1907 told the story of a Middle Fourth, caught without her gloves and tossed into the Thames by a Prefect,

Facing page (from top): *The Art room; Language laboratory with the current head of languages; Drama class for the younger students.*

Sketch of a Paulina from 1964. The usual attire has become more casual since the School's foundation.

*1919 Cricket team with Miss
Wolton.*

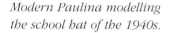

*Modern Paulina modelling
the school hat of the 1940s.*

who was then given hemlock to drink for a misuse of power. According to Margaret Powell (St Paul's, 1933–40) even by her day the rule over gloves was more honoured in the breach than in the observance. For Beatrice de Cardi (St Paul's 1924–31, now a leading archaeologist of the Middle East), however, 'it would have been inconceivable to have been seen in town without one's gloves'. School hats also had to be worn on the daily journey. The winter hat was in beautiful black felt from Scotts; the summer one was originally a wide-brimmed golden boater and later a small panama. For Grisell Roy, the boater was 'pretty', for Dodie Smith it was 'a brute of a hat . . . hideous and uncomfortable'; Vera Woollcombe (Mrs Royal-Dawson) wrote that it was 'unbelievably ugly and uncomfortable . . . but I adored my queer hat'. For Hermia Mills (St Paul's, 1917–20) the hats were 'rather comfortable' unless a girl had 'very frizzy sticking-up hair'. (The mother of one such girl wrote to Miss Gray asking for a dispensation from the hat, as it would only 'perch' on her daughter's head. Miss Gray's response was: Perch it must!) *Tot puellae, quot sententiae.* In 1964, Paulina undertook a consumer survey: 'Do you always wear your school hat going and coming to school? Do you maltreat it?' It has to be recorded that only half of the population surveyed wore their hats when supposed to, 'and this was often because they came into school with Prefects or teachers'. Paulina criticised some of its respondents for, illogically, both wanting a more attractive hat and opposing the principle of wearing one. 'Our (winter) hats', said Margaret Powell, 'were bashed into a suitable shape.' Monica Dickens (St Paul's, 1928–33) made a more dramatic gesture over uniform when, after a period of internecine warfare with Miss Strudwick, she, by her own account, took her 'hated Gym tunic and black coat and hard round hat and brown stockings and knickers to the middle of Hammersmith Bridge, dumped them into the Thames and turned up the next morning in my High Street Ken finery and was Asked To Be Removed'. Joan Harris was unaware of the episode, though she did recall that Monica wore her school hat 'at a rakish angle'. Rather splendidly, having resisted (Monica wrote in 1977) Miss Strudwick's suggestion that she become a 'Sanitary Inspector' and after decades as a best-selling novelist, she founded in 1988 the St Paul's Monica Dickens Short Story Competition.

What gave the sense of a uniform, however, was the tendency of younger Paulinas to wear the navy-blue games tunic and blouse (white and then blue and white striped) throughout the day. There was also a tunic, usually beige, for Gym. For decades, the gymslips were made on the premises by the same two long-serving seamstresses. Wearing the gym slip was for convenience, but soon became well-nigh universal amongst the first four years or so. One Paulina of the thirties, indeed, declares that if the gym slip was not compulsory for the autumn and winter terms, 'that must have been the best kept secret of all time'. Gymnastic stars also wore the white girdle, not abolished until the 1990s. This dated from the eight white girdles given to the gymnasts who had performed before the Princess of Wales during the official opening,

15 April 1904. Girdles were tied by the High Mistress with a complex knot during a ceremony curiously pagan in tone. Miss Murray on white girdles is irresistible: 'Miss Strudwick carried off the White Girdle ceremony easily with an aloof dignity, the suggestion of a smile and considerable dexterity. Miss Osborn was less successful. The children had a tendency to stand just a little short from her and to lean imperceptibly back as she worked on the knot. Little by little Miss Osborn was drawn away from the centre of the platform. One longed for her to haul the candidates in – as she could so easily have done with the girdle.'

Paulinas of any age could, however, wear clothes of their choice if they had sufficient nerve to defy convention. Dodie Smith has left, in *Look Back with Mixed Feelings* (1978), an account of how things could pan out in practice. At first she wore dresses made by her mother 'beautifully in soft woollens of pleasant colours'. When she realised that games tunics were the order of the day, Dodie's mother compromised with a 'rigidly conventional navy dress with a chokingly high neck . . . . But my well-bred, ill-mannered form-mates were no nicer to me, so I soon reverted to pretty dresses and skittish hair ribbons.' At one point, Miss Gray said that Dodie might have fewer colds if she were to wear longer dresses, at which 'I replied, I hope not too pertly, that as my mother chose my clothes it would be best to write to her.' It was not until the mid-1960s, with the arrival of knee-boots and

Hockey on the field behind the School, circa *1910.*

miniskirts, that an accepted notion of what was conventional dress was seriously challenged. 'Boots were discussed *ad nauseam*,' remembers Mlle Monique Boudier, until, eventually, Mrs Munro allowed girls to wear them. No one was wearing jeans when Miss Gough left St Paul's for her brief spell in Manchester and Worcester; when she returned, 'they were everywhere'. If there is a school uniform, *Paulina* remarked in 1976, it is jeans. So, with a few sartorial experiments along the way, matters have remained. Writing in 1996 ('The Best School in Britain', the *Daily Telegraph*, 2 October), John Clare simply observed that Paulinas 'dressed without fuss for the most part in jeans, trainers and sweatshirts'.

Discipline and deportment at St Paul's reflect the general pattern of London society but also the understated liberalism of the school. Compared with English schools now, St Paul's may have been strict. Miss Gray insisted that Paulinas were not to speak on the Marble, or in the corridors, or to Paulines in the street. This last rule applied even to Paulines who were brothers of Paulinas, for fear that casual conversations might be misinterpreted by passers-by. The High Mistress also could not abide loitering at the school gates. 'The mark of well-bred girls is that they would never by any possibility allow themselves to be seen loitering about', she declared in 'Dangers of Loafing' (1913). If a girl were early, she should come in and take a brisk turn around the grounds. Moreover, girls should learn to cough silently: 'Your shoulders may shake but there is no sound so that no one need know you are coughing' ('Manners', 1913). In a talk entitled (unfortunately) 'Prisoners' (1912) Miss Gray had the highest hopes of her girls: 'I wish it to be impossible for you to walk with your Form into the Hall and wish to talk before Prayers begin.'

Group of girls at the main entrance in the 1980s.

But by the standards of its time, St Paul's was far from oppressive. 'Few rules, so we kept them, "no running", so no tumbles or clashes,' wrote Phoebe Weismann (Mrs Lean; St Paul's 1911–21) emphatically in 1997. 'No talking on the stairs meant that we didn't stop and chat and block the staircase!' St Paul's never had the elaborate system of punishments and deterrents developed by so many other schools and is unusual in not awarding detentions for misbehaviour. Prefects, who were the whole of the Eighth Form, were expected to keep order when staff were not present, but had to rely on moral authority. As Charis Frankenburg (née Barnett, St Paul's 1907–11) wrote in *Not Old, Madam, Vintage* (1975), 'We tried, therefore to maintain discipline by personality alone. My mother said that the school was run on Prefects' nerves.' Some Paulinas were amazed at the array of school ordinances they encountered at Wycombe Abbey during 1939–40. 'We resented what seemed to us the petty rules', Professor Miers said in a talk (May 1995) to St Paul's on her wartime experiences. 'We were used to travelling freely around by ourselves and Wycombe Abbey only allowed us out for two hours once a week and in fours.' Moreover, precept and practice often diverged. 'I frequently breached the prohibition on talking in corridors', confesses that model Paulina, Grisell Roy (St Paul's, 1929–33). Indeed, the sanction on talking in the changing rooms was officially dropped by Miss Gray in 1925, which suggests that it had been impossible to enforce. In one of her speeches, Miss Gray told girls who felt faint during Prayers not to leave but quietly to put their heads between their knees. Dodie Smith's account of the sequel suggests that even Miss Gray was not as intimidating to all girls as posterity was to suppose: 'I had never seen a girl leave Prayers, but from that day on many of them took to putting their heads between their knees or even, disobediently, staggering out.' At their best, relations between staff and pupils have been remarkably happy. Brigid Brophy (St Paul's, 1943–4; Lady Levey) found the school to be 'thoroughly civilised' and, memorably, described the staff as 'scholarly and unfierce'. 'The bearing and behaviour of the girls call for unstinted praise', recorded the University of London Report of 1925.

Waiting for staff outside the staff-room, shown here in the 1950s, was a tradition continued until the early 1980s.

A tradition that encouraged conversation between pupils and staff was the carrying of books to lessons. From 1904 it was habitual for girls to meet their teacher at the staff-room door and escort her to the class, taking with them whatever she wanted carried. This custom, remarked the Inspectors of 1965, was 'surprising when first encountered', but allowed pupils to have a quiet word 'without fuss'. Paulinas seemed to have liked the tradition, but by the 1970s some staff felt that it slowed down the school day and allowed some girls to win too much attention, so it was discouraged. Meeting at the staff-room door, however, took a long time to disappear and could still be observed in the early 1980s.

Edwardian preoccupations with deportment and anxiety over 'curvature of the spine' did make their mark on the young St Paul's. Indeed, at the official opening of the school, the Princess of Wales congratulated the Swedish Gymnastics Mistress, Miss Arbman, on detecting so many cases of 'incipient curvature of the spine'. Miss Gray did her bit by declaring that morning break should be devoted to 'drill' in the playground, but drill seems to have disappeared fairly quickly. To help posture, the original Form Room chair had a movable slat to provide lumbar support. Something that lasted until the 1960s was 'position marks'. Periodically, the PE staff would patrol the Form Rooms looking for girls who were slumping in their chairs. 'Whenever one caught sight of a member of the Gym staff', remembers Grisell Roy, 'one drew oneself up into a rather unfeminine guardsman-like posture.' Those girls seen either hunching forward or, by contrast, negligently leaning backwards, would all receive 'posies'. The Form which ended the term with the fewest position marks would be praised or even receive a modest prize. Deportment lessons continued for many years and *Paulina* recorded in November 1921 that 'bowing and general carriage showed improvement . . . but the curtseying was weak, and many marks were lost for un-natural rigidity whilst moving'.

Deportment aside, Paulinas showed the same zest for games as for their

Girls playing Lacrosse in 1999.

other activities. It is wholly wrong to suggest that St Paul's has not been a sporting school. The first sports were basketball, gymnastics, cricket, hockey, swimming and tennis. Early Paulinas carry reports on the performance of individual players: 'A keen, though immature player', was Evelyn Sharp in 1919, the future Permanent Secretary of the Ministry of Housing; 'She must learn to be less rigid and more adaptable in the field.' Cricket was a much-loved game for decades and it is surprising that it was abandoned after the Second World War. Mrs Munro did not share her predecessor's passion and told the *Evening News* (10 July 1963): 'I'm strongly against girls playing cricket . . . When I was at St Paul's I remember having to play and loathing every minute. I'm all for sport, but there's a limit.' It is ironic that her much-admired Deputy Head Mistress, Miss Sheila Hill, was a renowned cricketer and is (1999) the first woman Chairman of the Association of Cricket Umpires and Scorers. In the spring of 1999, she also became one of the first ten women to be elected honorary members of the MCC and to have the right to join the men in the Long Room at Lord's. Basketball was replaced with net-ball, Gym became allied with athletics. Hockey was first joined with and then supplanted by lacrosse, which became immensely popular, and the First XII were National Finalists at the Schools Tournament of 1997–8. Wartime did not deter the lacrosse players, and Suzanne Doyle remembers that, as a hole in her lacrosse stick could not be mended because there were more urgent things to do, the ball became lodged in her stick 'and only came out when I wanted it to – I had a meteoric career as a player'.

The Great War inflicted tragic losses on the families of Paulinas. The magazine carried a Roll of Honour and in December 1916, for instance, six lieutenants, two captains and one private soldier from Paulina families were reported killed in action. In practical terms, the First World War did not disrupt deeply the pattern of school life. Moreover, no Paulinas died in World War I from enemy action, as did Letitia Emanuel (St Paul's, 1915–21) in October 1940. The Second World War was another matter. A pupil's poem in the Paulina of March 1939 ran thus:

But still our lives are governed by a Fear
The Fear that those who died
At Somme, Marne, Vimy, Ypres, Gallipoli
Have died in vain.

No one escaped the impact of the war when it came. As a German, Lisalotte Heyman (St Paul's, 1939–41; Mrs Montague) was interned, as were two other Paulinas. Mrs Montague remembers a frightening journey from London to Liverpool in a locked train and walking through the Liverpool streets to the taunts and even spitting of passers-by. Her first night there was spent in a boxing ring without toilet facilities. Miss Strudwick, she believes, then went to the Home Office and 'moved heaven and earth' to get the girls released.

After eight weeks, they were sent back to the school.

As a previous chapter has told, Paulinas on the roll in September 1939 were evacuated to High Wycombe. Others were scattered to schools abroad, or elsewhere in the country or in London itself. Wycombe Abbey gave a warm welcome to the Paulinas, but their loyalty was to Brook Green. 'Neither the Paulinas nor our staff were happy', says Suzanne Doyle. 'Wycombe girls looked down on us socially, we looked down on them academically.' There were some compensations. When St Paul's reopened in May 1940, some seventy Paulinas remained at High Wycombe, which was in startling contrast to London: 'the beeches just bursting into leaf, Daws Hill carpeted with cowslips . . . our breath was taken away' (*Paulina*, July 1940). One hundred and fifty-three girls, however, resumed their classes at Brook Green and, like all Londoners, worked and studied in the midst of air-raid warnings: 'The only time the Paulina loses her usual equanimity is when the aeroplanes roar overhead during a netball or lacrosse game and the siren forces her to descend into the air-raid shelter . . . There we have lessons as usual, concentration being one of the best qualities we have acquired since the war . . . Above the general hum of the dining room the urgent and repeated blasts from the whistle upstairs cause a general rush for second helpings and migration to the shelter. There we dine in comparative comfort.' At night, those on fire-watching would often hear the sound of Miss Rosamund Jenkinson's oboe, as she practised in the dark dining room.

With reduced numbers, several teachers had to go, and Miss Strudwick had the difficult task of naming those to be dismissed. The Chairman of the Governors was sympathetic, writing on 29 November 1940: 'I understand how painful to you must be the drastic reduction which circumstances . . . oblige us to make in the teaching staff of the Girls' School, but these reductions are equally painful to the Governors as a whole and to myself in particular.' Those who had been dismissed were offered their former posts as soon as it was possible for the Governors to do so and some, such as Miss Winifred Pasmore and Miss F. L. Partridge, came back while the war was still on. All teachers were worked intensely hard; heavy teaching loads were combined with shortages, fire-watching and anxiety. The correspondence of those years bears constant reminders of lives disrupted or destroyed by the conflict. In Mercers' Hall is an anguished letter from Dr E. Harpner, LLD Vienna, a former member of the Vienna Bar, whose father had been President of the same. Asking for help with the school fees of his daughter, he wrote, shortly after the war (January 1948): 'To escape further persecution (which had included imprisonment by the Gestapo) I fled in 1938 to England. I have been trying hard to offer my two children an education similar to the one I had been given by my parents . . . And I am also trying to help, though in a modest way, to rebuild a shattered world.' It is, however, consoling to notice that Rosalind Franklin chose her first field of research, on carbon crystals, because 'she wished to do something connected with the

The Dame Colet House Food Van, part of the Stepney Charity Services provided by the School.

151

The Infant Welfare Centre at Dame Colet House, 1927.

war effort and there was a need to learn to make better use of coals and chars' (Sir Aaron Klug, opening the Rosalind Franklin Workshop).

Paulinas' charity work was one thing that was not stopped by the war. 'Dame Colet House,' said Miss Strudwick in December 1944, 'now standing quite alone in a sea of desolation, is still serving Stepney.' Since Miss Gray's time, the school had maintained an extraordinary complex of charities in the East End of London. Miss Gray's own account is that she drifted by chance into Stepney one day in 1905 and was struck by the deprivation she witnessed there. It also meant much to her that it was Stebenhith where Dame Christian Colet had lived and where John Colet had been Vicar towards the turn of the fifteenth century. By 1912, Miss Gray was ready to act, and was urged on by Helen Gladstone, then Warden of the Women's University Settlement in Southwark. At a crucial meeting of Paulinas current and former (7 July 1912), Miss Gray proposed Stepney as the target for the main charitable drive of St Paul's. Some of the audience, however, wanted somewhere close to home. So the High Mistress put it to the vote but offered Hammersmith, North Kensington or Stepney. This split the opposition: Stepney did not gain an absolute majority but won first-past-the-post (10:7:7). So Miss Gray, wrote Charis Frankenburg (*née* Barnett, St Paul's 1907–11) in *Not Old, Madam, Vintage*, 'gave us our first lesson in manipulating a vote. I went home seething with indignation.' With that, the SPGS Union for Social Work (later 'Service') was founded.

Its achievement over the next half-century or so was remarkable and was, as Miss Osborn rightly said in 1948, 'a triumph of the voluntary principle'. In 1917, a house was bought in St Helen's Terrace to act as a base for the charity. Six years later, the Union converted a derelict pub in Duckett St to 'Dame Colet Cottage' and used it as a clinic. In 1926 a new Dame Colet House, a disused kipper factory, opened, also in Duckett St. By the late 1920s and using these buildings, the Union was supporting an Infant Welfare Centre, a Baby Weighing and Children's Care Centre and a Dental Clinic. Cases of neglect were reported to the NSPCC. It also provided an office for a Poor Man's Lawyer (Miss E. A. Berthen, a solicitor living in Stepney, who gave her services free). Paulinas also ran Brownies, a Girls' Club, Girl Guides, Wolf Cubs, took their friends on camps and gave tea and Christmas parties at St Paul's. A Women's Club accompanied the children's groups and husbands were offered 'Fathers' Health Talks'. Working girls who chose to be confirmed at St Paul's Cathedral and thereby lost a day's pay had their cut in wages recompensed by Paulinas. Bazaars were held to raise money, and long-suffering parents donated things from home and then travelled to Stepney to buy them back. Mrs Alexandra Roudybush remembers dolls, dressed in the St Paul's gymslip and wearing white girdles and Scotts' hats, for sale in the fair of 1927.

Then, ambitiously, the school charity launched a housing trust and was the first girls' school to do so. Mrs Phyllis Carew-Robinson (*née* Hardy, St

Paul's 1907–9) master-minded a money-making drive which culminated in the formation of Stepney Housing Trust (1930). This built a block of flats, named in honour of the first High Mistress, which offered family accommodation at heavily subsidised rents. 'Frances Gray House', reported *Maternity and Child Welfare* in September 1933, 'stands among mean streets like a promise of better things for the future. Built in restrained red brick, with long balconies running across the front and a courtyard at the back, it has space and dignity.' This was opened in March 1933 by the then Duchess of York, now HM the Queen Mother. In order to buy a holiday home in Langford Cross, Maldon, Essex, described at auction as a 'Detached Freehold Commodious Semi-Bungalow', hundreds of Paulinas signed charitable covenants. At Langford Cross, people from Stepney could have a seaside holiday at a negligible cost. Housing remained a priority and the Trust went on to built Paul House (1934) and Searle House (1938), 'fresh and new, green-painted railings, grass plots, window boxes gay with daffodils, lofty rooms flooded with light and air', as ran a contemporary description. During the war and because of the bombing of the East End, the Union bought a 'Food Van' which took snacks and hot drinks from the school to Stepney. After 1945, the Stepney Housing Trust poured money into Duckett St, which had been heavily bombed. Eventually, the Union and the Trust co-operated to build a third Dame Colet House, which was opened in Ben Jonson Road by Princess Margaret in 1957. This combined flatlets for the elderly with accommodation for the Clubs.

Yet St Paul's, 'still a name to conjure with among the people of Stepney' (*Paulina*, 1955), withdrew from its East End charities in the 1960s. There did seem to be good reasons for this. Some Paulinas felt that post-war rates of taxation were punitive and that private subsidies of housing were both unnecessary and difficult to fund. Muriel Walmsley wrote on these lines to Miss Elizabeth Poyser on 28 April 1950: 'I'm rather uncertain how much of the Stepney work is still essential in these days of high wages. For the most part they can probably afford better clothes and furniture etc. than I can – not to mention television, beer and cigarettes!!! . . . as the State does so much, parents feel they have no responsibility towards their offspring and are content to sit back and let the taxpayer do everything. . . . When the middle class is struggling against the Government's efforts to lower their standards I'd like the help to be given there.' In fact, the Langford Cross holiday home was closed in 1951 partly because mass tourism was taking off and partly because, a policy memorandum stated, 'it has become clear that the home was being used for a cheap holiday by people who could well afford other accommodation'. More significantly, the National Insurance Act of 1946 and the creation of the National Health Service two years later seemed to make the medical work of the Stepney Charity redundant.

Shifting social attitudes also made some Paulinas uneasy with any implication that those providing the charity were superior to those receiving it. In

Official opening of Frances Gray House by the Duchess of York, 23 March 1933.

December 1916 a Paulina could write confidently of 'the unconscious refining influence which is the outcome of upbringing and education' and that 'it is up to us to give this influence'. But another Paulina, of the 1930s, who made several friends amongst the Stepney girls, writes that the Stepney operation 'reinforced our sense of social superiority and enabled us to ease our consciences by playing Lady Bountiful'. For disparate reasons, therefore, the St Paul's-Stepney connection ended in 1967, though many Paulinas were less than happy with the decision. A policy statement from Mrs Munro, of 29 August 1967, indicated that Stepney would be better served by entrusting the school's charity to a Frances Gray Memorial Fund. Paulinas who had signed covenants were given the choice of terminating their covenants or transferring them to the Memorial Trustees. The Union dissolved. Charity work in general, however, has blossomed. Not only do Paulinas raise tens of thousands for many charities, the older girls visit local people and offer swimming for the disabled in the school pool. And Dame Colet House still flourishes in Stepney.

Little of the Stepney work would have been possible without the League, the Paulinas association. This was formed by Miss Gray, who had an intense feeling that Paulinas should form one great family, united across the globe. In retirement, she wrote chiding letters to *Paulina*, urging her former charges to correspond more fully and more often with the editor. Indeed, at one point (1920) she had a plan of photographing the entire League with their offspring and she was fond of throwing parties for Paulinas and their little children, if available, in the Library. At the League's first meeting, 7 February 1908, twelve Paulinas defined its 'Objects' as:

> To bind together the past and present of the School.
> To succour any former Members of the School who may be 'in danger, necessity or tribulation'.
> To assist the Charities of the School.

The badge of membership dates from 1916, creating, as Paulina wrote in December 1916, 'the Freemasonry of the League Brooch'. A beautiful version of the brooch was produced by Ernestine Mills, the famous enamellist and mother of Hermia (St Paul's, 1917–20). If Paulinas have not, through force of circumstance, deliberate choice or weight of numbers, been quite the single body which Miss Gray imagined, they have nonetheless been remarkably close-knit alumnae, and the League has drawn together many of their activities. Apart from providing the delights of social contact and annual reunions and the *Newsletter*, the League maintains a benevolent fund to help Paulinas in need, and (since 1980) the Rowan Education Trust, to provide scholarships for Paulinas.

In touching upon the world beyond school, it is natural to ask whether St Paul's embodies a feminist tradition. Until recent times, successive High

Paper chain made to raise money for an AIDS charity, 10 December 1986.

Mistresses were hardly feminist in that they took it for granted that some legal and economic differences should exist between men and women. It was unremarkable that the 1904 form of registration required the 'name of father' and his profession but no information about the mother. Miss Strudwick, her friend Mary Strachan noted, 'silently disapproved' of suffragette marches, though by the time she became High Mistress the issue of votes for women had been resolved. It was a commonplace with Miss Gray that it was a noble ambition for a girl to be a wife and mother, and a helpful Lower Fifth expressed this sentiment in 'The Vision of the Future' (*Paulina*, March 1915): 'the truth that School-taught knowledge trains, not spoils, for the homelife / No Paulina is found wanting as a mother or a wife'. Suzanne Doyle did not recall any militant feminism from her time (1935–41) nor discussion of issues like equal pay. 'We certainly all assumed that we would get married and have children.'

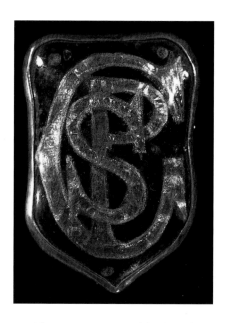

The League enamel badge of membership. Copyright Ernestine Mills, design: V Irene Cockcroft; photography: David Cockcroft. Badge kindly loaned by Polly Patullo.

Nonetheless, St Paul's tolerated and at times encouraged a certain degree of radicalism. Suzanne Doyle, comparing St Paul's with Wycombe Abbey, wrote (2 July 1994) that 'I do not believe that any of our staff would have asked as my House Mistress did after discovering some minor infringement of the rules: "How can I make you into good wives and mothers when you behave like this?"' Many pupils and staff and a few parents were associated with the suffragist and suffragette movements. Indeed, the Association of Head Mistresses resolved in 1906 to support women's suffrage and sent a petition in 1909 to Asquith, then Prime Minister. Ernestine Mills was a suffragette and, as Irene Cockcroft, author of the definitive study of this artist, tells us, 'enamelled the purple, white and green emblematic badges for the Suffragette Movement and banners were embroidered at sewing parties held in the infant Hermia's nursery'. The school's first Head Girl, Mary Mackenzie, worked with the National Union of Women's Suffrage Societies after coming down from Cambridge. According to Charis Frankenberg (*née* Barnett, St Paul's 1907–11), the *Saturday Westminster Gazette* in 1909 had judged one of her articles to be the best entry in an essay competition and then refused to publish it when the editor discovered that the essay was 'Votes for Women propaganda'. Winifred Giles told *Paulina* in April 1924: 'I belong to the Socialist parties of Australia, Greece and England – likewise to the feminist parties . . . in years to come I hope to find Paulinas in the Cabinet and scattered throughout the embassies of Europe.' It is interesting to compare the warm tone of a John Colet Society report (1930) of a talk by Mrs Oliver Strachey on Millicent Fawcett and votes for women with the dry irony of an account of A. H. Fox-Strangways' paper on music for the Society: 'We heard that women were incapable of attaining to the first rank in any creative Art, but we were consoled by the assurance that we all excel in collecting and cataloguing music, and in organising concerts.' This was shortly after the premature death in 1929 of Jane Joseph, a distinguished young composer and associate of Holst, and when Joan Cross was developing an international reputation as a soprano.

Miss Patrick admired the early women's movement and, as *Paulina* recorded in 1963, 'impressed on us with great fervour that we must fight to maintain the status which the suffragettes and campaigners for women's education won for women at the beginning of the century, in case we find that, with democracy, it has slipped from our grasp'. A decade later, Alexandra Clarke, as Head Girl, had an exciting year when she resolved to support Willie Hamilton's Private Member's Anti-Discrimination Bill. Her experiences are vividly captured in Miss Etain Kabraji's *Looking Back*. With Mrs Munro's agreement, Helen wrote to 900 schools across Britain to canvass support for the bill; Mary Quant bankrolled the cost of postage. Publicity gathered pace and Alexandra was interviewed, *inter alia*, by the *Guardian* and *Cosmopolitan* and took part in a discussion on Radio London and on the ITV 'Today' programme.

Mrs Munro did not call herself a feminist, but supported civil rights in the precise and legal sense and approved of career ambitions. She also liked to drop the odd gem for the benefit of the press: 'I'm on the side of the girls . . . A man gives his wife a dishwasher as if he's giving her the crown jewels' (*Evening News*, 10 July 1963). It was wildly inappropriate for Paula Davies in the *Catholic Herald* (31 October 1969) to entitle an article on Mrs Munro and Paulinas 'Enviable Dollies'. However, as Mrs Munro explained in her Speech Day address of 1965, marriage and home-making would, 'very rightly', have priority at some stage for most women, but should not eliminate a career. 'There is no conflict of career versus marriage or brains versus femininity. They all go together into the making of the whole woman.' Women had to make individual choices about competing demands.

The achievements of one of the school's most famous former pupils, Rosalind Franklin, have been caught up in the feminist debate. Disturbed by the picture of Rosalind given by James D. Watson in his celebrated *The Double Helix* (1968) – a portrait described by Jenifer Glyn in *Cambridge Women* (1996) as a 'cruel and absurd caricature' – Anne Sayre responded with *Rosalind Franklin and DNA* (1975). The comment of the publisher on the dust-jacket told it all: 'A Vivid View of What it is Like to be a Gifted Woman in an Especially Male Profession.' The book sought to show that Watson had tried to reduce Rosalind Franklin to 'Rosy', an embittered and unimaginative blue-stocking who obstructed rather than helped the greater gifts of Watson himself. Against this image Anne Sayre set the true Rosalind: an intellectual but one who had many friends, loved France and mountaineering, walking and cycling and was devoted to her family. Similarly, the *Jewish Chronicle* (5 July 1968) sprang to her defence. Anne Sayre was careful to insist that the 'general notion of raising the status of women was never more than peripheral to Rosalind. She was "feminist" only in the widest philosophical sense.' It was, however, difficult not to draw feminist inferences from the book and the other studies it helped to inspire (including

DNA model created by members of the VIIIth, dedicated to the memory of Rosalind Franklin.

'The Dark Lady of DNA' on BBC Radio 4, 1987 and 'Life Story' on Horizon, BBC, 1987) especially as Sayce herself concluded that 'Certainly she has been used, thanks to *The Double Helix*, to menace bright and intellectually ambitious girls.'

Some evidence has been played against Anne Sayre. Horace Freeland Judson, in particular, has tried to lay to rest the 'unquiet legend' that Rosalind Franklin was a victim of sex discrimination and that her career suffered as a result (*Science Digest*, January 1986). Freeland Judson puts his case shrewdly, and it may be that the difficulties between Watson and Rosalind Franklin arose from his failure to understand the intellectual integrity of someone who was from an academic and close-knit London family and who had been taken completely seriously at St Paul's and at Cambridge. Peter Given wrote perceptively in the *Guardian* (12 May 1987): 'In his book, *The Double Helix*, James Watson makes it evident that he did not take Franklin seriously. I doubt if she had ever been treated like that before and would not have tolerated it.' It is, however, easier to be philosophical after rather than during a struggle. Whatever Rosalind's personal position, the simple fact was that no women were elected Fellows of the Royal Society until 1945 and that Cambridge University did not officially award degrees to its women graduates until 1947, the year she joined the Laboratoire Centrale des Services Chimiques de l'État in Paris as a *chercheur*. What the debate did do was to prompt a reconsideration of Franklin's achievements and in three distinct areas: her early research on carbon compounds, her mastery and application of X-ray diffraction in the study of DNA and her closing work on tobacco mosaic virus with Aaron Klug. Arguing on the side of the angels, Judson insists that to say her career was damaged by sexism 'diminishes what she [had] accomplished' by the time of her premature death at the age of 37. J. D. Bernal's comment in his memorial article in *Nature* (vol. 182, 19 July 1958) has often been quoted but bears repeating here: 'As a scientist Miss Franklin was distinguished by extreme clarity and perfection in everything she undertook. Her photographs are among the most beautiful X-ray photographs of any substance ever taken.'

Rosalind Franklin was an example of those Paulinas who took it as read that they should pursue a rewarding career. Although in some respects the professional life followed by Paulinas beyond school shadowed changes in society at large, the school was at the cutting edge of careers for women. For the *Graphic* (18 February 1922): 'At St Paul's . . . every girl is being prepared for a career. The High Mistress considers that no woman has a right to exist who does not live a useful life' (though she would naturally have included motherhood therein). Summing up a school debate on the motion 'That the Entry of Women into Public Affairs and Industry is to be Deplored', Miss Strudwick declared that women should not 'be relegated to the home'. After the Second World War, assumptions about career expectations became so strongly entrenched that they could produce the post-modernist reaction of

Newfoundland Memorial Park, visited as part of the 1998 Battlefields Tour.

157

Rachel Johnson (St Paul's, 1981–3) in the *Daily Telegraph* (21 February 1998): 'The whole basis of education for females in the 1980s was to prepare us to compete with men in what was still a man's world of power breakfasts, golden handshakes and City bonuses. I do not remember anyone at St Paul's ever mentioning the possibility that some of us, at some stage, might have to interrupt our high-flying careers for domesticity.'

Careers advice followed in the slipstream of Paulinas entering professional life. On the eve of the Second World War, *Paulina* ran a series of articles on women in the professions. The paper on 'Social Work as a Career for Girls' (July 1939) contained some practical information on the Probation Service and on care for tuberculosis sufferers and directed Paulinas to the Women's Employment Publishing Company. From 1948, Paulinas were offered careers lectures and a decade later an allowance was given to a Mistress to take responsibility for giving the right advice. A careers room came with Mrs Munro, who observed in 1965 that most of the information available, 'although paying lip-service to opportunities for girls, is written wholly from the standpoint of the boy'. Her years as High Mistress saw a rising proportion of Paulinas going to university, so that by the mid-1970s virtually the entire Eighth was proceeding to university degree courses. It is no coincidence that *Paulina* dropped advertisements from secretarial firms about the same time. By contrast with this pattern of university entrance from, say, 1976, fifty of sixty-five leaving Paulinas had gone to university in 1950, thirty-three of fifty in 1951, thirty-two of fifty-eight in 1961, although many of the college courses then undertaken would now be university degrees.

At first, teaching seemed to offer the obvious pathway to a respectable salary and position. Miss Gray believed that this was 'the profession' but even from the earliest days many Paulinas did not agree with her. Vocational horizons lifted year by year. Elisabeth Benjamin (1908–99), the modernist architect (St Paul's 1922–8) determined in her teens upon her chosen path. Miss Gray, she told Lynne Walker for *Twentieth Century Architecture* (2: 1996), 'wanted me go to Oxford or Cambridge, just to be a statistic, and read Modern Languages which I was interested in. She was horrified that I became an architect.' Careers were either 'risky' or 'safe', wrote Margaret Cole (*née* Postgate, historian wife of the socialist historian G. D. H. Cole) in *Paulina* (December 1938); the first group included teaching and the civil service, the second journalism, writing and all the Arts, but plenty of Paulinas opted for the latter. As early as 1920 twelve of the twenty-seven Prefects (the Eighth Form) planned a career in medicine, according to the University of London Inspection. Miss Strudwick's comment in 1947 would sound familiar now: 'I must warn parents that there is a real danger of overcrowding in the London medical schools.' Fifteen years later, the Inspectors noticed that only fourteen of the seventy-four girls in the Seventh and Eighth had not made a decision about their careers and that their chosen professions included accountancy and publishing. In 1946, of thirty-one Paulinas mentioned in the League news

In the Andes: the World Challenge Expedition of 1999.

item, nine were housewives and the remaining twenty-two scattered over a variety of occupations, including that of 'sportswoman' (Janet Morgan, winner of the USA Squash Championship of that year). When the Foreign Office opened to women after the Second World War, a Paulina (Grace Rolleston) was the third woman to qualify (1947) and came joint top (with a male candidate) in the examination. An attempt by the League in the late 1940s to identify professional Paulinas listed actresses (including Celia Johnson), architects, artists, five bankers, civil servants, four gardeners, many doctors, a few journalists, four masseuses, two missionaries, eight Head Mistresses, musicians, five novelists, two nuns, two poultry farmers, scientists, secretaries, singers, solicitors, teachers and also owners of private schools, and, in solitary splendour, Kathleen Kenyon as the Archaeologist. Looking across Paulina occupations today, their range is remarkable, as is the facility with which some women move from one profession to another. Amongst the many Paulinas in the traditional rôles of doctor, lawyer or scientist, there are Paulinas making films, starring in them, directing plays or acting in them, painting pictures or signing contracts of their sale, running companies, restaurants, glossy magazines or academic journals, and more of their words appear in printed, recorded or electronically transmitted form than any person could trace.

Community work in Peru during the World Challenge Expedition.

'Enter the infant Paulina', were the opening words of the first issue of the school magazine. The editor, Henriette Massé, wondered then whether her journal would last. Succeeding editors kept the faith, and *Paulina* has never missed an issue. Even during the evacuation to Wycombe Abbey and throughout the rest of the war, the school magazine appeared. Its cheap brown paper and rusting staples, for binding was not possible, are now a mute reminder of wartime restrictions. Nearly a hundred years later, we can only admire what has come of 'the infant Paulina' and wonder what our successors will make of us at the end of the first century of the third millennium. From the outset, St Paul's Girls' School has offered exceptional opportunities to the young and so far as possible, the school, its parents and its Governors have tried to open the gates to gifted students whose families could not afford to send them here. To leave the last word with one student who came to St Paul's on a scholarship endowed by parents: 'Tomorrow term starts at Cambridge. I shall be the first person in my family to attend university.'

159

SELECT BIBIOGRAPHY

CHIEF SOURCES OF UNPUBLISHED INFORMATION

(a) Minutes of the Meetings of the Governors of St Paul's Girls' School. The school holds a complete set of these, from 1903 onwards, with the text running to some 8,000 pages. For the period 1876 to 1903, I used the St Paul's School Minute Book at Mercers' Hall.

(b) Mercers' Company Archives: files relating to St Paul's Girls' School. There is a wealth of information in these records, beautifully organised by the Company's archivists. I consulted many of these files but many others remain to be exploited. For the chapter on the school's origins, the Acts of Court, 1872 onwards, is a necessary source.

(c) Notices in the press: most of these are cited in the text.

(d) School records apart from the Minutes of the Governors' Meetings. These are too varied to specify in any detail: records of interviews, the correspondence of successive High Mistresses, notes of staff meetings, memoranda, information sent to the school by parents, Paulinas and others (including photograph albums and scrapbooks), records of examination results, prize lists, programmes and so on.

(e) *Paulina*, the school magazine, which has appeared continuously from 1904; the *Saint Paul's Girls' School Book*, a handsome collection of essays produced by the school in 1925; *St Paul's Girls' School 1904–54*, the Jubilee book edited by Miss M. G. Hirschfeld and printed for the school; *Looking Back*, a collection of reminiscences edited and privately printed by Miss Etain Kabraji to celebrate the school's ninetieth anniversary; *Ethel Strudwick*, a collection of tributes to the second High Mistress, edited by K. C. Harrison, (1955); Elizabeth Bushnell and Linda MacGilp, *St Katharines School* (1994).

PUBLISHED WORKS

AVERY, Gillian, *The Best Type of Girl: A History of Girls' Independent Schools* (Andre Deutsch, 1991)
BAGGULEY, *Harlequin in Whitehall: A Life of Humbert Wolfe* (Nyala Publishing, 1997)
BOLT, Christine, *Feminist Ferment: the 'Woman Question' in the USA and England, 1870–1940* (UCL Press, 1995)
BURSTALL, Sara and DOUGLAS, MA, *Public Schools for Girls* (Longmans, 1911)
CAINE, Barbara, English *Feminism 1780–1980* (OUP, 1997)
CANNELL, George, 'Resistance to the Charity Commissioners: the Case of St Paul's Schools, 1860–1904', *History of Education* (1981, vol. 10, no.4)
CARDEN, Joan, et al., *Daughters of the City: A History of the City of London School for Girls* (James & James, 1996)
DELAMONT, Sara, and DUFFIN, Lorna, *The Nineteenth-Century Woman* (Croom Helm 1978)
DICKENS, Monica, *Mariana* (Persephone Books, 1999; first published by Michael Joseph, 1940)
DOOLITTLE, Ian, *The Mercers' Company 1579–1959* (the Mercers' Company, 1994)
DUNN, Jane, *Antonia White: A Life* (Jonathan Cape, 1998)

EVANS, Jean, *Not Bad for a Foreigner* (Safari Books, 1996)

FLEMING, Kate, *Celia Johnson* (Weidenfeld & Nicolson, 1991)

FLINT, Lorna, *Wycombe Abbey School* (Wycombe Abbey School, 1989)

FRANKENBURG, Charis, *Not Old, Madam, Vintage* (Galaxy Press, 1975)

GIRLS' PUBLIC DAY SCHOOL TRUST 1872–1972 *A Centenary Review* (GPDST, 1972)

GIROUARD, Mark, *Sweetness and Light: The Queen Anne Movement 1860–1900* (OUP, 1977/Yale, 1984)

GLENDAY, Nonita, and PRICE, Mary, *Reluctant Revolutionaries: a Century of Head Mistresses 1874–1974* (Pitman, 1974)

GRAY, Frances, *And Gladly wolde be lerne and Gladly teche: a Book about Learning and Teaching* (Sampson Low, 1931)

GREENWOOD, *Holy Terrors: A Theodora Braithwaite Ecclesiastical Whodunit* (Headline, 1994)

GROVE, Valerie, *Dear Dodie: The Life of Dodie Smith* (Chatto & Windus, 1996)

HARCOURT, G. C., 'Joan Robinson 1903–83', *Economics Journal*, (105, September 1995)

HICKLAND, Susan, *Polished Corners 1878–1978* (Francis Holland School, 1978)

HIRSCH, Pam, *Barbara Leigh Smith Bodichon* (Chatto & Windus, 1998)

HOLLOWAY, Sally, *A School of Dolphins: The History of Godolphin and Latymer School* (the Book Guild, 1995)

HOLST, Imogen, *Gustav Holst* (OUP, 1938/1969; published as an Oxford Lives paperback, 1988);
A Thematic Catalogue of Gustav Holst's Music (Faber Music Ltd in association with G. & I. Holst Ltd, 1974)

HOOPER, Barbara, *Mary Stocks 1891–1975: An Uncommonplace Life* (Athlone Press, 1996)

HOPKINSON, Diana, *The Incense-Tree* (RKP, 1968)

HUGHES, M. V., *A London Girl of the 1880s* (OUP, 1946/78)

MATTHEW, H. C. G., *Gladstone 1809–74* (Clarendon Press, 1986) and *Gladstone 1875–98* (Clarendon Press, 1995)

MEAD, A. H., *A Miraculous Draught of Fishes: A History of St Paul's School 1509–1990* (James & James, 1990)

PALMER, Christopher, *Herbert Howells – A Centenary Celebration* (Thames Publishing, 1992)

ROTHMAN, Patricia, *Women in the History of Mathematics from Antiquity to the Nineteenth Century* (UCL, 1996);
'Grace Chisholm Young and the Division of Laurels', *Notes Rec. Royal Society*, London (50 (1), 1996)

ROWBOTHAM, Sheila, *A Century of Women: A History of Women in Britain and the United States* (Viking, 1997)

SAYRE, Anne, *Rosalind Franklin and DNA* (W. W. Norton, 1975)

SCOTT-JAMES, Anne, *Scenes from a Life* (Michael Joseph, 1993)

SHILS, Edward, and BLACKER, Carmen (eds.), *Cambridge Women: Twelve Portraits* (CUP, 1996)

SHORT, Michael, *Gustav Holst: The Man and his Music* (OUP, 1990)

SHROSBEE, Colin, *Public Schools and Private Education: The Clarendon Commission, 1861–4, and the Public Schools Acts* (MUP, 1988)

SKINNER, Lydia, *A Family Unbroken 1694–1994: The Mary Erskine School Tercentenary History* (Mary Erskine School, 1994)

SMITH, Dodie, *Look Back with Mixed Feelings* (W. H. Allen, 1978);
Look Back with Gratitude (Muller, Blond & White, 1985)

SONDHEIMER, Janet, *Castle Adamant in Hampstead: A History of Westfield College: 1882–1992* (Westfield College, 1983)

STRICKLAND, Margot, *Angela Thirkell: Portrait of a Lady Novelist* (Duckworth, 1977)

SUTHERLAND, Gillian, 'The Movement for the Higher Education of Women: Its social and intellectual context in England, c.1840–80', in P. J. WALLER, (ed.), *Politics and Social Change in Modern Britain* (Harvester, 1987)

SUTTON, Anne, *I Sing of a Maiden: The Story of the Maiden of the Mercers' Company* (the Mercers' Company, 1998)

THANE, Pat, 'Late Victorian Women', in T. R. Gourvish and Alan O'Day (eds.), *Later Victorian Britain 1867–1900* (Macmillan, 1988)

VICINUS, Martha, *Independent Women* (Virago, 1985)

WATSON, Nigel, *Latymer Upper School: A History of the School and its Foundation* (James & James, 1995)

WEINBERG, Samantha, *A Fish Caught in Time: The Search for the Coelacanth* (Fourth Estate, 1999)

WISEMAN, T. P., 'Elizabeth Donata Rawson', *Proceedings of the British Academy* (84, Lectures and Memoirs, 1993)

A Few Well-Known Paulinas

ALEXANDER, Helen, 1957–: St Paul's 1967–74; Chief Executive, *The Economist*.

ARDEN, Annabel, 1959–: St Paul's 1970–7; theatre director, founding member of the Theatre de Complicite.

AYRES, Gillian, 1930–: St Paul's 1943–6; painter, works in many public collections, RA 1991.

BARNETT, Charis (Mrs Frankenburg), 1892–1985: St Paul's 1907–11; expert and writer on nursery education.

Helen Alexander.

BEAUMAN, Nicola: see MANNING.

BENJAMIN, Elisabeth, 1908–99: St Paul's 1922–6; modernist architect.

BICKERDIKE, Rhoda: see DAWSON.

BINYON, Nicolete (Mrs Gray), 1911–1997: St Paul's 1924–9; medievalist, international authority on lettering.

BLANCH, Lesley: St Paul's 1915–21; romantic biographer and writer.

BOTTING, Eirene (known as Antonia White), 1899–1980: St Paul's 1914–16; author, known especially for *Frost in May* (1933)

BOWDEN, Ruth, 1915–: St Paul's 1928–34; anatomist, doctor, scholar and writer.

BRINTON, Mary (Baroness Stocks), 1891–1975: St Paul's 1904–8; academic,

Dr Shirley Williams.

social reformer and writer, the Principal of Westfield College, London, 1939–51.

BROPHY, Brigid (Lady Levey), 1929–95: St Paul's 1943–4; writer.

BURKE, Lady Rosalind: see NORMAN.

CARUS-WILSON, Eleanora, 1897–1977: St Paul's 1912–17; medieval economic historian, Ford Lecturer (1965).

CATLIN, Shirley (Mrs Williams), 1930–: St Paul's 1943–4 and 1945–7; stateswoman, co-founder of the Social Democratic Party in 1981.

CONRAN, Shirley: see PEARCE.

CROSS, Joan, 1900–93: St Paul's 1912–16; soprano, interpreter of Britten.

Jocelyn Herbert.

DAWSON, Rhoda Nelson (Mrs Bickerdike), 1897–1955: St Paul's 1910–16; artist, Quaker.

DE CARDI, Beatrice, 1914–: St Paul's 1924–31; OBE, FSA, archaeologist, especially of Afghanistan, Iran and Oman.

DICKENS, Monica, 1915–92: St Paul's 1928–33; novelist.

DONALD, Alison (Dame Alison Munro), 1914–: St Paul's, 1931–3; senior civil servant, High Mistress of St Paul's Girls' School, 1964–74, Chairman of the Chichester Health Authority, 1982–8.

DOYLE, Suzanne (Mrs Oliver, Professor Suzanne Miers), 1922–: St Paul's 1935–41; historian.

FOSTER, Megan, 1898–1987: St Paul's 1910–16; soprano.

FRANKENBERG, Charis: see BARNETT.

FRANKLIN, Rosalind, 1920–58: St Paul's 1932–8; scientist, made major contributions to the discovery of DNA.

Harriet Harman MP.

FRASER, Flora, 1958–: St Paul's 1971–6; historical biographer.

GARNETT, Jane, 1957–: St Paul's 1969–76; historian, editor of the women's section of the *New Dictionary of National Biography*.

GOUGH, Rachel, 1966–: St Paul's 1982–4; bassoonist.

GRAY, Nicolete: see BINYON

GUPTA, Smt. Mona: see PRASAD

GLUCKSTEIN, Hannah (known as Gluck), 1895–1978: St Paul's 1910–13; outstanding portraitist.

HANDLEY, Carol: see TAYLOR.

HARMAN, the Rt. Hon. Harriet, 1950–: St Paul's 1961–8; Labour politician.

HASTINGS, Lady Selina, 1945–: St Paul's

Dame Celia Johnson.

1953–62; biographer.

HENREY, Blanche, 1906–83: St Paul's 1920–3; botanical writer.

HERBERT, Jocelyn, 1917–: St Paul's 1928–32; theatre designer.

HOGG, Mary (the Hon. Dame Mary Koops), 1947–: St Paul's 1958–65; barrister, High Court Judge.

HOLST, Imogen, 1907–84: St Paul's 1921–5; composer, musicologist, conductor, tireless proponent of her father's music.

JOHNSON, Celia, 1908–82: St Paul's 1919–26; actress, film star.

JONES, Eirene, (Mrs White), Baroness White of Rhymney, 1909–1999: St Paul's, 1920–28; Labour journalist and stateswoman.

JONES, Karen, 1965–: St Paul's 1977–83; flautist.

JOSEPH, Jane, 1894–1929: St Paul's, 1909–13; composer.

KELLY, Rachel, 1965–: St Paul's 1976–83; journalist.

KING, Catherine Stevenson: see PECKHAM.

Susan Kramer MP

163

Baroness O'Neill.

KENYON, Kathleen, 1906–78: St Paul's 1919–25; archaeologist, especially of the Middle East and the ancient city of Jericho, the Principal of St Hugh's College, Oxford, 1962–73.

KOOPS, the Hon. Dame Mary: see HOGG.

KRAMER, Susan: see RICHARDS.

LABOVITCH, Carey, 1960–: St Paul's 1973–8; publisher, founder and editor of *Blitz*.

LANCASTER, Lady Anne: see SCOTT-JAMES.

LANGDON, Beatrice, 1898–1986: St Paul's 1911–16; artist.

LASKI, Marghanita, 1915–88: St Paul's, 1929–32; broadcaster, critic and novelist.

LEVEY, Lady Brigid: see BROPHY.

LOUSADA, Jocelyn: see HERBERT.

MACKAIL, Angela (Mrs Thirkell), 1890–1960: St Paul's, 1904–6; romantic novelist, perhaps as prolific as Monica Dickens.

MACKENZIE, Mary, 1891–1953: St Paul's 1904–8; medievalist, royal archivist.

Sonia Proudman.

MADDOX, Bronwen, 1963–: St Paul's 1973–8; journalist, Foreign Editor of *The Times*.

MAIR, Lucy, 1901–86: St Paul's 1913–19; prolific anthropologist, especially of Kenya and Uganda.

MANNING, Jessica, 1937–: St Paul's 1948–55; novelist.

MANNING, Nicola (Mrs Beauman), 1944–: St Paul's 1955–62; biographer, publisher of Persephone books.

MANTON, Irène, 1904–88: St Paul's 1918–23; botanist, pioneered use of microscopy, FRS.

MANTON, Sidnie (Mrs Harding), 1902–79 : St Paul's, 1917–21; zoologist, FRS.

MAURICE, Joan (Mrs Robinson), 1903–83: St Paul's, 1918–22; major Cambridge economist.

Natasha Richardson.

MIERS, Suzanne: see DOYLE.

MORGAN, Janet (Mrs Shardlow), 1921–90: St Paul's 1932–9; Women's squash champion, President of the WRSA (1954–87).

MORTENSSON, Brita, 1916–58: St Paul's 1925–35; Scandanavian scholar, expert on Strindberg.

MORTIMER, Emily, 1971–: St Paul's 1982–9; actress.

MUNRO, Dame Alison: see DONALD.

NORMAN, Rosalind (Lady Burke), 1908–94: St Paul's 1922–5; aviatrix, and aircraft factory manager during the Second World War.

O'NEILL, Baroness, Onora, 1941–: St Paul's 1953–8; major moral philosopher, Principal of Newnham College, Cambridge, since 1992.

PEARCE, Shirley (Mrs Conran), 1932–: St Paul's 1942–7; writer, famous for

Dodie Smith.

Superwoman (1975).

PECKHAM, Catherine Stevenson (Mrs King), 1937–: St Paul's 1949–55; scientist, academic, expert on child medicine, Professor of Paedriatic Epidemology, University of London (1985–).

PRASAD, Smt. Mona Chandravati (Mrs Gupta), 1896–1984: St Paul's 1910–13; humanitarian, social reformer, awarded the Padma Shri Medal (1965).

PROCTER, Joan, 1897–1931: St Paul's 1908–16; biologist.

PROUDMAN, Sonia, 1949–: St Paul's 1960–67; barrister, QC.

QUIRK, Jessica (Mrs Rawson), 1943–: St Paul's 1949–54; authority on ancient China, the Warden of Merton College, Oxford, since 1994.

RAWSON, Elizabeth, 1934–88; St Paul's 1945–51; classicist, Roman historian.

RAWSON, Jessica: see Quirk.

REYNOLDS, Barbara, 1914–: St Paul's, 1928–32; Italian scholar, translator of Dante, editor of the letters of Dorothy Sayers, general editor of the *Cambridge*

Imogen Stubbs.

Italian Dictionary.

RICHARDS, Susan (Mrs Kramer), 1950–: St Paul's, 1961–68; London mayoral candidate for the Liberal Democrats, 2000.

RICHARDSON, Natasha, 1963–: St Paul's, 1974–9; actress.

ROBINSON, Joan: see MAURICE.

SCOTT-JAMES, Anne (Lady Lancaster), 1913–: St Paul's 1923–31; writer, editor, broadcaster.

SHARP, Baroness, Evelyn, 1903–85: St Paul's 1916–22; civil servant, Permanent Secretary at the Ministry of Housing and Local Government 1955–66.

SHARDLOW, Janet: see MORGAN.

SHULMAN, Alexandra, 1957: St Paul's 1969–76; journalist, editor of *Vogue*.

SHULMAN, Nicola (Marchioness of Normanby), 1960–: St Paul's 1972–8; journalist.

Shirley Summerskill.

SMITH, Dodie, 1896–1990: St Paul's 1911–13; novelist and autobiographer, famous for her Dalmatians.

STUBBS, Imogen, 1961: St Paul's 1972–7; actress.

STOCKS, Baroness: see BRINTON.

SUMMERSKILL, the Hon. Shirley, 1931: St Paul's 1945–50; doctor, Labour politician, novelist.

TAYLOR, Carol (Mrs Handley), 1929: St Paul's 1945–48; Head Mistress, Camden School for Girls, 1971–85.

TENNANT, the Hon. Emma, 1937–: St Paul's 1949–53; novelist.

THIRKELL, Angela: see MACKAIL.

THORNTON, Dora, 1961–: St Paul's 1973–80; scholar of the Renaissance.

WALLIS, Helen, 1924–95: St Paul's 1934–45;

INDEX

Numbers in **bold** refer to illustrations

PICTURE ACKNOWLEDGEMENTS

All pictures are from the St Paul's Girls' School Archives, with new photography [by] Alan Owen except: The Cheltenham Ladies' College 20, 27; City of London Scho[ol] for Girls 81; Girls' Day School Trust (photographer: Peter Warne) 26; The Mistr[ess] and Fellows, Girton College, Cambridge 16, 100; Hammersmith & Fulham Archi[ves] and Local History Centre 23, 25, 32, 33, 35, 39 (lent by Miss Cowie), 65, 74, 120, [?] (Photo Reportage Ltd), 147; Hulton Getty Picture Collection 21, 30 (top); Lond[on] Metropolitan Archives 87; Sandra Lousada 162 (bottom); Mary Evans Picture Libr[ary] 12 (both), 14; Reproduced by courtesy of the Mercers' Company 15, facing page [?]; The Principal and Fellows of Newnham College, Cambridge 28; North Lond[on] Collegiate School 17; Queen's College 18; Roedean School 19; Royal Institute [of] British Architects 29, 30 (bottom); St Katherines School, St Andrews 71; St Pa[ul's] School 13.